# HOW I KNOW WHITE PEOPLE ARE CRAZY

## and Other Stories

# HOW I KNOW WHITE PEOPLE ARE CRAZY

## and Other Stories

Notes from a
Frustrated Black Psychologist

DR. JONATHAN MATHIAS LASSITER

NEW YORK BOSTON

Excerpt of "The five things no one will tell you about why colleges don't hire more faculty of color," by Marybeth Gasman (https://hechingerreport.org/five-things-no-one-will-tell-colleges-dont-hire-faculty-color), was produced by *The Hechinger Report*, a nonprofit, independent news organization focused on inequality and innovation in education. Used under a commercial use license.



Legacy Lit, an imprint of Grand Central Publishing
Hachette Book Group
1290 Avenue of the Americas
New York, NY 10104
HachetteBookGroup.com
Twitter.com/LegacyLitBooks
Instagram.com/LegacyLitBooks

First Edition: November 2025

Grand Central Publishing is a division of Hachette Book Group, Inc.
The Legacy Lit and Grand Central Publishing names and logos are trademarks of Hachette Book Group, Inc.

The Hachette Speakers Bureau provides a wide range of authors for speaking events. To find out more, visit hachettespeakersbureau.com or email HachetteSpeakers@hbgusa.com.



Some names and identifying characteristics have been changed.
Some dialogue has been recreated in parts.

Library of Congress Cataloging-in-Publication Data has been applied for.

ISBNs: 978-0-3068-3305-2 (hardcover); 978-0-3068-3307-6 (ebook)

Printed in Canada

MRQ-T

1 2025

*To all the Black psychologists of yesterday and today, thank you.*
*I see you. I affirm you.*

*To all the future Black psychologists, you are not the problem.*
*You are the solution.*

*To all the folks seeking mental health care, you deserve better.*

# Contents

## Part 3
## Whiteness Is a Mental Health Problem

# Prologue

## Whiteness Makes Us All Crazy

I'm not even mad anymore. I'm simply frustrated.

The whiteness of psychology and mental health has become old hat. I refuse to let the limitations of the whiteness mindset steal my peace. I am frustrated by the whiteness mindset that empowers white people to dictate how society defines mental health and the "legitimate" methods by which we treat mental health problems. I am frustrated because the mental health system that the whiteness mindset has wreaked is a narrow, Eurocentric, Western-culture-bound paradigm that is treated as universal. It is the whiteness mindset and its resultant mental health system that keeps Black and other people from the global majority[1] (e.g., Indigenous peoples across the globe, Latine, Arab, Asian, South Asian, Asian American) out of the mental health field. It is this whiteness mindset that keeps all of us unwell.

The latest statistics from the American Psychological Association showed that only about 20 percent of the psychologist workforce is composed of people from the global majority. Black people only make up 5 percent of the psychologist field. Black men like me are particularly rare, making up .86 percent of the psychologist workforce. And you know that's a damn shame.

Latine people make up about 8 percent of psychologists, and Asian Americans make up 3 percent. A testament to the effectiveness of the whiteness mindset that centers itself, American Indian/Alaska Native and Native Hawaiian/Pacific Islander Americans make up less than 1 percent of psychologists. These numbers are far lower than the percentages of these groups in the general population, according to the US census. Meanwhile, white people account for 81 percent of psychologists in America. They are overrepresented in the field compared to their numbers in the general population. This is disgraceful. And it is exactly what the whiteness mindset, which privileges white ways of understanding the world and concentrating power among white people, intends. I am not surprised. I read books. I know history. This is not new.

I am frustrated for my young students from the global majority who hope to become psychologists but feel discouraged because they do not see themselves represented and centered in psychology classrooms or books. I am frustrated for my clients who must search high and low for a Black therapist and under every rock for a Black male therapist. I am frustrated for therapists who want to help their clients from the global majority but only have psychological theories and techniques created by their oppressors at their disposal. Too few psychologists from global majority communities are welcomed in the field and receive funding to support creating culturally grounded healing methods. So even most culturally sensitive therapists are just adapting the master's tools. I am frustrated for everyday Black people and others from the global majority who are trying to heal but are hamstrung by the whiteness mindset in themselves and their families.

I am frustrated. But I am not mad. I am not hopeless. In fact, I am exercising my power in writing this book. I am using my vision to write to you. I am walking in my purpose as I write these words. The passion with which I discuss the whiteness mindset in this book was first shaped by my father—a Black person born in 1950s Georgia. He would often say to me after experiencing some racial injustice like being denied for a promotion after training the white man who was promoted instead: "White people crazy." I used to think my father was just bitter and mean. But now as a fortysomething Black, same-gender-loving man whose feet have been singed on the roads of an anti-Black and heterosexist world, I fully understand.[2] My father's fervor is kindling for my own fire. My knowledge is personal. I have been assaulted by the frenzied, entitled domination[3] of white people who have alternatively desired, hated, and terrorized me. My knowledge is also professional. As a clinical psychologist, I have witnessed some of my white clients struggle to let go of cultural beliefs that, on one hand, harmed them and, on the other, provided scapegoats—non-white, nonheterosexual, non-cisgender, poor people—for their suffering.

Now I, too, know that white people *are* crazy—and in turn the whiteness mindset has the power to make us all crazy. There are countless examples of this, including voting for politicians who slash the government programs they need to live; believing that civilization started in Greece; watering down cultural-spiritual rituals like mindfulness and meditation and then marketing them to white women as evidence-based health practices; arguing against gun control; and refusing to listen to Black women about their bodies and thus risking their lives and those of their fetuses. The dismantling of *Roe v. Wade* is an example of the whiteness mindset shaping our society. We can see the craziness of the whiteness mindset in advocating for foreign aid for white countries while ignoring anti-LGBTQ violence in African countries; hiring diversity, equity, and inclusion (DEI) officers only to ignore their recommendations, and then ultimately lay them off en masse when hordes of legislators call for DEI bans. The list goes on and on.

But white people are not alone. Black people and other people from the global majority suffer from the crazy, too. They show evidence of an internalized whiteness mindset when they self-diagnose as having imposter syndrome; engage in colorism and anti-Blackness; encourage their children to abandon their native languages so that they can fit into English-speaking environments; kick transgender and gender nonconforming children out of their homes because they believe it is what a white god would want them to do; and abuse their own children in hopes of sparing them from the abuse of white people.

We are crazy because we have all been infected with the whiteness mindset. We are in critical condition and many of us are *dying of whiteness*. As Jonathan M. Metzl[4] argues, the policies meant to restore and maintain white power and privilege contribute to injuries and death for many white people. Whiteness in law enforcement and school districts leads to police brutality and anti-woke campaigns, which leads to more death of the bodies and minds of

Black people. Maybe most alarming is that due to the ubiquity of the whiteness mindset, effective treatment for this condition is nearly impossible. In fact, as I will explain throughout this book, most mental health treatments themselves are grounded in whiteness.

So what is the whiteness mindset and why does it have the potential to make us crazy? And why do I, a mental health professional, use the term "crazy" to describe it? *The whiteness mindset* assumes that the world and the people in it are limited, fragmented, and at risk of destruction or annihilation. Specifically, the whiteness mindset assumes that we exist for a limited time and that what matters most is our lifetime, not our legacy or the lives of those who come after us. By limiting the definition of human life to simply physical experience, and denying the importance of spirituality or the possibility of any eternal experience, this mindset encourages people to consider only their own individual lives, without concern for the legacy they may leave. This belief can result in people "living for the moment" without considering long-term, generational impacts. Living for the moment may look like ignoring climate change because "that will be someone else's problem to deal with, I won't be here." It may also look like not investing in teaching our children an accurate history of their world because "what does the past have to do with today?" It may look like hoarding money, houses, food, and other resources because one believes that just as their own life is limited, so too are the resources available to them.

I am often frustrated because our minds and the world we live in were not always structured by the whiteness-based assumption of limitation, and they don't have to be. There is copious evidence from the fields of anthropology, Egyptology, and archeology—among others—that a different mindset once predominated. It was a mindset that focused on "living for eternity." It emphasized a harmonious relationship with the Earth, resources, and other human beings. This mindset, originating among the peoples of East Africa, southern Africa, and the Nile Valley regions,[5] promoted responsibility for not just oneself but also the people that would come after. This mindset is still evident among many communities of the global majority. For example, the Latine concept of *familismo*[6] highlights a commitment and loyalty to one's family. This value, which prioritizes healthy relationships, is related to the idea of collectivism, which also emphasizes the group over the individual.

A worldview of limitation disrupted this. A whiteness mindset either forgets or ignores the principle of conservation of energy: Energy is neither created nor destroyed. According to ancient African philosophies, to be human is to be the physical manifestation of spirit.[7] Therefore, we are always existing and all actions are consequential not only for our children and grandchildren but for the future versions of the bodies that our spirits will inhabit. Consistent with this mindset, ancient peoples understood that among those who may come after us could be ourselves, although in a different physical form. Therefore, our stewardship of natural resources and operating with an ethic of care for each other was not just about the other, but was also intricately tied to our future selves in a future time. In a very real sense, "living for eternity" meant preparing the world and those who would be in it to warmly welcome us back.

A whiteness mindset distorts this process and convinces people that they have only one life to live (limitation/scarcity) and the purpose of that is to gain material things that will give them a sense of security and worth (materialism). In its purest form, a whiteness mindset holds that material-based security and worth are the only things that matter. Love for people—even spouses and children—lags behind whiteness-fueled materialism. Those with a whiteness mindset find it hard to see the innate value in themselves and thus deny or ignore it in others. We all know people who perpetually work late nights and weekends. Some board plane after plane, excusing their absences from family events and dodging criticism because "It's work, and I have to be there." When one centers their life and self-worth around prioritizing the material, which is itself finite, they cut off their infiniteness and their humanity.

The assumption of limitation is connected to the assumption of fragmentation. Fragmentation is the belief that as human beings we are separate entities from God, other sacred forces, and each other. There are interactions between individuals, but we are all separate with our own features and goals. Due to this separation, we have no real responsibilities to each other, only to ourselves. The limitation and fragmentation assumptions are evident when people act with an "every person for themselves" mentality. We also see these assumptions manifested in the individualistic cultures of many Western countries. Fragmentation contributes to a selfishness that centers one's individual desires regardless of the consequences for others. Indeed, it's the basis for one of the great fuels of capitalism: competition. Not only do we serve ourselves, but we must do it better and be more richly rewarded than anyone else.

The final assumption is that as human beings we are metaphorically and physically at risk of being destroyed, defeated, or annihilated. We fear losing our way of life, our values, our culture, our rights and privileges, and our power, convinced that these things can be destroyed or taken away at any moment. This assumption of annihilation and its resultant fear contributes to wars both physical and cultural. It contributes to anxieties about preserving an "American way of life." The assumption of annihilation convinces people that if their opinions, cultural norms, and values are not being centered, then those things are at risk of being supplanted.

Recent examples of the assumption of annihilation include the debate over critical race theory being taught in schools, book bans, bathroom bills, and the "don't say gay" law. These initiatives reveal some people's concern that their beliefs and values are being attacked. In this worldview, the existence of difference represents a threat—if your ideology is not dominant you risk annihilation. Not to mention the grim rallying cry "Jews will not replace us" chanted by white nationalist protesters at a "Unite the Right" rally in Charlottesville, Virginia, in August 2017. Protesters decried the removal of Confederate iconography from public spaces. Their chant, a stark recitation of the assumption and fear of annihilation, echoed the "Great Replacement" theory espoused by French novelist Renaud Camus.[8] Whereas Camus decried what he perceived as Europe being overrun by African and Muslim immigrants who were replacing native Europeans, Charlottesville protesters feared being substituted by Jewish people. Going on the offense, they shouted their fears of annihilation into the streets, one of them running down counterprotesters with his car. Thirty-five people were injured and one killed. Instead of making space for various viewpoints and ways of being to thrive, the assumption of annihilation convinces people that they should kill or be killed metaphorically and, sometimes, literally.

I label this whiteness mindset as crazy because of the effects that it has on all of us, individually, collectively, and as a society. A few individual people from the global majority may reap some benefits when they internalize and perpetuate the whiteness mindset, like promotions in whiteness-based workplaces. However, communities and countries composed of people from the global majority will always be subjugated by whiteness, which works to ensure that white people are the center of all aspects of lived reality.[9] The whiteness mindset, with its focus on limitation, fragmentation, and annihilation, contributes to emotional and, ultimately, physical death. Yet, whiteness has and continues to convince its adherents to hold on to it, even as it is killing them and the world around them. Believing and acting to perpetuate something that is killing you is my definition of crazy.

A whiteness mindset, rooted in limitation, fragmentation, and annihilation, leads people to develop and maintain systems of oppression based on a variety of differences, which are too often used to justify the brutal methods whiteness employs to gain psychological, social, and material benefits. In short, the whiteness mindset allows perpetrators to label those they oppress as different and other, thus neatly justifying the oppression that enriches and empowers the perpetrators.

Dr. Linda James Myers points out in her book *Understanding an Afrocentric World View* that these differences have primarily been based on sex, gender, race, ethnicity, religion, class, and ability status that have resulted in a large group of "isms." These isms have been codified by bell hooks as imperialist white supremacist [capitalist hetero-ableist] patriarchy.[10] They include but are not limited to such oppressive societal systems as imperialism, racism, capitalism, sexism, ableism, religious marginalization and persecution, and heterosexism. These isms are not mutually exclusive, affecting people one at a time, but often overlap and have a compound effect on people like me—a Black, same-gender-loving man[11] with sickle cell anemia—who lives at the intersection of multiple marginalized identities. Clearly, the whiteness mindset is one of the most detrimental and ubiquitous mindsets harming people across the globe.

Yet, in all my years of training and practice as a clinical psychologist, the destructive mindset of whiteness was never taught to me as a mental health problem or disorder. Although it meets all the criteria for abnormal psychology—it's dangerous, deviates from most spiritual and cultural norms, causes distress, and promotes dysfunction—a comprehensive overview of its features was never presented. To get an understanding of this mindset I had to go off the beaten path and study the works of psychologists like Dr. Linda James Myers, Dr. Lisa B. Spanierman, Dr. Kenneth M. Tyler, and others who have written eloquently about whiteness. These scholars are not taught widely in mainstream Eurocentric/Western psychology classrooms. But their work has been essential in helping me focus in on the whiteness mindset and examine its effects in my own life and society. Several components of the whiteness mindset have been described in different ways, as a suboptimal worldview, the psychosocial costs of racism, and cultural value-based attitudes. However, these features of the whiteness mindset have yet to be presented as a set of diagnostic criteria like I share below.

## Whiteness Mindset

### Diagnostic Criteria*

The onset of the whiteness mindset typically occurs at an early age and lasts throughout the lifetime. The prognosis is usually poor with substantial remission rarely seen, particularly for those racialized as white due to the benefits bestowed upon them through the codification of this mindset in societal systems. This diagnosis represents a distortion of the spiritual reality of oneness. It is akin to what Dr. Linda James Myers and Dr. Kobi Kambon have respectively described as a suboptimal worldview or cultural misorientation. The following set of criteria must be present for more days than not.

A. Possessing a mindset that is primarily oriented to at least one of the following three **assumptions** about the nature of life:
   1. Limitation or scarcity
   2. Fragmentation
   3. Annihilation

B. Evidence of this mindset can be seen in a person's behaviors that demonstrate prioritizing at least one of the following **values**:
   1. Individualism
   2. Competition
   3. Materialism

C. Due to this mindset a person **benefits** from at least one of the following:
   1. Purpose
   2. Power
   3. Protection

D. A person experiences at least one of the following **symptoms** due to an internalization of the assumptions, values, and benefits of whiteness:
   1. Distorted and/or psychopathic thoughts
   2. Negative emotion and/or lack of emotion
   3. Oppressive behaviors and/or inaction in the face of wrongdoing

---

**Note:** The whiteness mindset is not a diagnosis that is only limited to people who are phenotypically white or who are considered white by society. A person can be diagnosed with the whiteness mindset regardless of their racial or ethnic background.

**Note:** The whiteness mindset does not only have racial and ethnic implications but can also—and often does—structure society in both subtle and pervasive ways that contribute to oppression based on gender, physical and neurological ability status, class, religion, and other social identifiers.

**Note:** Although whiteness has been described here as a mindset, this mindset has ripple effects in society and often not only plays out within and between individuals but also influences society's policies, laws, and cultural norms.

**Note:** The whiteness mindset does not necessarily cause significant functional impairment in the context of a society that is structured—in its laws, policies, and cultural norms—by it.

In fact, most people who evidence whiteness will have their behavior reinforced and rewarded by societies structured by the whiteness mindset.

---

* This diagnosis has been constructed based on the works of several scholars, including Dr. Linda James Myers, Dr. Kobi Kambon, Dr. Bobby E. Wright, Dr. Erylene Piper-Mandy, Dr. Taasogle Daryl Rowe, Dr. Frances Cress Welsing, Dr. Kenneth M. Tyler, Dr. Judith H. Katz, Dr. Lisa B. Spanierman, and Dr. Mab Segrest.[12] In addition, my own personal and professional experience informs this explication of the whiteness mindset.

---

This set of diagnostic criteria is a first step toward acknowledging a serious problem. And acknowledging the problem is a first step toward healing. This book serves as a public acknowledgment. It is a reckoning. It is a revolution. This revolution will be psychoanalyzed.

And that's what makes this book special.

The whiteness mindset has a negative effect on us all. I, too, must constantly fight to keep it in check. Having grown up as a Black boy in a low-income home and neighborhood, I struggled with self-worth. People suffering from the whiteness mindset solely seek confirmation of their value from outside sources, in things that they do, not who they are in relationship with. This way of being separates us from others and our sacred essence. It also stems from the assumption of limitation. Instead of understanding oneself as eternal and linked to those who have come before and who will come after, one feels a desire to make an impact on the world through material means.

The scary, and perhaps most distressing, thing about the

whiteness mindset is that formalized treatments are pretty much nonexistent. The whiteness mindset harms not just our minds but the mental health profession and the study of psychology from which we derive our mental health practices. The mental health field has yet to effectively dismantle the whiteness mindset at the roots of psychology and society. The whiteness mindset promotes a patchwork approach to mental health. Providers attend to the symptoms of the whiteness mindset but not the whiteness mindset itself. Therapists have theories and techniques that can help teach us how to cope in an oppressive environment. Some therapists may even have the skills to help their clients discuss internalized racism or sexism. However, they are likely less equipped to aid their clients with recognizing when they are using the whiteness mindset in their behaviors and emotions. Many therapists do not adequately consider their clients' sociopolitical context when diagnosing and doing therapy. Therapists are often only treating some small discrete part of a person focusing on symptom reduction, not well-being and, god forbid, thriving. The goal of a whiteness-based mental health system is to get the patient well enough to be productive for corporations or family.

My hope is that after reading this book, you will have a better understanding of what the whiteness mindset is and how it harms the mental health of Black people and other people of the global majority. You'll be able to see how the whiteness mindset plays out in psychology and the mental health field and how that has harmed us all.

This book is for everyone. In order to heal, we must all start by recognizing, diagnosing, and treating the whiteness mindset in us.

# Part 1

# My Life "Ain't Been No Crystal Stair"[1]

## CHAPTER 1

# The Impact of Whiteness

My father loved us toughly. It was a love that was hard to see on the surface, but it was there. To protect us from the indignities inflicted by white people, he taught us to be strong at all costs. It was as if he believed that having no emotions meant that they could never be bruised. A barrier was better than a breakdown. But barriers are not cheap. The biggest cost: I grew up unsure if my father loved me. I knew he took his role as my father seriously. He was stern, protective, and stalwart. Yet, I seldom sensed gentleness, warmth, or affection. Was he proud of me? Did he like me?

As a child, I thought I alone carried this cost. But as an adult, I realized that my father carried it, too. He grew up guessing about his parents' love and passed the guesswork along. The cost was generational. The cause was the whiteness mindset.

✦✦

The tale was imagined and passed down like this.

The year was 1957, the sun was pressing down on Sardis, Georgia. Ninety-one degrees of heat with a faint breeze that brushed the townspeople as they went about errands. My father, Joshua, who had just turned seven, stepped down the sidewalk to the movie theater with his family. His birthday had been five days before. But since it fell on a Monday, he wasn't able to celebrate as jubilantly as he would have liked. Joshua hated when his birthday blew by on a weekday. At least his mother had baked him a sweet vanilla cake to cap off dinner that night.

The weekend after, Jasper and Minnie, Joshua's parents, decided to take their six children for a family outing in the next town over. To commemorate his belated birthday, Joshua had the honor of deciding which movie they would see. The short, skinny boy with chicken arms and a bird chest loved westerns and was eager to see *Gunfight at the O.K. Corral*. It had been released a few months back and tickets would be discounted now.

Jasper, a forty-one-year-old man, was stoic as he watched over his family. His days were spent toiling on the land he leased from the white family whose name was on the deed. Jasper, like many men in Georgia at that time, was a sharecropper. His hands were calloused, and his heart was shielded to fend off a dangerous world. His lungs were scarred from childhood asthma and now smoking tobacco. To his children, he spoke with authority in a voice that sounded like thunder.

With Minnie, he barely spoke at all. They exchanged words and exclamations related to household tasks, the children, and playing the numbers at J's Drug Store. Straightforward, matter-of-fact words were for tasks and children. Exclamations were for when the numbers hit.

Jasper was dutiful. He never missed work. He was up with the roosters every day, except for Saturday and Sunday. Every payday, he presented his earnings to his wife, sans a few dollars for the numbers and a drink at Church's Beer Garden. Jasper would get dressed up slicker than a nickel and make his way to the shack that used to be a general store out in the woods of Millen, Georgia. At Church's Beer Garden, he let his guard down just a little to engage in the common pastimes of telling lies and fanning flies. Jasper nursed Gordon's gin in his glass as he played bones and spades. The smell of oak and liquor swirled together while Jasper and his neighbors let the booze do its work, slackening their backs and soothing their stress.

The reality of working with no hope of reward and relying only on a prayer for survival was too heavy for Jasper. To shield his family from the weight, Jasper stayed away most evenings soothing himself with drink and leisure. After supper, he left and did not come back until late. This tactic was not entirely effective. All the Lassiters felt the weight Jasper carried punching down on them.

Minnie, seven years her husband's junior, was forced into maturity long before she met Jasper. As the youngest of nine—seven boys and two girls—she was used to being unseen. When she was born, her parents were already tired from eight other children and struggle. They had little energy to engage with her. She learned early on to be self-sufficient.

She was nineteen when she had her first child, a little girl with onyx skin. When Polly was a baby, Minnie polished her daughter's skin with petroleum jelly and powdered her butt with talcum. But after the baby's father disappeared, Minnie grew distant from her daughter. Heartbroken by her first love and abandoned with a baby, she ceased to look deeper than the skin. She gave up searching for glints of joy in her baby's eyes or her own.

Maybe Minnie was afraid Polly would disappear, too, and take any remaining joy away with her? Minnie decided to keep her hopes close, deep in the pit of her stomach, twisted up like sheets in the wash. She remained guarded after marrying Jasper. I'm sure that somewhere inside of her lived affection for him. But that warmth was barely seen.

When she met Jasper, she was happy to have a man who placed duty over passion. He seldom asked about her desires. He needed a mate, a partner, and Minnie needed the same. The load of surviving in the white man's world was better carried by two than one. Side by side, they cultivated cotton and created a family. Jasper allowed her distance, to keep her fortress around her emotions.

When the children were born, a part of her wished they would give her distance, too. She wished they would not need her so intensely. She often did not see them as they really were. She saw them through the eyes of the ill-intentioned white people who might try to injure them. She worried well into the night about their safety. She wanted them to be well-mannered, clean, hardworking—all the attributes that might buffer them from white people's abuse. But their inner lives were invisible to her. She did not know their dreams. She did not encourage them to imagine a life of their own. How can a mother give something to her child that she does not have for herself?

Minnie went through the motions. The only place she lit up was in the presence of God and the hosts at Sand Hill Baptist Church. She was a straight-up Christian woman attending church with her children every Sunday. She was on the usher board, always in pressed, starched Woolite-white dresses and gloves. She was quick to admonish children and adults for chewing gum. Her outstretched, gloved hand and sternness struck people straight. She was a good housekeeper and strict disciplinarian. Her children feared her but did not know her. She held so much down.

Each member of the Lassiter family was in their own world as they progressed to the movie theater. Jasper, his face a shield, looked straight ahead. He made note of his surroundings out of the corners of his eyes. Minnie, weathered by life, looked in shop windows as she passed them. Did she need any new fabric for one of the girls' dresses? She ran through her mental list of tasks.

My father's older sisters, Polly and Lena, were chattering about what candy they would share.

Polly pondered aloud. "Maybe chocolate?"

"Maybe sticky taffy?" Lena replied, licking her lips.

"You got enough from cleaning Mrs. Walters's house to get a soda, too?" Polly asked.

My father's two older brothers, Wally and Ray, were a little ahead, whispering about girls.

"Did you see Phyllis on Friday?" Ray grinned with a glint in his eye.

"Her skirt hit her in all the right places," Wally said with his lips pursed, eyes narrowed as he recreated the memory.

"You ain't got a chance. You might as well keep dreaming," Ray teased.

Hank, the youngest Lassiter, wobbled down the street, still getting used to moving on two limbs instead of four. Joshua, my father, was kicking a rock down the dusty sidewalk a little ways behind his siblings but ahead of his parents.

Joshua was quiet and compliant. His siblings thought of him as laid-back. It was as if he was born carrying secrets conceived in a previous incarnation. As was customary, he rarely spoke to adults unless spoken to. If someone had ever actually asked him what he was thinking about, he might have produced the word *playing*. He wanted to climb trees, skip rocks across the pond, and ride horses. But his parents, determined to keep their children safe from the destructive effects of racism, made sure that Joshua and his siblings stayed close to home. Folks would often find Joshua sitting, staring off into the distance, sucking his thumbs.

Inside his home, he was his mother's helper. He would share the load of cooking and cleaning with his siblings. It was because of his mother that he learned to cook corn bread with a whole stick of butter in the batter and then another one melted on top after it came sizzling, in a cast-iron skillet, from the oven. He loved his mom's recipes and Sunday feasts. Her stewed beef and rice filled the house with a savory, peppery aroma that he often smelled in his sleep. His mother did not ask him about his hopes. But she made sure he was not hungry or harmed.

Joshua knew less about his father. At least his mother was mostly physically present in the home. On the weekdays, his father was gone when Joshua got up. He did not appear until the day's last meal. Despite the physical absence, Jasper occupied a large space in Joshua's heart.

"I loved my daddy. He was a good man." Those words were worn onto my father's tongue from being uttered whenever someone asked him about Jasper.

Years later when I would press my father about what it was *specifically* about his father that he loved so much, he could not articulate it.

To my father, some things did not need to be spoken or speculated. He respected his father and wanted to be like him: a powerful provider.

About a block away from the theater, the Lassiters were stopped mid-step as two white men lumbered toward them. They had red eyes and sweaty skin, pale and plain. They were not seasoned men as my grandfather was, but fresh in their arrival to adulthood. Their manhood was frail and needed to be fortified.

They called out to Jasper:

"Hey, *boy*, what you doing on the sidewalk? You know you're supposed to be off the sidewalk when we come by."

The white men flashed yellowish-brownish grins to each other. One spit chewing-tobacco juice into the street. All the Lassiters, except baby Hank, felt tightness creep into their chests. Their bodies went into autopilot and stepped off the sidewalk. Minnie grabbed Hank and hurried beside her husband into the street.

Without saying a word, they continued to the movie theater. As always, my grandfather swallowed the assault. Challenging them would have meant either jail or lynching or both. Justice was not an option. My grandfather rushed the family along the final block to the theater so that they could seek shelter in front of the screen.

They may have been physically safe, but they were emotionally harmed. No one dared to reveal the realness of their emotions. The fear, humiliation, anger, hatred, hopelessness. They all held their breath in the dark, colored-only balcony of that theater. It was not until Doc Holliday fired his first round that they let the air escape their lungs.

All the Lassiters were traumatized that day. If they could have received psychotherapy from a culturally informed therapist, they may have been able to be accurately diagnosed and receive the care they needed to recover from that assault. They may have been able to reject the barbaric display of the whiteness mindset expressed in those men's oppressive behaviors that disregarded the humanity of a whole family. A culturally skilled therapist may have been able to help the family understand that those men's need to feel powerful and superior was an example of distorted and delusional thoughts not connected to reality. Those men used the power of their white skin and status in that time and place to bestow purpose upon themselves—a perceived right to exist above others. A therapist experienced in diagnosing the whiteness mindset could have helped the Lassiters appropriately narrate the incident as a problem with the white men and not them. If the Lassiters could have received therapy from a whiteness expert, they may have had the chance to process their pain and speak their shame. However, no such opportunities were available.

Instead, the verbal assault deeply wounded my father. He witnessed his father rendered irrelevant by those white men. The white men, who were younger than his father, had the power to block a Black family's path. Joshua saw the man whom he respected, loved, and cherished more than any other man turned into a boy. A silenced boy who swallowed fear and anger to ensure survival. The silence was a mask for the shame. But Jasper knew the shame was there. And Joshua knew it, too.

Submerging one's hurt emotions only causes them to bloat and take up too much space. Those emotions swell and leave no room for anything else. That's exactly what happened with my father. Although never diagnosed, I believe my father suffered from *Post*

*Traumatic Slave Syndrome* (PTSS).[1] Dr. Joy DeGruy, a Black woman with a PhD in social work research, defines PTSS as a condition stemming from multigenerational trauma due to experiencing chattel slavery and subsequent anti-Black oppression. This condition influences Black people's beliefs and emotions throughout their lives. Dr. DeGruy identified three primary characteristics that are associated with this condition: vacant esteem, ever-present anger, and racist socialization. A person with vacant esteem carries a sense of inferiority in reference to others, particularly those whom they perceive as powerful or more desirable than them. Vacant esteem equals little intrinsic self-worth. Ever-present anger is rage that Black people feel as a result of the almost constant experiences of subtle and overt acts of violence, degradation, and humiliation targeted at Black people, our ancestors, our children, and our culture. This rage frequently simmers and sometimes boils over. Racist socialization occurs when anti-Black stereotypes are taught to Black people and then subsequently internalized and further disseminated by those same Black people. My father's behaviors suggested that he suffered from all three of these symptoms.

Although a proud Black man in a lot of ways, my father possessed a vacant esteem that noticeably haunted him in his later years of life. Deep down he believed he had little inherent worth. This belief was reinforced by blatant and subtle societal messages of inferiority and sub-humanness from an anti-Black society. His own mother often told him that he "would never be nothing." He often felt "less than a man" when he had difficulty financially providing for his family. The whiteness mindset had convinced him that his worth was wrapped up in what money he made.

My father had an ever-present anger. His rage always seemed to simmer just under the surface, the product of having his goals blocked repeatedly and the fear of never being able to reach those goals. My father's anger at the attempts of annihilation, fragmentation, and restriction of resources enacted by non-Black people often turned inward on himself and outward on his family. My father was also a victim of racist socialization that subtly reinforced his adoption of the whiteness mindset that values individualism, competition, and materialism. This racist socialization was evident in his anti-gay comments, adherence to whiteness-based masculinity that included domination and violence, and harsh self-criticism when he couldn't provide for his family in the way he wanted.[2]

To a person watching the event my father and his family experienced, it may have looked mundane. In some ways, it was. White people being white people: forcing their will regardless of others' desires. They demanded deference they didn't deserve or earn. Those men took up space and squeezed my father's family onto the street. Black people always had to beware of brutality born of the whiteness mindset and enacted by white people.

Common as this story might be, this tale is an origin story of poor mental health. I imagine it as the genesis of my father's hurt and hatred. It was the beginning step on a road that led my father to become a hardened man who was hard on his family.

That dehumanizing moment was what my father's parents were trying to protect him from. They were trying to preserve seven-year-old Joshua's innocence. But rarely are Black parents successful in that goal. Few Black parents can spare their child from speeding to maturity. The barbarity of whiteness turns everyone into warriors.

So our Black parents teach us early to fight not just for physical survival, but for dignity. They teach us to guard our emotions, shield our tongues, and keep our eyes open. Black children cannot afford to avert their gaze. We must see even when it hurts to do so. We must restrain ourselves even when we are wronged.

My father grew up ingesting these lessons. He hated white people's ability to inflict cruelty without consequences. The older he grew, the bolder he was in his rebellion. At school, he would flatly refuse to listen to white teachers. They looked down on him with thin noses and crooked frowns and labeled him a problem. In 1964, he was arrested for snatching Sambo snapshots from downtown city hall's walls. And in 1975, he cursed out a young white man who dared call him *boy*. The white man refused my father's direct orders, although my father was his supervisor at the pest control company they both worked for.

"I almost stomped a mutthole in his ass," my father would relay to me years later.

Witnessing my grandfather belittled by whiteness had a profound effect on my father. It shaped how he understood the ways white people could rob Black people of dignity and freedom. Joshua developed a reactive hatred. He needed the hatred to hold out against the white world.

I also grew up with the impact of that hatred—and the hurt beneath it. My father taught me and my younger brother his hatred. He tried to hide his hurt from us, but the hatred was evident. Hatred is hard to turn off at five o'clock. Its acidity was corrosive, even at home. There was no tenderness for his family when he walked through the door. The acidity scarred the bonds between us, making them tough and brittle. Instead of welcome-home hugs and smiles, my father seemed to only desire quiet time, a family seen but not heard.

As a child, I loved my father *some* but did not know him. He was a demigod, sometimes benevolent and sometimes wrathful. His love of playing must have died long before he had my brother and me. He would often warn us, "I may laugh and joke, but I don't play."

Based on the way my father described my grandparents, I believe that my father was kinder and more emotionally visible than them. My father was not unloving. He was not hateful toward my brother and me. He was not physically neglectful. He always kept food on the table, a roof over our heads, and clothes on our backs. Throughout my childhood, he kept a job. My father loved us in the ways he knew how. My father's love was like fire to remove impurities, pressure to produce a diamond. But I was too delicate. I was made of flesh. I wished that my father would try tenderness more than strictness. This conflict of interests created a barrier between us. While my father valued protection and strength, I was much more drawn to the world of fantasy, the arts, and emotions.

Like my father as a child, I was short and skinny with chicken arms and a bird chest. I was quiet, too. But my idea of playing was escaping into a world of books. The *Reading Rainbow* theme song could have doubled as the theme song for my early childhood. I loved to read *Amelia Bedelia*, *Berenstain Bears*, and the Little Critter collection. In my free time, I would cuddle with a book. It was my way of imagining a world outside of the pain of illness and want. It was my way of imagining an emotionally close, gentle relationship with my father.

In *Berenstain Bears*, Papa Bear may have been stern at times. But he always let Brother and Sister Bear know that he loved them. He was tender in teaching the lessons of life to his cubs. He volunteered at their school. And even when he and Mama Bear had disagreements, they rarely were angry. Papa Bear was able to do something my father never seemed good at—admit when he was wrong. Although stubborn, Papa Bear was no stranger to saying sorry and sharing heartfelt hugs in concession. Papa Bear was the type of father for which I prayed. But my father wanted me to be a different type of boy. He wanted me to play sports, have sex with girls while maintaining a powerful emotional distance, and be physically aggressive. This type of boy would develop into a strong man who could lead and shield his family from the harms of white people no matter the emotional costs. My father wanted me to mimic him as he emulated his father.

My father led his family from a space where he simultaneously fought white people's brutality and internalized the whiteness mindset. Being exposed to the norms of white manhood, his own manhood looked like a combination of his father's emotional distancing and the disregard for the fullness of others' humanity that was demonstrated by those white men on that Saturday morning in his youth. After generations of intentional cultural suppression and demonization by the white world around him, Joshua's ancestors' African values were largely unfamiliar to him. My father was culturally misoriented.

Dr. Kobi Kambon, a Black psychology pioneer, defined *cultural misorientation* as the predominance of a Eurocentric self-consciousness within a person of African descent. Black people essentially become white.[3] The whiteness mindset had restricted my father's emotions, and he impressed the same restrictions on me.

Dr. Linda James Myers, a pioneering Black female psychologist, explained in *Understanding an Afrocentric World View* that materialism, competition, and individualism sever interpersonal relationships. My father's preoccupation with my power and protection put walls between us. He was trying to protect me in his way. But his way was painful. His way was the way of whiteness. The whiteness mindset convinced him that the only legitimate way for me to be a man was to stand on my own two feet through individualism and strive to be the king of my own castle through competition and materialism.

These values of the whiteness mindset have shaped the world around Black people for generations. Instead of a collective of families connected in their care of children, which was customary in many pre-colonial African societies, the whiteness mindset has been used to fragment, pathologize, and brainwash Black families into familial relationships structured by gender-based domination instead of cooperation. The perceived benefits of appropriately assimilating the values of whiteness have been dangled on a stick like a carrot. On one hand, Black people are told to gain wealth, control their families, and only worry about themselves. However, they are often thwarted in doing so by systems derived from whiteness such as capitalism, patriarchy, white supremacy, and racism.

When people are kept from gaining access to the things that they are taught give them worth, they can develop vacant esteem and ever-present anger, which can metastasize into self-hatred. Self-hatred is commonly destructive to the self and those who are the closest to that person. It's a vicious and painful cycle. By accepting a vision of success informed by the whiteness mindset, only to be deprived of the means of reaching that success by that same whiteness-informed society, many marginalized people are left blaming themselves for an impossible situation.

This way of life informed by the whiteness mindset is a learned way of being among Black families. Pre-colonial African societies viewed gender performance, masculinity, and femininity in very different ways than Black American families are now socialized to perceive them. In his book *Seeking the Sakhu*, Dr. Wade Nobles suggested that a more culturally aligned and health-affirming structure for the Black American family would be one based on the Kemetic principles of Ma'at. Ma'at is an ancient Egyptian goddess who represented several virtues that provided a road map for a moral life.[4] Such virtues, like harmony and balance, open up the space for Black families to hold gender-related role definitions but not gender-based performances. This means that the definition of male and female may be linked to anatomy, yet family members operate flexibly in the roles they perform, with men and women performing similar functions for the overall well-being of the family unit. Regardless of whether one identifies their gender as male, female, something else, or nothing at all, Black families are healthiest when they prioritize the unity of the family over the differences of the individual members. Because of generational oppression, my parents were disconnected from their African roots and raised my siblings according to a whiteness mindset.

They did not know that some African groups, like the Dagara tribe in West Africa, de-emphasized gendered anatomy and prioritized harmony between one's masculine and feminine energy instead.[5] The Dagara people, who are closely tied to present-day

Ghana, Ivory Coast, and Togo, knew that suppression of one energy in service of the other was a detrimental practice. People in their villages engaged in rituals and rites of passage that cultivated harmony among one's masculine and feminine energy. Men participated in all-male rituals where they engaged in male-to-male emotional exchange that was similar to a mothering process. They cried together and comforted each other to get in touch with their vulnerable emotions and release themselves of the burden of *male* responsibility. Women also engaged in activities such as hunting and warrior rituals to balance their masculine and feminine energy. The goal was not gender domination or erasure, but rather to create a collective where all genders appreciated and honored each other.

My father had no knowledge of Dagara customs that defined sex, gender, and sexual orientation according to one's divine purpose. To the Dagara, sex, gender, and sexual orientation were not solely about physical anatomy and actions. They occurred as part of the divine plan for one's life. One's particular sex, gender, and sexual orientation designations contributed to the experiences and distinct events that shaped their life. Furthermore, intersex people and gatekeepers (i.e., people identifying as lesbian, gay, or bisexual in the contemporary world) were believed to have a spiritual purpose as the intermediaries between the spiritual and physical worlds. These people were exalted, not oppressed, in many pre-colonial African societies.

My father and his ancestors' ties to their African ways of being shifted drastically with the introduction of the whiteness mindset by colonizers and enslavers. Black people went from prioritizing harmony and healing to centering domination and defense. This shift played out in Black families across the United States. Witnessing the brutality of white enslavers indoctrinated many Black men into believing that violence and gender-based domination was an acceptable avenue to establish control of their families and mandate manhood in their sons. Many Black fathers have forced their sons to feel pain and then punished them when they expressed emotions. Mandating manhood requires what bell hooks has referred to as *soul murder* in her book *We Real Cool: Black Men and Masculinity.* This soul murder is exercised using verbal and physical aggression to force emotional suppression that eventually contributes to chronic depression. This depression is not always evident, as it often does not look like sadness. It often appears to be anger or irritability, or silence and obedience. Yet, the root is repeated suppression. To my father's chagrin, my spirit resisted his brand of suppression. However, I was still often depressed because of his forcefulness and rejection of my tenderness.

I couldn't help but be vulnerable. Maybe part of my softness was genetic? I was born a month earlier than expected, diagnosed with sickle cell anemia. Due to sickle cell, I was hospitalized several times as a toddler. My red blood cells were not able to hold oxygen. They turned into a sickle shape. When too many of them gathered in one place, they stopped oxygen flow to that area of the body. The lack of oxygen caused organ tissue to die. This happened to me a lot as a child. It affected my lungs, legs, arms, chest, and pelvis. No part of my body was left in peace.

My mother and father were not people with four-year college degrees. They did not understand the detailed medical explanations for my disease. But they aimed to protect me from my ailment as much as possible. My mother did this by sheltering me. She made sure I was always well hydrated, which was supposed to help blood flow. She made sure I did not overly exert myself. Exercise could demand too much oxygen and stress my cells. So I was shielded. And, in some ways, stunted. I was stunted by never having to face things deemed too hard in the physical world. I didn't develop the skills to navigate peers' rejections, and instead prioritized comfort in my internal world of imagination.

My father, with his emphasis on strength, despised it. His way for me to heal was to face it. To get outside, fall down, get up, and grow sturdy skin. But I was much too delicate for that. I failed at meeting my father's requirement for fortitude: Deny all displays of weakness. But my body was often weak despite my father's disdain.

✦✦

In 1991, I was seven years old and hospitalized for five days due to a sickle cell anemia pain crisis. One moment I was reading, the next overtaken with agony. The torture took all logic and form from my mind. I existed only in affect, images, and sensations. My cells were like maroon crescent moons, crimson curves stuck together like fingers in Elmer's glue. My inhalations sounded like tires on gravel. The pain felt like boulders crushing me, like being bludgeoned and simultaneously squeezed from the inside out. A thousand ice picks pierced me all at once. A sonic boom bashed my bones, and I prayed for peace.

That peace came in a syringe of opioids. The affect washed away, images went dark, and all sensations were transformed into relief. Nothing mattered anymore as I drifted into sleep and away from the anguish.

Recovering, four days later, I stared up at a drop ceiling. The twelve-by-twelve squares with neat, straight lines made a mockery of me. My life was not orderly. My cells had rebelled. My mind fixated on my body. I was on a mechanical bed. The pillow beneath my head was too soft. I seemed to be sinking under the double layer of thin mint-green blankets.

*I'm thirsty* was the thought that slid in and out of my head. Quickly, my attention moved from my thirst to the thin, hollow butterfly needle inserted in and taped to my right hand. The skin underneath the tape itched. White, chalk-like ash coated the webby parts between my fingers. I couldn't move my hand freely. It was fixed to a white board beneath to prevent me from bending it. My chest and side itched, too. There were sticky round pads on me to monitor my vital signs. One on my sternum, a few on my ribs, and one on each side. I squirmed. My thirst came back.

My father—short, dark, and silently transfixed by the television screen—sat sucking his thumbs. He was in the pull-out chair next to me. He had come earlier that morning to watch over me while my mother took a break. She had gone home for a shower, food, and rest. She had been there all night praying, patrolling, and pampering.

My dry mouth returned to the front of my mind. I wanted something to drink. I thought of tart, sweet purple liquid that made my lips pucker.

"Dad, I want grape juice."

My father got up. He went over to the tall, right-angled table and pulled the seal off the plastic container of juice and poured it into a Styrofoam cup. He grabbed a bendy straw, peeled the paper down the thin, long tube, and placed it in the cup. He presented the beverage to me. I took it into my left hand and clumsily tried to hold it steady with my useless right one.

"I want ice."

"I'll tell your mama to get you some ice when she comes back."

A levee broke. The emotions that had been pressing against my barriers cracked me open. I started crying. My impulse was to stop myself. The more I tried to stop, the more defiant my tears were.

"Stop all that crying. You're out of the woods now. You've got to be tough so you can go home." He seemed to think that I was crying out of physical pain, but the agony of that moment was emotional.

Just four days before, I was on the verge of death. At that moment, I lay in the hospital bed helpless. I had endured doctors and nurses poking, prodding, shining lights in my eyes, and injecting medicines into me. I needed to feel loved and nurtured. I wanted my father to take care of me. Instead, I was met with an impenetrable barrier, like so many times before. I could not control my cries.

Almost as if on cue, my mother materialized.

"What's wrong, baby?"

✦✦

As a psychologist, I now interpret my father's reaction on that day as a trauma response rooted in the damage of the whiteness mindset that started decades prior to his birth. Racism is one system of oppression that flourishes in a world structured by the whiteness mindset that reinforces individualism and competition based on individual differences—in this case, based on race. Experiencing chronic racism, starting at an early age, can contribute to hypervigilance and difficulties managing one's emotions. Chronic exposure to racism—and oppression of any kind—has long-term effects on the human body by dysregulating the central nervous system that is responsible for responding to actual and perceived threats. My father inherited the hypervigilance and emotional problems of the ancestors before him.

My grandfather's grandfather was born one year after slavery ended in Georgia. This man, whose name I do not know and whose story I never knew, was born into a chaotic world. In 1866, formerly enslaved African people exercised their talents in sharecropping, blacksmithing, and other work with their hands. But it did not provide much freedom or wealth for Black laborers. There was still an unequal balance of power. White people still exacted their cruelty and exploitation in every situation.

When Rufus Bullock was elected governor in 1868, white Georgians accelerated their terrorism in response to his promotion of Black equality. They tortured and tormented Black people. They could harm, so they did. They savored their skill at shattering Black souls.

Black families were seized with anger. Anger was the surface-level emotion that protected them from the tenderness of their gloom and blues. Underneath the rage, they were stricken with fear. They were afraid to be out after dark. They were afraid to be alone in the daylight. They were afraid to look too long at a white person's eyes. They were afraid to speak to them. They were afraid to offend.

They prioritized protection. Children were told:

"Don't talk too loud."

"Keep your head down."

"Don't linger."

"You have to know what white people want before they do."

These experiences and lessons were extended to each generation. My father taught them to me. He added:

"Don't ever tell white people the truth."

"Always keep your eyes open."

"Always sit with your back up against the wall."

"If you take three steps, they're going to try to push you back two."

"You can't be weak out there. The world will eat you alive."

I was born into a world stained with the stress of surviving while Black. Survival was all there was. It was more essential than emotional awareness and expression. Disclosing the depths of your emotions might put you at risk for being devoured by the world.

The beliefs and behaviors of my father came from the ancestors before him. Those beliefs and behaviors composed the undercurrent of *intergenerational trauma* in my family. Intergenerational trauma is the passing down of the harmful effects of an oppressive event or events from one generation to the next. Many families who suffer intergenerational trauma have emotional problems such as PTSS. The Lassiters' emotional problems stemmed from the oppressive events of white people's perpetual barbarity—the pressing down of my family's spirit through slavery, sharecropping, disrespect, and debasement. Surviving white savagery bred the belief that burying one's emotions was required to endure. This burying required my father—and his father and his father—to deny and minimize any emotion that did not communicate courage. Any emotions that might show vulnerability were dangerous. White people's ever-present barbarity made my father believe that a Black person could not live without armor. It was life-threatening.

Intergenerational trauma is common in a world structured by the whiteness mindset. The whiteness mindset, with its focus on securing power, purpose, and protection, sets up the conditions for genocides, wars, and colonial occupations that harm families across generations. History supplies several examples of historical traumas that have had generational effects, such as the Trail of Tears, the transatlantic slave trade, and the Rwandan genocide. More recently we have the Russo-Ukrainian War, ongoing conflict in the Democratic Republic of the Congo, and the Israeli-Palestinian conflict. The mental health outcomes from such horrific events could include a lack of emotion, possibly manifested as unresolved grief,[6] and self-destructive behaviors such as substance abuse to numb one's emotions. For many people, the effects of intergenerational trauma are quiet but comprehensive. The trauma victims may not overtly display their hurt but it impacts how they see, make sense of, and act in the world. These ways of reacting to the intergenerational trauma of whiteness are passed along.

My father used every tactic he knew to help me forge my own armor. He feared for me. He was scared that someone might use my emotions as an excuse to harm me. It did not matter if my emotions were justified. It did not matter if I had just survived a medical emergency. It did not matter if I was seven years old. In his mind, I needed armor.

That day, in 1991, lying in the hospital, I wanted my father to care for my emotions. He cared for my toughness, my survival. His inability to emotionally connect and treat my vulnerability with gentleness was a symptom of the whiteness mindset that harmed us both.

## CHAPTER 2

# Who God Wants Me to Be

*Who God Wants Me to Be* was spelled out in big bold black letters, backlit by the bright white marquee at the Bell Auditorium. The fifty-two-year-old theater with 2,700 seats loomed large among the short buildings of downtown Augusta, Georgia. My family and I stood in line waiting to see the Christian play. It was 1992. I was eight years old, staring up at my mother as she held my hand. Small for my age, I came up to her waist. She had on a teal peplum dress with fringe at the collar, and her short black hair was tightly curled. To me, she was the most beautiful person in the world.

The line moved and she pulled me forward, snatching me out of my trance of adoration. Inside the theater, a flood of footsteps surrounded us as people searched for their seats.

"Here we are," my father's voice cut through the crowd. My older sister, Thelma, scooted down the aisle first to her seat, and my mother motioned me forward to sit next to her. Thelma smiled as I settled at her side.

"You ready?" she asked as she reapplied her clear, cherry-scented lip gloss. Her Hershey's chocolate skin was smooth and blemish-free. At sixteen years old, she was a second mother and my best friend. From her, I learned how to play UNO and lip sync and dance along to the songs on the radio. Sometimes we would play school and she taught me fractions. At other times we played restaurant, and she would make double-decker sandwiches with extra juicy sour pickles. Next to my mother, she was the star in my world.

"Yep," I said. My eyes were big with expectation. I had never seen a play before, but I loved actors. The ones on TV transported me to awe-inspiring and sometimes terrifying worlds. My sister was a good actor, too. The way she tailored her voice for each character when she read stories to me was spellbinding.

My little brother, Nate, sat on the left of me eagerly awaiting the play. Although he was two years younger than me, we were the same height. "Your boys twins?" strangers in stores often inquired of my mother in their twangy accents. After a while, my mother started to tell them that we were. That response seemed to require less interaction. "They sure are cute," the stranger usually replied and moved on.

That night my brother and I were dressed alike in white oxford short-sleeve shirts and khaki-colored shorts that fell right above our knees. Our socks were pulled above our ankles and we had on black tennis shoes with Velcro fasteners.

Even my father had a warm expression as he settled into his seat. He took off his teal blazer and put his arm around my mother's shoulder. As we waited for the curtain to rise, the gold-plated arched ceiling seemed to glow above the audience. I scanned the room filled with people in their Sunday best. The mocha, sable, and sandalwood complexions of ladies in draped dresses and men in suit vests made the place sparkle. Ushers escorted people to their seats. Men greeted each other with firm handshakes and stern pats on the back. Husbands guided their wives between rows. Women complimented each other's outfits. Children laughed and teased one another. Gospel music played over the speakers, foreshadowing the occasion. My ears caught some of the lyrics to "He's Working It Out for You" by Shirley Caesar.

I pondered the presence of God as I tugged on my starched shirt. There definitely was a stirring energy in the place. The greetings and interactions of the people around me reminded me of how we mingled at church. Was God in this place, too? Was God watching us all now? Was God watching me? My Christian faith felt active and alive in that space.

I was not the first or last little Black boy beguiled by Christianity. The religion was and is a foundational and energizing force for many Black people. I grew up in a house where I was taught that the God of Abraham, Isaac, and Jacob was always present and all-knowing. Most Black families in the United States shared my family's religious beliefs. It's estimated that approximately 91 percent of Black Americans identified as Christian in 1991.[1]

Black people's history and relationship with Christianity is complicated. Prior to European colonialism, heterogeneous groups of people across the African continent practiced a variety of religions and spiritual traditions.[2] Most of those religions were rooted in traditional African spiritual systems and Islam. Christianity was a minor religion on the continent. Most African people were introduced to Christianity in the eighteenth and nineteenth centuries by way of colonization, abduction, and enslavement. Once bound in the Americas, African people were forbidden to evoke their indigenous spirituality. Christian indoctrination was used as a tool to separate African people from their spirituality in order to ensure their service to European colonists.

Many European colonists rationalized their crimes against African people as "God's work." They reasoned that although they may have been enslaving African people, surely it was a better fate for them than the one they would have had without European intervention. They believed that African people, in their own countries and tribes, were evil savages worshipping pagan gods, destined for hell. To many Europeans, African people were barely people at all; their very humanity was doubted. The whiteness mindset convinced many European enslavers that they were saving African souls and thereby bestowing humanity upon them.[3]

The problem was and is that the whiteness mindset narrows what salvation and humanity can look like. One of the benefits of whiteness is the power to define and enforce one's way of life—or in this case one's religion—as the only one that is normal and desirable. The whiteness mindset convinced Europeans that their ways of thinking about God and what it meant to be a human were the only natural options. The world according to this vision looked like Christianity. It looked like sacraments, soul revivals in shacks, and prosperous harvests. It looked like a hierarchy with a white father-figure God on top, white men second, and everyone else below. The whiteness mindset contributes to a humanity that is nothing more than a dehumanizing enterprise that pits people against each other. Christianity shaped by the whiteness mindset uses an image of God to justify colonialism, domination, and exploitation. With white people sitting just below God in their hierarchy, it is divinely ordained that they benefit from these systems of oppression. Other people are lesser beings who are divinely subservient.

By the time Christianity was passed down to me, I inherited a version altered by my ancestors' fights with the whiteness mindset. Many enslaved African people refused to accept Europeans' whiteness-informed version of Christianity that proposed that people are born cut off from the spirit world and could only obtain salvation in an afterlife. Some Africans morphed and reinterpreted Christianity in creative ways to aid their resistance to brutality. They infused European ceremonies with their indigenous African beliefs to create a truly unique relationship with the divine. They used their spirituality as inspiration for rebellion. Enslaved Africans formed their own churches, held their own rituals, and sang their own songs of freedom. In churches, enslaved Africans could gather without the gaze of their masters and overseers. Eventually, Christianity was often a guise for planning meetings about escape and restitution.

Enslaved Africans enacted their intellectual prowess by selecting and interpreting biblical scriptures in ways that affirmed them. For example, whereas many white ministers emphasized passages written by the apostle Paul—an author of several books in the New Testament—that instructed slaves to obey their masters, Black ministers focused on stories of liberation like the Hebrews' escape from Egyptian slavery with God's guidance to the promised land.[4] These stories inspired strength and hope for enslaved people in the face of tyranny, and provided courage that led to revolts on many plantations. Black rebels were often closely identified with heroes in the

Bible. For example, Harriet Tubman was referred to as Moses by many of the people she led to freedom during the American slavery period.[5]

Christianity continued to serve as a resource for Black Americans after emancipation. Black churches provided power, purpose, and protection for many people in the face of continued racism and discrimination.[6] In fact, many civil rights leaders began as ministers in Black churches.[7] Black churches have been and remain critical spaces for Black people's physical, mental, and spiritual liberation.

I was raised in a Southern, Black, Christian family. We held many of the beliefs of the enslaved African and free Black Christian people before us. We went to church to rinse the residue of whiteness off us each week. This cleansing was somatic, rhythmic, and melodic. My favorite Sundays were when the choir performed. My parents were both members, my mother an alto, my father a tenor. Cobalt-blue robes covered the saints from shoulders to shoes as they sang about suffering and salvation. Bodies stood and swayed as the piano and drums intertwined with three-part harmonies. The pianist's left hand played out the bass runs in my favorite songs, with "Order My Steps" at the top of the list. The bass line and lyrics carried me and the other congregants along to a place of hope. The soprano pleaded for guidance and release into the hands of a benevolent God, one who remained faithful even in a chaotic, crumbling world.

I was raised to have unwavering faith in that benevolent father in heaven. I was raised to believe that no matter what it felt like, God was concerned with all aspects of my life. God was concerned about my health. God was invested in how I treated others, the thoughts I kept, the deeds of my hands. I was taught that others could see

God's presence (or the lack thereof) in how my body moved and the sound of my voice. God was—and would be—with me throughout my whole life. God would be there when I died. Then, if I had lived right, I would walk on streets of gold and hurt no more.

I was also taught that God was vengeful. God could be jealous, so I should never love anything or anyone more than God. My parents taught me that God smites his enemies. He forsook those who did not listen and shortened the lives of the disobedient. My mother told me that God would allow my brain to rot if I sinned too much. I was at risk of going to hell for an eternity if I displeased God. This is the God that I lived with: a mercurial, all-powerful deity that wanted the best for me, but would let me suffer for sinning. A God who both exemplified and defied the whiteness mindset.

Back in the theater, as the lights dimmed and the crowd hushed, I felt secure in the sanctity of the space, already filled with the murmur of fellow Christians. The audience applauded as the first actor walked onstage. She had a strong presence as she strutted across the space. The setting was a hair salon, with four stylist chairs evenly placed on the left side of the stage and vanities that served as the stylists' stations, each cluttered with hair dryers, combs, and curling irons.

The sole stylist tied her apron on, smoothed her straight black bob, and opened the shop for business. Almost immediately other characters populated the place and the story began.

The all-Black cast was impressive. The actors' booming voices, big mannerisms, and evocative expressions captivated me. I wasn't the only one—the audience around me were responsive throughout the play, sharing laughter, sighs, and gasps as the plot turned, secrets were revealed, and God was praised. I watched as one character lost her job, another was trapped in an abusive relationship, and another suffered with an unnamed disease. In the end, all the characters gave their life over to Jesus.

It was James, a flamboyant male character who contracted the mysterious disease, who turned my excitement for the play into terror. Four months earlier, Magic Johnson had announced that he was HIV-positive. HIV was the virus that caused AIDS. AIDS was what killed all those white men on the news. AIDS is what I heard my mother say those men deserved for "fucking each other in the ass." Somehow, in my eight-year-old mind, I knew the unnamed disease that James had was AIDS. And somehow, I was convinced that if James could get it, I could get it.

I had not yet referred to myself as "gay." But I knew that I was like James. I was fond of hanging out with girls and gossiping. My stomach felt funny in the presence of the athletic boys at school. I had not yet thought about sex with a boy. I barely knew what it was. But I dreamed of a male friend holding my hand one day. Did that make me doomed to die? I already had sickle cell anemia that could kill me at any time. Was God going to kill me even earlier because I was like James? I was afraid.

Sitting in the dark theater, scared that I had been uniquely and permanently marked for divine retribution, I was, in fact, just the latest victim in a long, painful history of folks othered and reviled by religion narrowed and structured around the values of the whiteness mindset.

Although many Black people had worked to reject the belief that they were inferior in the eyes of God due to their skin color, the oppressive behaviors of a world structured by the whiteness mindset made them hypervigilant in protecting their humanity. It was as if they believed it could be taken away or diminished. This is part of the racist socialization that Dr. DeGruy highlighted as a symptom of Post Traumatic Slave Syndrome. Unfortunately, too many Black people believed that sexual and gender diversity beyond heterosexuality put their humanity at risk. Religion interpreted and enacted with the whiteness mindset was used to keep Black sexually and gender-expansive people in check. Because the whiteness mindset assumes we live in a world of scarcity, competition becomes an act of survival ensuring access to limited resources, whether material, psychological, or spiritual. Effectively, some heterosexual Black people used religion to justify fragmenting their families and communities based on sexual orientation and gender identity, and to annihilate behaviors and beliefs outside of heterosexuality.[8] By condemning others based on sexual orientation, they were able to place themselves higher up in a whiteness-constructed hierarchy—they would be more worthy, more beloved by God than "those people." Just as Christianity was used by European colonists to justify the enslavement of Africans in the colonies, it was and is still used by some Black Christians to condemn sexually and gender-expansive people. This *horizontal oppression*—oppression of one marginalized group by members of that same marginalized group—harms all Black people.

In the early nineties when I was child, approximately 83 percent of Black American people reported on the General Social Survey that they identified as either a fundamentalist or moderate Protestant.[9] Eighty percent of them believed that homosexuality was always wrong.[10] My parents agreed. I agreed.

I sat in that theater fearful, not of something I had done, but of what I believed lived silently inside of me. I thought of James as the ghost of me yet to come. He was the only male hairstylist in the salon. A tall, skinny man with a light complexion, he wore tight pants and shirts that exposed his lower stomach while sashaying around calling everyone "chile." He was fun-loving, gentle, and the butt of several jokes. Overall, you got the sense that everyone liked him, although they thought he was misguided.

Despite being disowned by his family and being warned by a few "true Christians" to change his ways, he did not heed their warnings and continued to dress as he did and shared vivid details about his male sexual partners with the female patrons in the beauty salon. Toward the end of the play, James was ill, scared, and outcast. In the penultimate scene, he went to church crying out to be saved during the altar call at the end of the service: "I want to be the man God wants me to be."

Everyone in the audience cheered and clapped at his repentance. I was horrified. After that play, I fretted about hell almost daily. Was hell in store for James? Was the lake of fire waiting for me? Twelve years would pass before I stopped fearing God's wrath.

✦✦

"There is nothing for you to be afraid of," the skinny, bald white professor told me.

It was 2004, I was a sophomore at Georgia College & State University. My best friend, Brenden, had convinced me to accompany him to his friend's house for dinner. Unbeknownst to me, his friend was an assistant professor in the religion department at our school.

Dr. David Banks smiled at me from behind his thin, rimless spectacles. I gripped the cool glass of water in my hand as my stomach fluttered in the immaculate kitchen that smelled like chocolate-chip oatmeal cookies. I was fascinated and nervous. His house was a treasure trove of books. Every room had shelves filled with texts from authors like Brad Gooch, Toni Morrison, James Baldwin, and Flannery O'Connor. It was like his house was his own personal library. I was enthralled.

But I also felt uneasy. Dr. Banks was a proud, openly gay man. I had never met one of those before. Brenden was the only gay person I knew, and he was my age. But Dr. Banks was an adult, a professor, a white man. And he was loud and out. He was not suffering from an unspecified disease. He seemed to be enjoying his life. He did not work in a hair salon. He did not say "chile" all the time. He was a nerd, like me.

Brenden smiled at me. His espresso-colored skin was flawless. His eyes were soft, comforting.

"But aren't you afraid we're going to hell?" I whispered to Dr. Banks.

"No," he said with more confidence than I had ever imagined having at that point in my life. "One, there is nothing wrong with being gay. Two, there is no such thing as hell."

I sat there in disbelief.

"But the Bible says..."

Dr. Banks held up his hand. He smiled.

"Follow me." He stood up and led me to a bookcase in his formal living room. He scanned the shelf and selected two books. The first one was *What the Bible Really Says About Homosexuality* by Dr.

Daniel A. Helminiak. The second was *Rescuing the Bible from Fundamentalism* by Bishop John Shelby Spong.

"Read these and then let's discuss."

As a good little bookworm, I did as I was told and devoured the texts in a matter of weeks. My mind was blown free of the clutter of sermons that made me believe my existence was a sin. The authors of those books provided compelling arguments against the fundamentalist literal interpretations of the Bible that I had grown up with. They even argued that homosexuality was not an abomination. Dr. Banks started me on my path of spiritual salvation through intellectual rebellion.

As I continued expanding the bounds of my knowledge, I read the work of Dr. Ronald Long, a former professor of religion at Hunter College, who challenged the argument that homosexuality was a sin in his book *Men, Homosexuality, and the Gods.* In conversations with Dr. Banks, I shared my amazement with the words on those pages.

Sitting on Dr. Banks's deep brown suede couch with Annie Lennox's "Legend in My Living Room" playing in the background, my mind opened as we dissected the scriptures in context, considering the cultural values and traditions that had shaped them—and how they had been misused in the modern day.

"Have mercy," I exclaimed and took a breath. My friendship with Dr. Banks blew up the walls of condemnation that scarred me as child. My scars began to heal and smooth as I continued to read more books from Dr. Banks's library.

As I learned more, my eyes began to open wider to the function of condemning difference, whether based on race, sexuality, or something else. Audre Lorde provides powerful insight in her 1984 book *Sister Outsider* when she discussed the actions often taken by people in response to difference.

> We have *all* been programmed to respond to the human differences between us with fear and loathing and to handle that difference in one of three ways: ignore it, and if that is not possible, copy it if we think it is dominant, or destroy it if we think it is subordinate. But we have no patterns for relating across our human differences as equals. As a result, those differences have been misnamed and misused in the service of separation and confusion.

While I do not propose that pre-colonial African people were free of bias toward same-sex-attracted or same-gender-loving people, or any people deemed different, the post-colonial treatment of sexually expansive people by Africans and their descendants across the globe mirrors the model set forth by European colonists in their treatment of African people and their differences. With their myopic focus on scarcity, fragmentation, and annihilation, European people began a process of defining and redefining African people. The definitions conjured by them and their offspring—white Americans—often cast Black people not only as other, but as a *deviant* other.

European explorers first defined African people as primitive. Dr. Stephen O. Murray and Dr. Will Roscoe reported in their 2001 book *Boy-Wives and Female Husbands* that the primitive African person served to highlight the differences between Western and non-Western culture. Whatever the African person was, the European person was not and vice versa. In contrast to the sophistication of European culture, African people were judged to be "close to nature, ruled by instinct, culturally unsophisticated... heterosexual, [their] sexual energies and outlets devoted exclusively to their 'natural' purpose: biological reproduction."[11]

Early European anthropologists bolstered this heterosexist claim with reports of the absence of same-sex relationships and practices among African people. When they did acknowledge it, they either explained it as a necessity due to lack of women available for men or a temporary phase among adolescents. However, historians and anthropologists have found evidence that clearly prove that the assertion is fictional.[12]

Several African tribes throughout the African continent had members who engaged in same-sex sexual practices and had same-sex romantic relationships. In Africa, however, egalitarian same-sex relationships—in which both partners have relatively equal social statuses and roles—were not as widespread as they were among Europeans.

Murray and Roscoe reported that the two most common and widespread types of same-sex relationships among males were age-based and gender-based. Age-based patterns of same-sex relationships featured a younger partner, who was receptive, and an older partner, who was usually the penetrator and often served as a mentor figure. In gender-based same-sex relationships, the penetrating partner was not considered to be anything other than heterosexual. However, the penetrated partner was expected to perform the gendered role of a woman. That meant dressing and behaving like a woman.

In some African societies, same-sex sexual activity was a rite of passage. For example, among tribes in Cameroon and in parts of West Africa, it was common among children and adolescents to engage in sexual activity with members of the same sex before marriage.[13] Some even continued their same-sex sexual activities into adulthood. It was more common for African women to enter same-sex relationships as adults than it was for their male counterparts. There were even tribes composed entirely of women who worked together and had romantic partnerships. It was not unheard of for widows to take the money left by their husbands and start symbiotic romantic relationships with other women—often younger—for whom they provided financially. Some scholars suggest that the Agojie, the all-woman army portrayed in *The Woman King*, were an example of women who lived outside of traditional feminine gender roles.[14] The evidence presented by Dr. Murray and Dr. Roscoe—and the other authors—in their anthology provide substantial proof that homosexuality is not a foreign transmission to African people and their descendants: Black people in the diaspora. Given this evidence, it is clear that too many Black people are misinformed when they repeat the tired line that "homosexuality is a white thing meant to destroy the Black family." My parents and fellow church members were part of the misinformed. Their misinformation had eight-year-old me scared out of my mind. I believed that my difference was a betrayal of my family and I would be disowned by them, my church, and my peers.

The European notions of African sexuality were codified among American enslavers and dictated the beliefs and behaviors of white people regarding Black people—both past and present. According to Murray and Roscoe, American enslavers conceptualized the enslaved Africans as "oversexed, to have animalistic large genitals and to be characterized by predatory sexual behavior." Enslaved African men were perceived as violent bucks, a word that conjures the image of a beast. This term had the effect of stripping enslaved African men of their humanity and linking them with the animal kingdom. Enslavers viewed African women as sexually deviant as well. They formulated African women as either asexual domestics or hypersexual seductresses. These depictions allowed enslavers to cast African women in the roles of cooks, maids, and nurses and to justify the rape and sexual torture inflicted upon these women. The sex-negative stereotypes of Black people have evolved over time to include such permutations as "soft man" and "Instagram model."

Considering this history and ongoing tensions, it is not surprising that the policing of sexuality is rampant in Black communities. Too many heterosexual Black people respond to the sex negativity hurled at them by white people by turning on Black sexually and gender-expansive people. Sexually and gender-expansive Black people become the scapegoats for the ills of the Black community.[15] "If only those people would act right and stop being ungodly or acting like dykes and sissies, us Black people could get somewhere in the world" becomes the vocal assumption.

Too many Black people have ingested the inherent lies that make up the whiteness mindset, the racist and pseudo-religious myths about sexuality. These distortions result in them living through the assumptions and values of the whiteness mindset. Living by these assumptions destroys Black unity. Some Black heterosexual people think of themselves as somehow better than Black sexually and gender-expansive people. They unconsciously compete for normalcy and power—as defined by the whiteness mindset.

This whiteness-constricted Christianity played out in my childhood home. God was the lawmaker, the Bible was the law, and my parents were the enforcers. Joshua and Joycelyn often communicated their disapproval of anything non-heteronormative.

"Take that wig off your head and put some bass in your voice," my father would scold when he thought I was talking like a girl.

"I don't want you watching that," my mother would say when she saw me laughing at the "Men on Films" sketch on *In Living Color.*

"Stop all that carrying on like a sissy," my father admonished when I did my Broadway jazz-style dance to the theme song of *The Nanny.*

"Elaine is out there sleeping with other womens now. She's gonna go straight to hell," I overhead my mother commenting to my aunt.

This policing of my sexuality and gender expression convinced me I was the deviant "other," and I responded by isolating myself, hiding my emotions and thoughts from others, feeling depressed, and believing that I was flawed and sinful. And as a flawed and sinful person, I believed I would eventually be disowned and disconnected from my family and God. Ultimately, I would be doomed to hell—the ultimate form of annihilation. As a child, I did not yet understand that religion was also something that was societally constructed. All I knew was that according to what I read in the Bible and what I was told by my parents, I was at risk of wretchedness.

After seeing the play, I was determined not to be like James. I fervently prayed to God every night to make me into the man he wanted me to be. I prayed to God to take away the tingly feeling I got in my genitals when I saw handsome boys at school. I prayed to be heterosexual more than I prayed to be healed from sickle cell anemia.

It didn't work. I still liked boys. And the more I prayed, the more hopeless I became. The more I hated myself for my failure to pray hard enough. By the time I was in middle school, I stopped praying for God to make me heterosexual and started to pray that he'd let me die in my sleep. It was better to die before I acted on my sexual feelings, before I contracted some deadly disease like James.

As a child, I thought that being like James would mean that not only would I be damned to hell, but I would be rejected by Black people, too. As Audre Lorde suggested, many Black Americans have given too much power to arbitrary differences such as sexuality and gender expression.[16] This false power is often destructive in nature, and its use is greatly influenced by European colonists and their whiteness mindsets. Europeans did not introduce same-sex sexual behaviors and attraction to Africans but, through the lens of whiteness-infused Christianity, encouraged Africans and their descendants to distrust and dehumanize sexually and gender-expansive people.

My parents' heterosexist attitudes and behaviors were rooted in the whiteness mindset. These harmful beliefs are oppressive and potentially fragment Black sexually and gender-expansive people from their loved ones and God, leaving them in fear of damnation. The whiteness mindset passed down through generations of religious and secular myths about the limitations of Black humanness made the full range of Black sexuality something to be despised. Some Black people really believe that it is unnatural for Black people to occupy every space along the spectrum of sexuality and gender expression. Every other race may do so, but not Black people. This whiteness mindset contributed to my parents' attempts to stamp out my authentic self and left me unable to explore and be who I really was. The years of fear and suppression left me depressed and suicidal for much of my youth—a painful inheritance created by the whiteness mindset.

As an adult, I eventually learned that it was not my sexuality or gender expression that kept me from being who God wanted me to be. Instead, it was the invisible whiteness mindset imposed on my family through religion and their misguided attempts to combat racist myths about Black sexuality that plagued me and many others in Black communities. But in 1992 as an eight year old, my mind had not yet been liberated by that knowledge.

✦✦

After the play, my family and I filed into the packed parking lot. Once inside our blue Buick, my father cranked up the car and pressed play on the Georgia Mass Choir's *Hold On, Help Is on the Way* cassette. My mother turned the volume down some. My father drove with a smile on his face, humming along to "Come On in the Room" while my mother sang softly. In the backseat, I was lost in my head, drowning in dread. My sister turned and looked down at me.

"What did you think of the play?" she asked.

My mother turned around to hear my answer. I looked at my sister and then my mother. I felt hot. My eyes watered. My vision blurred. I sat there willing myself to speak for what felt like forever.

"You liked it?" my sister offered with glee in her voice.

I nodded.

"Good." My mother grinned and turned back around.[17]

## CHAPTER 3

# You Can't Buy Whiteness

The high school locker room was where two separate worlds collided. Amid the clang of lockers and sea of bodies, both jocks and ballet boys undressed. The athletes switched from jeans to mesh shorts that hung and clung to bulges and buns—and made me nervous. As a ballet boy, I was scared that the tights I stretched and stepped into would reveal the secrets in my head and stimulation in my groin. I was filled with excitement at the sight of my peers' taut bodies, and tense with anxiety that those peers might catch me sneaking a look at them in their Jordans and tank tops. While my scrawny physique seemed to be struggling and stalling along the path of puberty, their bodies had reached a pubescent climax.[1] The smell they gave off was intoxicating, intimidating, and alluring. In the locker room, I averted my eyes.

Abercrombie & Fitch embodied my locker room fantasy, but there I did not have to guard my gaze. In the store on the second floor of the Augusta Mall, the scent of Abercrombie's inescapable signature cologne filled my nostrils. The smell of grain, cardamom, lemon, orange, and fir swirled together, exciting me, conjuring up the locker room, and I fixated, wide-eyed, on the large poster images of shirtless boys.

The guys on the posters were tall, muscled, handsome, and white. They were having fun and people liked them. They had cookouts and beach parties. They streaked on college greens holding up collared shirts to conceal their crotches. They did not fear consequences. I envied the joy and freedom on their faces as they flexed their muscles and roughhoused with each other. In one of my favorite pictures, twelve guys wore nothing but boxer shorts. Standing in a lake, they jumped on each other's backs. One guy had another in a faux headlock. Bare chests and six-pack abs slid against each other. I swooned.

Oh, how I wanted a boy to *see* me, to romp around with me, to hug me. No guy had ever hugged me against his bare chest as we smiled for the camera. The images sent me into a trance every time I entered the store. They allowed me to imagine a different life than the one I had. The life I had was that of a Black, five-foot-two, skinny, unathletic (ballet didn't count) nerd. No one seemed to find me attractive. I was an unpopular, poor, reduced-lunch kid. I had no real friends. And worst of all, I was a sissy.

In Abercrombie & Fitch, with the lights dimmed around me, my misery didn't shine so bright. The whirlwind of images enraptured me in promises of acceptance, attractiveness, and love. I wanted to believe that I could be like the boys in the posters: popular, virile, smelling great, looking good, being touched by strong hands. I wanted to live the image Abercrombie & Fitch was selling.

A&F's image in the late 1990s and early 2000s, according to their *Look Book*, was "natural, classic, and current" with an emphasis on style.[2] But what I saw advertised was a white, privileged life filled with fun and sensuality. I wanted to be white, rich, and desirable.

To be those things would mean that I had value in the world. The whiteness mindset had convinced my father that men were brutes who demanded respect. This type of maleness was exemplified by lawmen and vigilantes. The whiteness mindset persuaded me that men were affluent, trendy, and carefree. My ideal maleness was defined by materialism and exemplified by the Abercrombie & Fitch boys. Both versions left me feeling inadequate.

I thought that maybe I could buy my self-esteem at Abercrombie & Fitch. If I could buy a shirt or pair of ripped jeans, then everyone would think that I was stylish, classic, and current. Maybe even sexy? It would give me the benefits of whiteness that I needed to be accepted by my peers. But the benefits of whiteness I wanted had a cost. It was $229. So I went to work, teaching dance at a church camp.

It was the summer between my junior and senior year of high school. My shoulders shimmied and my hips swirled as I sang along with Janet Jackson's "Someone to Call My Lover," changing "girl" to "guy." I was tidying up the repurposed math classroom where I had taught hip-hop, jazz, and African dance to students all day. As I pulled desks from the edges of the room and pushed them back into the center, I took small breaks to ball-change and chest pop.

Alone in the room, I floated on Janet's syrupy, innocent voice, full of longing. I, too, ached for a lover. Someone who would love and protect me. Stick up for me and take care of me. He would rescue me from the closet and teach me how to live out loud, not hide my truth. He would think that my small, skinny brown body was cute, adorable, and sexy. His big hand would enclose my small one and he would lead me through the world, revealing all its splendor. Maybe I couldn't be the protector my father wanted me to be, but I dreamed of dating one.

"Hey, Jonathan, your mom's out there." I was jerked from my reverie. Roxanne stood in the doorway of the classroom.

"Oh," I said, trying to compose myself.

"Were you coming up with a new dance to teach the kids tomorrow?" Roxanne asked.

"Yeah," I fibbed. "Cute sneakers," I said, changing the subject, scared she might have noticed my effeminate moves and comment on them.

"I had to get out of those wedges. They were hurting my feet."

"Teaching Black history all day in those things has to be killer," I said as we walked out together. "I'll see you tomorrow." I waved to Roxanne and hurried to meet my mother out front in our minivan.

"How was your day?" my mother asked as I hopped in and buckled up. I saw her eyes look me over in the rearview mirror.

"It was good. I taught them a dance to Jessica Simpson's 'I Think I'm in Love with You' today. I'm thinking about using a Janet Jackson song tomorrow."

"How did you get to be so creative?" She beamed.

"I guess I get it from my mama." I cheesed back.

That Friday, I got my paycheck. It was $234 after taxes. After giving my mother $70 for gas money and saving $64 to buy food for my lunch for the week, I had $100 left over for the next two weeks. Out of that $100, I put away $40 for my dream wardrobe to be purchased at Abercrombie & Fitch. By the end of the summer, I had $240 to spend.

✦✦

Growing up Black, chronically ill, low-income, and gay, I did not think of myself as a prize. At least not a physically desirable one. I had pride in my intelligence. I was a bookworm and excelled academically. That didn't win me any friends though. It pushed me to the margins. The world around me—MTV, my classmates, and all the teen movies—told me that to be worthy of acceptance and desire, I had to be cool. To be cool, I had to be rich, athletic, heterosexual, masculine, good-looking, and funny. In the world around me, these traits were primarily found in white boys.

Black heterosexual boys could be most of those things. But they were rarely rich. Sure, I knew Black boys whose parents bought them Air Jordans. They may have shopped at Journeys and Jimmy Jazz, but their parents were not doctors, lawyers, or accountants. As far as I knew, maybe they were a nurse or supervisor at the local plant. They did not have the sort of prestige that I imagined the parents of the white boys in the Abercrombie posters had. And Black sissy boys like myself were even further away from the pinnacle of cool. My hunger for self-worth was wrapped up in the values and benefits of the whiteness mindset. I believed that clothes, money, and muscles would give me a sense of purpose and pride, protecting me from self-loathing and the punishments of a capitalist society.

The whiteness mindset influences one to think of life as a condition defined by limitation: limited goods, limited time, and limited life. If there's never enough to go around, the people who *have*—beauty, popularity, material wealth, power—are more valuable than those who do not. When the world has limited resources, the people who are able to compete and win them become the victors. The victors feel powerful and can use that power to protect themselves from competition and the risk of losing their material and psychological gains. The Abercrombie boys of the world win, while the skinny nerds lose.

At the deepest level, our psychological mindsets inform how we understand ourselves and the world around us. Since the 1970s, African-centered psychologists in the United States have proposed that human beings are spiritual beings having a physical experience.[3] Part of this inherent spiritual nature is understanding and living in a way that prioritizes the oneness of all other spirit beings. In contrast, the whiteness mindset does not perceive that a spiritual oneness exists, or ignores that oneness. A person infected by the whiteness mindset has an individual understanding of self and looks to find happiness through competition, material acquisition, and consumption. Said plainly, the whiteness mindset sets up the conditions for materialism and consumerism that undergird capitalism.[4] If we believe we are completely separate from others, competition becomes inevitable. If we are separate from oneness, our self-worth is no longer a divine, innate fact, but instead dependent on how much we succeed in life.

The whiteness mindset I possessed as a teenager convinced me that I needed Abercrombie & Fitch to be whole and valuable as a man. In a world structured by the whiteness mindset, all aspects of the self and the world get entangled, including ideas about what makes for desirable maleness.

Part of what I loved so much about the boys in the Abercrombie posters was that they exuded the *right* kind of masculinity. They played sports. They made girls blush and smile by picking them up or splashing ocean water on them. Their exposed six-pack stomachs and well-developed arms portrayed virility and vitality. These traits were things that I did not perceive myself as possessing.

The boys on the poster did not suffer from sickle cell anemia. They were not in and out of the hospital. They did not have to take medication every day. Their mothers did not encourage them to drink what felt like gallons of water every day in hopes of staying healthy. They were able-bodied, disease-free. The white boys whose images hung in the Abercrombie store were the right kind of boys. They were the winners who had reaped the benefits of whiteness, and I wanted to be like them.

In addition to the lure of the right kind of masculinity, individualism and materialism—values of whiteness—were also on full display by Abercrombie. The models in their ads played rich-people sports like rugby. They hung out at lake houses, beach resorts, and ski chalets in exotic locations. In my teenage mind, all of them were at least middle-class. They lived the good life of rich white people.

My father could not provide me riches but he micromanaged my maturation into manhood. As far back as I could remember, I was being told how to be a man. Not a boy, a man. There was rarely space to be frivolous or immature. Black boys don't get that luxury.[5] Manhood was a serious matter. In his mind, my father's main job was to protect me and teach me how to be a protector.

My father couldn't imagine maleness like mine: artistic, playful, light. Those things were not appropriate for a Black boy. That scared him. It might get me harmed. That softness made me a punk, a faggot. Being those things might get me killed. Like Sethe in Toni Morrison's *Beloved*, he'd rather kill me himself than have me wrecked by racists.

My father's internalized whiteness mindset hurt him.

Unbeknownst to him, his embodiment of manhood was psychologically white. He could not recognize that although he hated white people, he lived values consistent with a whiteness mindset. The whiteness mindset led him to pass the harm done to him on to his family. It left me afraid of my father and questioning how I would step into my own version of manhood. But my version was also distorted by the whiteness mindset.

✦✦

It was the last Saturday before I started eleventh grade, and my mother had already agreed to drive me to the mall. Today was the day. My mission was to buy an outfit from Abercrombie & Fitch. Normally, my mother bought my clothes from Kmart, Burlington Coat Factory, and Citi Trends. Truthfully, I thought the bargain clothes I got from those places were cute. But they did not win me popularity points. The trendy classmates I envied all seemed to shop at places like the Gap, Structure, American Eagle, A&F. Finally, my time had come. The new addition to my wardrobe would finally transform me into someone I wanted to be.

Guitar riffs from John Mayer's "Love Song for No One" glided into my ears as I entered the store. I was in a dream. I perused the polo shirts, solids and stripes in every color of the rainbow. My fingers brushed the soft cotton. I savored each second as I searched for just the right shirt.

My eyes must have been sparkling when the sales associate approached me. He was a poster model in the flesh. A preppy Josh Hartnett. He wore a white rugby polo with navy stripes and khaki cargo shorts with a broad blue fabric belt at his waist. He put his hand on the rack next to me. His toned bicep and forearm looked so strong. His shiny dark hair fell just below his ears and framed his face as he looked down at me.

"Hi, my name's Drew. May I help you with something today?" His voice was deep, masculine. He had a kind look in his eyes.

I was so happy. It was like I was being seen for the first time. He made me feel special.

The whiteness mindset had infected my beliefs about physical attraction and sexual desirability. Drew's dark brown hair and eyes, his middle-classness, and his whiteness-approved masculinity made him irresistible. He was everything I wanted to be. He was everything I wanted in the person whom I wished would want me. Scholars have often discussed white beauty standards in terms of physical aesthetics and characteristics.[6] But what made Drew and those white models so appealing to me went beyond the skin, nose, or hair. It was the power, purpose, and protection that the prevailing whiteness mindset gave them. They were able to walk through the world with their way of life affirmed as the normal and natural way of being. They got to live in a world that was set up to protect them from having to consider the harms of whiteness. They got to live in a world that empowered them to be assertive and center their comfort. The whiteness mindset structured the world to increase white boys' access to expensive clothes, beautiful places, and social esteem.

Their white maleness meant they belonged in all the best places. I wanted to be in all the best places with Drew.

Looking at Drew, my mind flew off into fantasy. I wrapped my arms around him. I could smell his teenage scent mixed with the store's cologne. My head rested on his chest. He embraced me.

"It's all right. I've got you."

"I never thought someone like you would even care about someone like me."

"What do you mean? You're perfect. I think you're beautiful. I love the way you look up at me. I'm going to take care of you from here on out. I won't let anyone hurt you. You're mine."

"Hey!" The sales associate's voice snapped me back to reality. He was right in my face. "May I help you with something?" he repeated with curious coffee-colored eyes.

"Umm, yes. I'm just looking at some shirts and maybe some jeans. Back-to-school shopping, you know?" I tried to recover.

"We just got these in," he said, motioning to the shirts. "I think you would look nice in this one." Drew picked up a solid dark green polo and held it up against my chest. "Yeah, that's your color."

I smiled.

"And over here, we have the jeans. Let's see what will look good on you." He led me to a wall across the store with jeans folded on shelves that went up to the ceiling. "You think you might want to try any of these on?"

After finding some jeans, I followed him to the dressing room. He pointed to an open stall.

"Let me know if you need anything else. And remember, if anyone asks who helped you, my name is Drew." He winked.

I left the store with two polo shirts and two pairs of jeans. I had done it. I had bought cool clothes. I had purchased a piece of whiteness: a sense of purpose and esteem sanctioned by materialism.

Long before I stepped into an Abercrombie, bent on buying my way to worthiness, I was internalizing whiteness in big and small ways. Whiteness had harmed my grandfather and my father by forcing them to live in a world that limited their access to basic resources. They coped by withdrawing or exploding in anger. Living in the emotionally tumultuous environment this created, I felt disconnected from them and believed that something was wrong with me. The world around me, peers and media, seemed to confirm that there was something indeed wrong with me.

My family did not succeed in the ways society judged to be valuable, namely earning a lot of money and possessing expensive things. According to the world around me, structured by the whiteness mindset, this made us losers in the game of life. I wanted to win, to possess all the things whiteness gave you. By the time I was a teenager, my internalization of the whiteness mindset had reached a critical point. I was poisoned by it.

My sanity was suffering because I was trying to operate in a model of insanity. Instead of resisting the narrowed materialistic and individualistic world of the Abercrombie white boys, I attempted to crush myself into those boxes. Dr. Amos N. Wilson, a Black psychologist and author of *The Falsification of Afrikan Consciousness*, posits that the whiteness mindset and its corresponding values (i.e., individualism, materialism, and competition) set up an unhealthy world. He warned that "we cannot use these [white] people who are criminals, who have the world on the edge of suicide... as models of normality!"[7]

Dr. Wilson explained, "This system is one then that on one hand teases and provokes, and on the other hand denies. Its individualistic sensibility encourages us to dream big dreams, to imagine the best of everything is within our grasp and within our reach, and at the same time it denies the possibilities for those dreams to become reality. . . . Once the victim accepts the ideology of individualism, he is then set (when he fails to make it in the system) to blame himself in a very destructive sort of way; to begin to question his or her competence, to doubt his or her ability, to doubt his or her worth and ultimately, to hate himself."

That summer, my internalization of the whiteness mindset tormented me as I tried to fight against structural odds created by it (e.g., racism, poverty). I was trying to live according to its values. The whiteness mindset convinced me that I needed a polo shirt with a moose logo embroidered on the chest to be valuable. And I believed the lie. The real proof of my success would be how my classmates responded.

✦✦

Through black wire-framed glasses, I stared in the school bathroom mirror at my pristine, perfectly ironed polo shirt. I had tucked the polo half in and half out of the straight-legged faded blue jeans that hung from my hips. My crinkly kneecaps peeked from behind the fray at the knees. I patted the mini afro that I was growing out so that I could eventually get it twisted. I'd spent all morning picking it out so that there were no naps. I smiled as I caressed the cowrie shell necklace around my neck. I liked the image in the mirror. For that moment, the inferiority and self-hatred I felt was staved off.

When the bell rang at 7:50 a.m., I sat down at my homeroom desk. No one had yet commented on my clothes. It would only be a matter of time. They had to have noticed. After we said the Pledge of Allegiance, the school announcements were broadcasted. My classmates chattered around me. My teacher busied herself with her grade book, peering at us from behind her desk every so often.

"Jonathan." A'Nya Johnson startled me from my preoccupation.

"Good morning, A'Nya." I turned to her, smiling. This had to be it. A'Nya was one of the pretty, popular girls who always wore Tommy Hilfiger and Charlotte Russe. She loved fashion. She must have noticed my outfit.

"I forgot my pencil today. Do you have one I can borrow?"

"Sure," I said, deflated. I reached into the top pocket of my book-bag and handed her a No. 2 pencil.

"Thanks." She smiled sweetly. "Oh..." she continued. "Is something different about you?"

I smiled back. My eyes were wide.

"I like those new Payless shoes you got, Jonathan." Bennett Langston laughed, sitting behind A'Nya. His silky cornrows were perfect, like curved arrows against his scalp. He was so handsome, so mean. His friends started to laugh around him.

# Part 2

# All I Want to Do Is Be a Psychologist

## CHAPTER 4

# "Cause We Niggas and That's All We Ever Gonna Be"

The Pussycat Dolls' "When I Grow Up" was blasting on my iPod nano as I rode on the Muni headed to Outer Richmond, in San Francisco. I tapped my feet as I sat on the hard plastic seat and shimmied my shoulders. The rhythm pulsed through me. On the two and the four, I felt excited and sexy. On the one and the three, I was nervous.

San Francisco, the land of rainbow milk and honey, was the setting of my new adventure. I was starting my doctoral education. After years of being an honor roll student, a dean's list undergrad, and an AmeriCorps Volunteers in Service to America (VISTA) member, I had finally been accepted into graduate school to become Dr. Jonathan Mathias Lassiter.

The study of the mind had become a calling after years of struggling with my own mental health due to my sexual orientation and sickle cell anemia that had led to recurrent storms of depression, anxiety, and suicidal ideation. Dr. Banks's mentorship, good friends, and developing my own personal spirituality allowed me to begin to heal, and inspired me to become a mental health professional to help other Black and same-gender-loving people like me.

So, there I was in San Francisco in 2008, taking the first step to becoming the first doctor in my family, and a healer for my people. In just six years, I was going to be a psychologist. But first, I had to find a place to live.

Outer Richmond was far out there. The train ride from where I was staying in Chinatown with my friend Jameson to the apartment I was scheduled to see took almost an hour. Jameson had arrived in San Francisco about a year before me to pursue his master's degree of fine arts in creative writing. He let me bunk with him as I got acclimated to the city. However, his landlord was not in a gracious mood. He gave me an ultimatum a week after I arrived.

"You pay rent, or you get out."

I was never planning on staying long-term with Jameson, but I needed longer than a week to secure housing. His landlord did not care. My search kicked into overdrive.

San Francisco was getting one of its 263 days of sunshine, but the temperature was an incongruously chilly 68 degrees. I was born and raised in Augusta, Georgia, where the average temperature is 92 degrees in July. Even New York summers got steamy. I didn't know what was going on with San Francisco, but this was a part of my whole new world.

I looked down at the MapQuest directions I had printed out before I left my friend's apartment and made note of the stop where I was supposed get off. Once off the train, I took in my surroundings.

The three-story houses all seemed so narrow and slammed against each other as I ascended the hill. Some of them looked as if they had been renovated not too long ago. Others looked like they could use a good power wash. I smoothed the hoodie that I was wearing. My black-and-silver metallic Converse high-top sneakers were not doing my feet any favors as I forged ahead. It was almost like I was strolling shoeless on concrete. I walked a lot in New York but those San Francisco hills were something different.

Finally, I reached my destination and rang the doorbell. A few minutes passed and there was no answer. I rang again and hoped they were home. *I have an appointment*, I reminded myself in my head. Someone peeked out of a window, their face like an owl staring out with dark eyes. I smiled warmly, trying to look as nonthreatening as possible. Pulling the MapQuest directions out of my pocket, I checked the address again. I was definitely at the right place at the right time.

"Yes?" A short, wrinkled Asian woman answered the door. She looked at me sternly. The way she stared without blinking made it seem as if she had consumed too much caffeine. She stood directly in the center of the doorway, as if to block me from entering.

"I'm Jonathan. We spoke on the phone earlier today," I said deferentially, the way I had been raised to interact with elders. She finally blinked. She didn't seem to know what I was talking about.

"What do you want?" No kindness was detected in her voice.

"I'm the graduate student. We spoke about the room you have for rent today," I said slowly and deliberately.

Maybe there was a language barrier? She didn't seem to have a hard time understanding me on the phone. But maybe my Southern accent was coming out.

"I'm Jonathan." I smiled again.

"Oh, you're Jonathan?" A note of recognition in her voice. She narrowed her eyes, taking me in.

"Yes." I grinned, thankful she now seemed to remember. "You said that I could take a tour of the house and if I liked it, we could discuss my moving in." Optimism coated my voice.

"The room has been rented," she replied and began to close the door.

"What? We just talked three hours ago," I protested.

"Things move fast. Goodbye." The door closed.

I stood there stunned, trying to make sense of what happened.

My inner voice said, "Get off this stoop, girl, you Black. She might call the cops." I wanted to cry but I heard my parents' voices in my head: "Keep it moving or you gon be homeless out here."

I took a deep breath and headed back toward the train stop. Hopefully, I would have better luck at my next appointment. Waiting for the train, I pressed play on my iPod nano and let Danity Kane's "Damaged" float into my ears. That slight would be far from the last I suffered in the Bay Area.

In San Francisco, I learned a lot about the intersections of whiteness, sexual orientation, identity, and power. I moved to San Francisco in July 2008 to begin my graduate studies in clinical psychology. I was excited about moving to "one of the most liberal cities in the US"—as I had heard it described by friends and colleagues. I had been told that people in San Francisco accepted everyone: people from the global majority, LGBTQ+ people, immigrants, everyone. However, upon arrival in the city, I found that acceptance was neither guaranteed nor unconditional.

My interactions with people in the city seemed to be colored by, well, my color. Specifically, it seemed that I was consistently being regarded primarily as a Black. Not Black American but just black[1] with all its negative stereotypes and connotations:

soiled or stained with dirt
gloomy; pessimistic; dismal
deliberately harmful; inexcusable
boding ill; sullen or hostile; threatening
without any moral quality or goodness; evil; wicked
marked by disaster or misfortune
undesirable; substandard; potentially dangerous
deliberately false or intentionally misleading

My skin color was that of a Black person. A lot of non-Black people I met in the city seemed fixated on that fact. Nothing else mattered. I was black first. My sexual orientation, spirituality, educational attainment, and aspirations all seemed to be secondary to my skin color.

Now, I was not naïve about racism and I knew it existed everywhere, even in the "most liberal" places. But I had let my guard down and expected a less racially burdened experience in San Francisco than in other places known for their blatant prejudice. In fact, the racial bias in San Francisco felt more insidious to me than the outright discrimination I had experienced in my home state of Georgia. In Georgia, you know where you stand. Black people in this neighborhood beware; in this neighborhood you are welcomed. Yet, San Francisco projected an air of acceptance while implicitly engaging in various forms of bias—not the least being racial.

"Oh, *you're* Jonathan?" This time those words came from a thin Asian man who looked too young to have the liver spots that dotted his face. His jet-black hair and beard ruffled a little as the breeze made its way into the house behind him.

That was my third appointment of the day, and I was greeted the same way by all the people to whom I had previously spoken on the phone. On the phone, landlords had encouraged my visit, approving of my arrival in the city as a graduate student. But when I showed up, they suddenly had other renters coming to view the apartment, ones they had never mentioned before. Before, we had discussed me moving in right away if I liked the place, but now they needed to get back to me.

Each time I arrived at an apartment, I was greeted with "Oh, *you're* Jonathan?," the clear emphasis suggesting that while they'd expected someone named Jonathan, they certainly weren't expecting someone who looked like me.

Some landlords asked, "Are you sure you want to live in this neighborhood? It's far from your school, no?"

Another commented, "What is the name of the school? Do you have student ID?"

No one ever came out and said, "I don't want to rent to a Black person." But their consistent changes of heart, inflection, and tone revealed their bias.

I was hurt and worried. Would I be homeless in a foreign city? This city was supposed to be a social justice sanctuary. Yet, it seemed that no one wanted to give me a chance. I felt trapped in their race-defined boxes.

I expected racial prejudice from white people. Getting that kind of racism from Asian people was startling. I grew up in a world of

Black and white people in Augusta, Georgia. Asian people were a rarity. When I did interact with them, it was in Chinese restaurants on pleasant lunch outings with my mother and brother. In New York, I had not experienced this type of treatment by Asian people in Chinatown or anywhere else. But in San Francisco, it was clear that Asian landlords were not fond of my Black ass. This was the beginning of my education about the promiscuity of the whiteness mindset. The whiteness mindset can be internalized and perpetuated by anyone, regardless of their racial or ethnic identity or appearance.

The whiteness mindset fragments human beings from each other on the basis of difference. These people are then forced to compete for the small crumbs of resources available to them, while those at the top of fabricated hierarchies hoard the vast majority of resources. In such circumstances, many align themselves with white people and white cultural norms, and participate in their systems to gain access to resources, whether financial, political, social, or psychological. Many times, to ensure their survival and proximity to the benefits of whiteness, non-Black people from the global majority perpetuate anti-Blackness. It is often the case that Black people are the least valued group of people from the global majority.

I grew up hearing my Black elders recite a common rhyme that illustrated the racial hierarchies in the United States.

*If you white, you all right.*
*If you yellow, you mellow.*
*If you brown, hang around.*
*If you black, get back.*
*If you red, you dead.*

This rhyme outlined the desired outcomes of the whiteness mindset. It encourages people to artificially construct social hierarchies, placing the powerful minority at the top and with the less powerful majority below. This hierarchy offers the benefits of power, purpose, and protection. You may not be at the top of the pyramid, but if you receive more benefits than those below you, you will be eager to maintain the limited privileges you have access to. The whiteness mindset convinces people that they are fragmented from each other—and thus have no responsibilities to each other. Instead of seeking to raise up others, social groups feel superior to or even compete with the very people who could be their allies.

One of the ways people living with a whiteness mindset keep their power is by institutionalizing bias in "invisible" organizational policies such as redlining and confidential pay rates that results in socioeconomic inequity.[2] Alongside these discriminatory systems, cultural and psychological ideas that seem innocuous, such as scarcity, meritocracy, and rugged individualism, justify doling out small, unequal portions of power, purpose, and protection, which then creates infighting among people. For example, labor unions have often excluded people based on race rather than welcomed them based on economic concerns.[3] The whiteness assumption of scarcity contributed to working-class white people perceiving working-class Black people and immigrants as competition instead of comrades in the fight against industry magnates who hoard resources. Guided by the whiteness mindset, people who would benefit from unifying together to dismantle the exploitative nature of capitalism often worked against each other and themselves.

A recent example of how the whiteness mindset turns people from the global majority against each other is the push of Asian Americans to have race-based college admissions overturned. The ruling of the Supreme Court from *Students for Fair Admissions, Inc. v. President and Fellows of Harvard College* and *Students for Fair Admissions, Inc. v. University of North Carolina et al.* decided that considering race in college admissions was unconstitutional.[4] Primarily Asian and white American students brought the case to the Supreme Court due to concerns that they were unfairly being denied admission to schools because presumably unworthy Black and Latine students were being prioritized due to their race. They argued for a race-neutral approach to admissions.

But such a race-neutral approach does not acknowledge the systemic barriers like whitewashed curriculums that alienate students, and privileges like legacy admissions—that were set up through centuries of whiteness shaping society—that do not allow equal access to resources and engagement in learning environments. Yet, the overturning of race-conscious admission policies still does not seem to be enough for those infected by the whiteness mindset.

According to *The New York Times*, even after the Supreme Court ruling, Students for Fair Admissions president Edward Blum threatened additional legal action because some schools such as Duke, Yale, and Princeton reported lower numbers of Asian Americans in their incoming classes compared to Black student admissions numbers, which remained about the same. The whiteness mindset has convinced some people, including those of the global majority, to scapegoat other marginalized people from the global majority as the cause of their disadvantage instead of naming and working to dismantle unfair systems of oppression.

Even before the Supreme Court ruling, people of all races and ethnicities seemed to have opposed affirmative action more than they supported it. This is a sign of the whiteness mindset at play. Whiteness convinced white students that their power was at risk and they needed to get rid of the competition. The whiteness mindset motivated Asian American students to prioritize proximity to the benefits of whiteness and work to stamp out the perceived competition. Some Black and Latine students infected by the whiteness mindset believed that affirmative action implied that they were not capable of gaining admission to colleges without special consideration.

The whiteness mindset had convinced some Black students that they needed to prove their academic abilities and refute negative stereotypes about their intelligence. Their worth was not intrinsic but had to be extrinsically defended. Whiteness had them fighting lies, myths, about their intellectual abilities, their worthiness. The whiteness mindset disconnected them from a knowledge of the genius in their blood that dated back millennia to the first healers on the planet, the civilizations with the first libraries, the pioneering inventors in their lineages, the skilled midwives who had birthed generations, long before white men started experimenting on enslaved African women and put their names on university buildings.[5]

In a world structured by the whiteness mindset, fabricated hierarchies keep people trapped in a fragmented, competitive way of being. This division and competition is not inherent or inevitable. Historical records have documented the harmonious interactions between Black and Asian people throughout the twentieth century. Many Black people sent food to Japanese people in internment camps during the 1940s.[6] Bay Area Filipino and Chinese activists learned from Black activists and modeled their civic organizational strategies on the ones used by the Black Panther Party.[7] Black and Asian students worked together during the 1960s to fight racial inequality by forming coalitions such as the Third World Liberation Front.[8] This collective led protests at San Francisco State University and University of California, Berkeley, to demand changes to racially exclusive admissions and curriculum policies.

There are countless examples of Black and Filipino, Chinese, Japanese, South Asian, and Korean Americans coming together for the success of their communities. However, the whiteness mindset promotes the fracturing of such coalitions to ensure the protection and empowerment of white people, their cultural norms, and their ideas.

In the decades since the 1960s, there have been countless news stories about Asian American cops involved in the extrajudicial killings of unarmed Black people, and Korean beauty-supply shop owners surveilling and striking Black customers.[9] There are also Black people who believe that Asian Americans are unfairly given opportunities for education and employment because they benefit from the civil rights that Black communities sacrificed themselves to achieve.

All of this serves white people and systems structured by the whiteness mindset. If people from the global majority are fighting among themselves, it saves white people time.

With people from the global majority fragmented from each other, systems structured by the whiteness mindset, and people benefiting from the power and protection of those systems, remain unchallenged. And so, I found myself standing forlornly on an apartment stoop.

By the time I was looking for housing in the summer of 2008, the whiteness mindset had already contaminated the Asian landlords' perceptions of me. They did not see me as an ally, part of their community, or as one of the global majority. Their internalized whiteness mindset had them perceiving me as separate from them, beneath them, and potentially dangerous. I was a threat that needed to be annihilated. They neutralized me by turning me away from their doors and maintained their perceived protection from someone without the whiteness they valued.

✦✦

Many LGBTQ+ people in San Francisco seemed to share the Asian American landlords' whiteness mindset. In fact, it seemed to be intensified in non-Black LGBTQ+ spaces. It felt like psychological warfare aimed at making me feel invisible and marginalized. When I encountered white, Asian, and Latine LGBTQ+ people, it often felt as if they were looking past or through me. Naïvely, I expected more from a group whom I assumed had common experiences of hardships and triumphs.

The Castro, the notorious "gayborhood" of San Francisco that served as a welcoming hub for many LGBTQ+ people, made me feel more like an intruder than a neighbor. Walking into bars and restaurants, it took forever to be seated and service always seemed to be lacking. Servers' smiles were reserved for skinny white twinks or muscle bears, not my Black ass. I learned that there was a hierarchy in the LGBTQ+ community: White men hold the highest position, white women come in a distant second, men from the global majority third—with Black men at the back of the pack—and women from the global majority dead last.

I found the promoted "gay agenda" and the LGBTQ+ community were primarily a white male agenda and a white male community.[10] My interests, ideas, and needs as a Black American same-gender-loving man were not reflected. When I tried to align myself with LGBTQ+ concerns, I often felt unwelcomed, pushed aside by non-Black people. I felt this at nightclubs, in bookstores and restaurants. The whiteness mindset was present everywhere, including at the heart of LGBTQ+ rights protests.

✦✦

It was 5:30 p.m. on the dot and I was in the hot spot on Market Street, one of a crowd of people gathered to protest inequality. Four days earlier, Barack Obama had been elected as the first biracial Black president of the United States. Unfortunately, Proposition 8 had also been passed, banning same-sex marriage in California. It was a bittersweet time for me as a Black, same-gender-loving man. There was a win for my race, but a loss for my sexual orientation.

Chants of "No on hate!" and "We will not be quiet!" cut through the chill of the evening.

Marching protesters carried colorful signs emblazoned with the slogan

= rights = love.

My friend Jameson looked over at me. I looked up at him with cautious curiosity. It was my idea to come to the protest. I wanted to *do* something in response to the injustice. Carrying no placards, we chanted along with the crowd on the way west to our destination of Dolores Park.

"This is a lot of people," I said to Jameson.

"It's a protest, girl. That's good. What were you expecting?"

"No, it's good a lot of people showed up. But you know how I am about crowds."

"I'm surprised you wanted to come outside," he laughed.

"Listen, this is for movement purposes only. Movement, movement," I said playfully with a singsongy rhythm, laughing along with him.

As we continued to chant and march, my mind wandered. *Is this what Bayard Rustin and James Baldwin felt like marching during the 1950s and '60s?* I felt proud to be out in the streets, putting my introversion aside for the evening. I thought of my ancestors who had protested in Augusta, Georgia, and St. Petersburg, Florida. I daydreamed about the drag queens and trans women at Stonewall. With each step, a sense of connection surged. I looked up at Jameson, who was at my side. I was happy to be sharing this moment with him, my brother from another mother. We were two majestic, Black, same-gender-loving men making our voices heard.

"We have the Blacks and Latinos to thank for this. You know they're all so homophobic." My magical musing was abruptly halted by ignorance. I looked around and saw that those words had come from a white protester with a salt-and-pepper beard and cargo pants.

As a result of the reckless and widespread dissemination of post-election polling data, many Black and Latine people were unfairly scapegoated for the passage of Proposition 8.[11] Amid the protests,

Jameson and I were suddenly seen only as representatives of our race, and thus as those who had voted for Proposition 8 and worthy of the protesters' ire. As much as we wanted to stand in solidarity for our LGBTQ+ rights, we were not wanted.

The whiteness-based behavior and comments loudly communicated to me as a Black, same-gender-loving man that, as it was for the Asian landlords, for many non-Black members of the LGBTQ+ community, I was one thing and one thing only: Black. For them Black equaled homophobic. And because of that, I had no place in the LGTBQ+ community. I had no right to march alongside them for justice. I was expected to apologize for and explain the perceived betrayal of all Black Californians for the passage of the ballot initiative. One Proposition 8 protester voiced that belief to the *SFGate* newspaper, saying, "To have the lack of support from the Black community is very painful to us. Fifty years from now, I think the Black community will be ashamed that they didn't support us."[12]

This protester and many others opposed to Proposition 8 centered their white lives and values in their critiques. Although I understood and empathized with the emotion behind that statement, the statement itself revealed that the man was suffering from the whiteness mindset. That statement exemplified two major symptoms of the whiteness mindset: (1) negative emotion and/or lack of emotion and (2) oppressive behaviors and/or inaction in the face of wrongdoing.

How many white members of the LGBTQ+ community were ashamed for failing to help low-income children from the global majority receive a high-quality and culturally affirming education in Bayview–Hunters Point—the largely Black, low-income, resource-poor neighborhood in San Francisco where I lived? Did they experience remorse for not using their privilege to help Black women access better maternal health care? Did they regret not speaking out against the prison industrial complex that disproportionately affects Black men? I am not suggesting that Group 1 *must* help Group 2 before Group 2 assists Group 1. Working toward freedom from oppression should not be a tit-for-tat negotiation. Yet, it is often the case that Black people are expected to be moral super-beings who are allies to *everyone*, but who are never aided in our times of need.

The white people at the protest were consumed by the perceived betrayal of Black and Latine people who had denied them their rights. Not too far from Jameson and me, a brawny white guy with short blond hair said, "We don't see race, but they see our sexuality as a sin."

He and another white man were holding hands and carrying signs. One read "Love is love." The other was stamped with "Same-sex marriage NOW."

"Did you hear that?" I stopped and tapped Jameson on the shoulder, an alarmed look on my face.

"That gym bunny? Yeah, I heard him. My friend also told me he heard someone say *nigger* at the protest last night."

"Why you ain't tell me before we got our Black asses out here?" I asked with shock.

"We already know how they are. We just have to stay away from those kind. It's our protest, too."

"Chile, this about to turn into a Klan rally in a minute," I joked uncomfortably.

"You ready to go?" Jameson asked, already knowing my answer.

I nodded. Truthfully, I was a little scared. Could things turn hostile?

"We been here long enough. Besides, I could use a cocktail." He laughed, putting me at ease for the moment.

"All right, let's go before it goes from Abercrombie & Fitch to dump a nigg*er* in a ditch."

"Before the American Eagle comes off and the sheets go on."

Shielding ourselves with humor, we hurried to safer ground. Jameson wanted to go to Badlands, a well-known gay bar, to have a drink. I wasn't enthused given the establishment's sordid history. Not too long before, the San Francisco Human Rights Commission had conducted a formal investigation and found that the owner of Badlands consistently violated the civil rights of people from the global majority through racially discriminatory admissions policies and hiring practices as far back as 2001.[13]

Unfortunately, Badlands was hardly an outlier—Black people have often reported feeling excluded in the Castro. One Black American female activist expressed her experience of mistreatment in the Castro to a newspaper reporter. She said, "When you go to a bar, you get the feeling that the prices are being adjusted. It takes forever to get served, and the wait staff watches you like a hawk."[14]

The only nightclub that provided a welcoming place for Black American LGBTQ+ people to gather, the Pendulum, was closed in 2005, pushing Black LGBTQ+ people further out of the Castro. This discrimination affected youth as well; Jovida Guevara-Ross, executive director of Community United Against Violence, disclosed to the *Los Angeles Times*, "Young Blacks are dismissed as thugs, gang members who aren't welcome in the Castro."

As someone in a committed, monogamous relationship, the bar and club scene was not a joyful place for me. I was much happier spending time with Benjamin, the man I had started dating earlier that year while I was living in New York and working as an AmeriCorps VISTA member at the Bronx-Lebanon Hospital. Although I had moved three thousand miles away to become a clinical psychologist, we decided to commit to each other and do the long-distance thing. The bar scene also brought up insecurities related to my small body and lack of physical features that seemed to be hot commodities in the gayborhood. In addition, I was not in the habit of knowingly supporting institutions that did not support me. So I was definitely not feeling the Castro and its clubs. But Jameson was a big fan of Badlands' two-for-one happy hour drink special, and I didn't want to argue with my friend that night. So I followed along.

"We'll be fine. I know the doorman and the bartender," Jameson assured me as we crossed the threshold into the dark space illuminated by multicolored, circular LED lights on the wall. TV screens recessed into the walls played music videos. A techno version of Pink's "So What" was thumping throughout. The dance floor was starting to fill with mostly white and Asian guys. They sang along with Pink, expressing their defiance. Their bodies jumped, twitched, and swayed along with the melody as we made our way to the bar.

"Todd," Jameson yelled to get the bartender's attention.

"Hey, Jameson," the shirtless, smooth-chested, and burly white guy said as he turned and smiled. Todd leaned over the bar. He and Jameson shared a peck on the lips.

"I'm going to open up a tab." Jameson handed Todd his debit card. He turned and looked at me. "What do you want?"

"A Shirl on the rocks." I smiled at my nickname for a Shirley Temple.

Jameson rolled his eyes. He ordered the Shirley Temple and a Smirnoff Cranberry Apple. After we got our drinks, he led me to a tall table by the brick wall near the bar. Almost immediately two white men came over to us. I watched as they approached, coming up behind Jameson. One of them, a sandy-blond guy with skinny legs and a broad chest, put his hands over Jameson's eyes. The other one, a pale, muscled brunet, put his index finger over his lips and winked at me.

"Chad!" Jameson exclaimed. The guy removed his hands and laughed. Jameson exchanged hugs with the two men.

"Jonathan, this is Chad and Hugo. We go to the same gym. Chad, Hugo…this is my friend Jonathan. We went to college together." The three of us shook hands.

"So, what are you two boys up to?" Hugo asked with a mischievous smile. He winked at me again.

"Just having a drink," Jameson replied.

"We just left the Prop 8 protest," I said.

"We heard about that. If they have another one, we'll probably go," Hugo said. He put his hand on my shoulder. "So, what are you drinking?"

"A Shirley Temple," I replied, slightly annoyed by his touch.

"We'll have to get you something stronger. Don't worry. I won't take advantage of you."

I feigned a smile. The sirens from Britney Spears's "Womanizer" blared through the speakers. More people flocked to the dance floor.

"You want to dance?" Hugo asked.

"No, thanks."

"What's the matter, you don't like white guys?"

"No, I have a boyfriend," I replied bluntly, hoping to put an efficient end to Hugo's overtures.

"Is he here?" he asked, leaning in closer as I shifted uncomfortably.

"He lives in New York."

"Well, I'm sure he won't mind if you have some fun."

"I'm having fun right here," I bit out, abandoning any pretense of politeness and turning to look at my phone.

Although Hugo's behavior may seem like typical drunk-guy-at-the-bar antics, they are actually symptoms of the whiteness mindset: distorted and/or psychopathic thoughts. Dr. Bobby E. Wright described the *psychopath* as someone who is "constantly in conflict with other persons or groups. [They are] unable to experience guilt, [are] completely selfish and callous, and [have] a total disregard for the rights of others."[15] Hugo's disregard for my romantic relationship and boundaries was an indication of his expression of the whiteness mindset. He seemed to feel comfortable sexually propositioning me and joking about getting me too drunk to object. Researchers have found that white gay men regard same-gender-loving and bisexual Black men in the most hypersexual, stereotypical ways—aggressive macho thugs with large penises.[16] I was not interested.

Black LGBTQ+ people have consistently been sidelined, not just in San Francisco but also across the nation. From the closure of Black American–centric bars in Brooklyn, to harassment of Black LGBTQ+ youth in the West Village, to racial profiling in Chicago, Black people across the nation have reported being made to feel unsafe and unwanted by non-Black members of the LGBTQ+

community.[17] Many non-Black LGBTQ+ people seem to have little use for Black, same-gender-loving people outside of the bedroom. Hugo made me feel unsafe, a part of his attempt at sexual conquest. I resisted. Thankfully, Hugo got the hint and excused himself.

"Where is Hugo going?" Chad asked me, taking a break from his conversation with Jameson. I shrugged.

"Probably went to the bathroom," Jameson offered.

"Hey, so Jameson told me that you're a psychologist."

"Psychology student," I corrected. "I'm becoming a psychologist."

"Close enough," he said. "Let me ask you something."

"Okay," I said slowly, bracing myself for what was about to come out of his mouth. Experience had taught me that "let me ask you something" is usually followed by bullshit.

"So, what makes a person who has experienced oppression turn around and then oppress somebody else?"

"What do you mean?"

"I mean, all those Black and Latino people voted for Proposition 8. I was surprised because they know what it's like to be discriminated against and then they discriminated against the LGBT community. I guess gay really is the new Black. Gay people are at the bottom."

I looked at Jameson and smirked. *Is this dude serious?* Jameson shook his head, shrugged his shoulders, and grinned. I slurped the last sip of my Shirley Temple.

"I have to get up early tomorrow to study. I have an exam next week. Y'all have a good night."

"What did I say?" Chad asked with a look of bewilderment on his face.

"Talk to you tomorrow, girl," Jameson's voice trailed behind me as I stepped outside.

Walking out into the night air, I was annoyed at how many white LGBTQ+ people were invoking Blackness in the service of their push for marriage rights. They eagerly linked the fight for racial equity and marriage equality. Yet their actions demonstrated little to no commitment to using their privilege to address the actual concerns of Black Americans and other people from the global majority.

Social scientists have found that for Latine and Black American LGBTQ+ people, economic issues are of greater concern than marriage equality and rights for domestic partnerships.[18] Yet, a survey of reports in major news outlets during the 2008 election cycle, from *Time* magazine to *The New York Times* to MSNBC, would make you think that the biggest, and maybe only, concern of LGBTQ+ people was marriage equality.

Dr. Janet Helms, a psychologist and pioneer researcher on white racial identity, wrote in her book *A Race Is a Nice Thing to Have*, "Power is the capacity to define people in or out of existence."[19] Chad's assertion that "gay is the new Black" was a display of that power to center his reality over that of others, which is a benefit of whiteness. After hearing the racist remarks of protesters and warding off unwanted sexual advances, I was not in the mood that night to have to defend Black people and combat the distorted thoughts of someone I did not know.

"Gay is the new Black" was not new in 2008. It was also not solely a machination of white LGBTQ+ people. There were people from the global majority who had taken up this mantra long before Chad and those like him. In fact, Bayard Rustin, a Black American pacifist who orchestrated the 1963 March on Washington for Jobs and Freedom, may be the first person to highlight the similarities of the struggles for LGBTQ+ people's rights and civil rights for Black Americans in a speech he gave in 1986.[20] However, the energy of that assertion coming out of Chad's mouth was an erasure rather than a claim of relatedness. It rendered all Black Americans heterosexual and homophobic, and all LGBTQ+ people white and innocent.

"Gay is the new Black" is a flawed strategy that invokes hierarchies of oppression, as if we can quantify who is the most grievously injured. The naivete of the slogan is that it fails to realize all oppression is oppression. Equating your own hardships, however real, with another's minimizes the experiences of those you compare yourself to—thus, the very comparison is an oppressive act. In the bizarrely competitive world of the whiteness mindset, even oppression becomes a type of competition.

*I'm more oppressed than you now,* Chad seemed to be saying. His words suggested a whiteness mindset invested in hierarchy.

"Gay is the new Black" privileges the whiteness mindset and white LGBTQ+ people. Black people and those from the global majority are also promoting the whiteness mindset when they exclaim "Gay is the new Black!" The phrase renders obscure and, in some cases, attempts to erase the ongoing discrimination against Black Americans. In reality, both things can be and sadly are true: LGBTQ+ people continue to be discriminated against even as Black Americans face ongoing structural oppression. Moreover, people, like myself, can be both Black and LGBTQ+. We experience oppression based on people's disdain for our race, sexual orientation, and gender identity.

The whiteness mindset warps the fight for equality into a fight for equal access and expression of individualism, materialism, and competition. Although the real enemies are the systems of oppression conjured by the whiteness mindset, like racism and classism, people who are driven by whiteness turn against each other, pushing other marginalized groups further away to secure privilege for themselves. True protest and liberation are doing the hard work to heal from the whiteness mindset. This means acknowledging and accepting that the assumptions of the whiteness mindset—fragmentation, limitation, and annihilation—are false. Rejecting the terms of whiteness frees us up to pursue other values like harmony, balance, and reciprocity. It sets the conditions to imagine and build worlds beyond a preoccupation with power, purpose, and protection that always results in oppression.

San Francisco seemed to be telling me that no matter how much I tried, all that people would see was my race. I thought of "The Uncle Ruckus Reality Show" episode of *The Boondocks*. After Uncle Ruckus found out he was 102 percent African with a 2 percent margin of error, he lamented: "Cause we niggas... and that's all we ever gonna be." He felt trapped inside a box by the stereotypes heaped onto Black people. The Asian landlords, non-Black LGBTQ+ protesters, and white boys in the San Francisco bars seemed trapped in the whiteness mindset. They tried to crush me into it, too.

✦✦

Outside Badlands, I pressed play on my iPod nano. "Swagga Like Us" by Jay-Z, T.I., Kanye West, and Lil Wayne poured into my head, inducing a bop. Walking toward the Muni station, I pulled on my skullcap and zipped up my hoodie. The marquee of the Castro Theatre seemed to light up the whole sidewalk beneath it. The crisp air wafted the smell of cookies into my nostrils. Hot Cookie was still open. I stopped in to get a couple of oatmeal white-chocolate-chip cranberry cookies before heading home, hoping the tangy, sweet flavor could replace the bad taste the night had left on my tongue.

## CHAPTER 5

# A Good Match Is Hard to Find

### UNMATCHED.

The air was still. The bedroom in my boyfriend's New York City apartment was dark, with outlines of light peeking from behind window shades and around the door. The glow from my laptop was bright in the room. That word, *Unmatched*, crushed me. That prefix made all the difference. I was fixed to the bed, staring at the screen. I tried to will away those two letters. That *U* and *n* paralyzed my prefrontal cortex.

The melancholy melody of Drake's "Over My Dead Body" came to mind and rippled through me. These muthafuckas were trying to take away my dreams of being a clinical psychologist. How could this happen?

Getting a doctoral internship is a critical step in the journey to graduating with a PhD in clinical psychology. After three years of taking four to five classes per semester in San Francisco, doing psychotherapy for eighteen hours per week in Oakland clinics, completing a thesis, and successfully getting approval to start my dissertation research, I now had to complete an internship. Internships are secured through a process called matching.

With the advent of the Association of Psychology Postdoctoral and Internship Centers (APPIC)—the central and largest accrediting organization for psychology internships and doctoral programs in the United States and Canada—came the computerization and centralization of the match process. This replaced the more informal and unregulated approach to finding and filling internship positions. One of the changes associated with APPIC's regulation was the addition of multiple fees for the training site: requirements of membership dues, application fees, matching fees, and mandatory intern stipends that, as of 2024, could total upward of $16,000 per year.[1] These changes had some positive effects such as ensuring training standards and providing a small living allowance.

However, the stipends were not nearly enough to cover an intern's living expenses and many still took out loans to make ends meet. The changes also made it financially impossible for many training sites—most likely those in underserved communities that need mental health services most—to host psychology doctoral interns. These sites, which are often minority run, are exactly the types of sites that many Black students like myself preferred, even if we had to take out loans in order to serve there. Although such sites may not have been lucrative, they would have made it more likely that students would be trained by mental health professionals and work with clients who were both part of the global majority. The familiarity and sense of belonging that comes with training in an environment where I was one of the majority instead of a perpetual minority would have provided a level of comfort and confidence, encouraging me to take more risks and grow as a professional. Instead, being a minority made taking well-reasoned clinical risks seem like opportunities to be negatively judged.

I felt discouraged from the outset of the internship process. I wanted to be optimistic. Yet, there was little to help me hold that hope. While researching internship sites, I often looked for signs of Blackness. Most of them had some generic statement about valuing individual differences. Many of them rang hollow, especially when I studied the pictures of their current faculty and previous interns. Those photos planted doubt in my mind. It seemed like every portrait featured white female supervisors, two to three white women interns, and sometimes one Asian woman intern. Rarely did I see men. When I did, they did not look like me. Those photos revealed that many of the internship programs I was interested in had not trained Black men before, let alone a Black, same-gender-loving man with a chronic illness. How could these internship programs understand my needs?

I did my best to secure an internship in a place that would allow me to work with Black clients and live in a place where I felt safe and supported as a Black, same-gender-loving man. I had been encouraged by my doctoral advisor and previous clinical supervisors to apply to a broad range of sites all over the country in order to increase my chances of matching. A body of research on the matching process suggested that they were right. However, that advice hits different when you're Black and in the minority.

Matching with an internship site was not just about getting a position that would allow me to complete a year of training in providing psychotherapy and psychological tests to clients. It was not just about finishing the last requirement for earning my PhD. Those things were essential. But I needed to do those things in a place where I did not feel scared to exist. I needed to be in a place where I was less likely to face discrimination when house hunting. I needed to be in a place where I would not feel hyper-surveilled when I went shopping at the grocery store. I needed to feel safe walking down the street with the unkillable swish in my hips that marked me as a homosexual. I needed to be in a place where I had a chance of finding a doctor who had experience working with patients with sickle cell anemia.

Sure, there was a plethora of well-respected training sites to choose from in the APPIC internship directory. Many had awesome-sounding specialties like "mindfulness-based cognitive behavioral therapy with cardiovascular disease patients." But what good were those opportunities going to do me in places like Omaha? I had just started to feel comfortable walking the streets at night in Harlem, New York, as a Black, same-gender-loving man. What would I do in Wheeling, West Virginia? How would I make it in Mobile, Alabama? The standard advice for finding and applying to internship sites is not made for Black doctoral students, same-gender-loving students, or students with a chronic illness.

I ignored my mentors. I respected them as clinical psychologists, professors, and researchers. But they were not Black. I had to prioritize my well-being. So when I applied to sites, I applied to a large number—fifteen, to be exact. But most were in New York City.

One was in Boston. I was interviewed by three. Two were hospitals affiliated with prestigious New York City universities. The other was a community clinic in Boston. I hoped, prayed, and wished that I would match to one of them.

*To be equal or suitable; to harmonize with.* According to Dictionary.com, that is one of the common meanings of *match.* Yet, how can organizations that have few to no Black psychologists on their training committees and have seldom trained Black interns be suitable for Black students? It's not the Black trainees who are unfit, but the internship programs themselves. When you're a Black psychology doctoral student, a good match is hard to find. I knew this going into Match Day, when internship pairings are announced. I had an uneasy feeling the night before but I didn't want it to be real.

"God, please let me match," I pleaded silently right before logging on.

I had avoided checking the match website all morning. The results had been available since 10:00 a.m. but I was too scared to learn my fate. Twenty-one minutes after noon, I stared at *Unmatched.*

"Will I ever graduate?" The question ballooned in my head. "I know I did well in my interviews. I've trained in two hospitals and one community center. And I have clinical research experience at one of the top HIV prevention research centers in New York City. My letters of recommendation are impeccable. And I emphasized that I'm a Black, same-gender-loving man with a chronic illness. They claim they value diversity."

My mind rattled off all the reasons I should have matched. How could I not have matched?

I lay in bed for two days wondering what I would do if I could not be a psychologist. Benjamin, my boyfriend, came into the bedroom, letting sunlight in along with him. I squinted at the sudden light.

"How are you feeling today?" he asked with a concerned look, caressing my face.

"What am I going to do, Benjamin?" I asked, not really expecting him to have an answer.

"Mat," he called me by my abbreviated middle name. "I'm sorry. I know it hurts right now."

I sat up in the bed, rested my back on the headboard. I stared past him, my mind nowhere. His hand on my shoulder brought me back to the moment.

"You think you might want to talk someone about this? See a therapist?" he said hopefully.

"Maybe I should see a therapist," I considered as Benjamin pulled me to his chest. "The professors at school did recommend that we see a therapist since we're going to be one. I guess now is the perfect time."

✦✦

According to Dr. James M. Stedman, a white male clinical psychologist from the University of Texas Health Science Center at San Antonio, there was a shortage of internships as early as 1976.[2] Data from APPIC indicate that this shortage got worse from 1999 to 2013 with an 8 percent decline in matching, dropping from 84 percent to 76 percent. Some scientists have suggested that the shortage was due to several factors, ranging from internship programs not having enough funding for interns and thus reducing intern slots, to some doctoral programs accepting too many students that created higher demand for internship positions.

In 2012, 22 percent of all applicants did not match. Of the Black students who applied that year, 26 percent were not offered a doctoral internship position.[3] The Black psychology trainees made up just 5 percent of all the psychology students who were matched to internships that year, compared to the 13 percent of Black people in the United States that year. Concretely, that means that in 2012, 124 Black psychology doctoral students were able to get the required training opportunity they needed to graduate and become a professional psychologist. One hundred and twenty-four *new* Black psychologists to help serve the estimated 39,696,000 Black people in the United States that year.[4] I was not one of those new professionals.

Unbeknownst to me, I was the victim of a problem that was present long before I applied for an internship in 2012. The whiteness mindset structured the match system according to its values. APPIC and the American Psychological Association's (APA's) membership and accreditation, respectively, are prioritized as the standard of quality in professional psychology education. If one does not complete an internship at a site that is an APPIC or is APA accredited, one is typically seen as less qualified for the profession. There is a lot of stigma associated with forgoing an internship unaffiliated with APPIC or the APA. Not completing an APA-accredited internship can lead to ineligibility for certain jobs, such as working as a staff psychologist at a Veterans Administration medical center or a psychology professor at some universities. This is a major problem not just for psychology doctoral students but for the wider public who may need mental health services.

By prioritizing training at an APPIC member site or APA-accredited internship and simultaneously stigmatizing training at other sites—that may be just as or more clinically rigorous and culturally appropriate—mental health standards of care are determined by organizations that often do not look like the communities most in need of care.

This means that predominately white organizations are positioned to determine what constitutes the proper training for all mental health professionals, and thus mental health care for all people. This training and these standards of care may or may not be appropriate for the communities the mental health professionals will serve. It seems to me that due to the lack of cultural diversity in staff and culturally informed practices offered in predominately white, cisgender, and heterosexual APA-accredited training sites, mental health professionals are often not trained to serve clients in ways that center non-white, cisgender, and heterosexual ways of being. Clients from the global majority are effectively being provided mental health services sanctioned and, largely, provided by their oppressors.

I witnessed this as a graduate student. One of my clinical placements was at a nonprofit mental health clinic that served predominately Black and Latine children and their families. However, 99 percent of the staff was white. As one of the two Black students, I was appalled by the ways in which my clinical supervisors—who were licensed psychologists—often pathologized families due to their perceived failure for not living according to white family norms (i.e., two-parent household, middle-class). It was not uncommon to hear some of my supervisors and classmates use the term "lack of a father figure" as a possible explanation for "aggressive behavior" when discussing Black children who were referred to their services for misconduct in school.

The whiteness mindset maintains its power to determine what is normal, right, and desirable by positioning white ways of being on a pedestal, and white organizations as the arbiters of what constitutes appropriate mental health training and services. White mental health care becomes the only acceptable form. Simultaneously, the whiteness mindset perpetuates mental health disparities in marginalized communities by ensuring that the standards of training and care are culturally misaligned with marginalized communities. Instead of finding their own values and needs respected and understood, people in marginalized communities are offered treatments that don't speak to their lived experiences. These treatments and providers may be approved by whiteness but not by them.

For example, the mis- and overdiagnosing of Black children with disruptive behavior disorders rather than ADHD, a mood disorder, or no diagnosis at all may be due to cultural misalignment between mental health professionals and the communities they serve.[5] Black children often display a preference for high levels of verve—or physical stimulation.[6] This can look like attending to several different tasks at once, using expressive body language, and moving around a lot. Many Black children are raised in households with high energy levels, with music playing in the home, friends and family coming and going, and communal activities like dancing and storytelling, all of which have their roots in African and Black American cultural dimensions.[7] Though not exclusive to Black families, verve is much more commonly observed in low-income Black households compared to middle-class white families.

However, whiteness centers the norms of middle-class white families. When Black students, used to busy homes and expressive ways of being, bring their norms into the classroom, teachers and therapists who have been trained in an educational system structured by the whiteness mindset are less likely to understand. Instead, they interpret their student's actions as behavioral problems. Too often this results in the child receiving a stigmatizing mental health diagnosis, such as conduct disorder, that often leads to poor educational and disciplinary outcomes for the child.[8]

Similar patterns of misdiagnosis are present for people who are Latine, Native Hawaiian, and Asian American/Pacific Islander.[9] They are also more likely to receive stigmatizing diagnoses such as substance use disorder, alcohol use disorder, and schizophrenia. Relatedly, many youth from the global majority do not seek the mental health services they need. For example, Dr. Alfiee Breland-Noble's team at the AAKOMA Project found that over half of Asian American/Pacific Islander youth did not seek mental health treatment even when they believed they needed it.[10]

Whiteness makes it harder for people who may be suffering from mental health problems to get the help they need. Instead, they may be diagnosed as problematic or threats to themselves and others. Instead of mental health professionals offering help, police may be activated to confront mental health crises that have been interpreted as criminal behavior. This is exactly what happened in the cases of Ryan Gainer, Nichole Clayborne, and Walter Wallace Jr.[11] All of them needed mental health care and were met with death.

Ryan Gainer was a fifteen-year-old Black boy with autism who was shot dead in 2024 by two San Bernardino deputies within five seconds of seeing him after they were called by Ryan's family members. They labeled his behavior as attempted murder. Nichole Clayborne, a Black woman with a schizophrenia diagnosis, died after being taken into police custody in 2020 in Memphis, Tennessee. According to news coverage, cops were called when Nichole was reported as yelling, singing, and praying in a pet store bathroom. The manner of death was deemed "natural" but the family questioned exactly what happened that led to Nichole's demise. Walter Wallace, a twenty-seven-year-old Black man in Philadelphia, was fired at fourteen times and killed by police in 2020 after his family called for help while he was experiencing a mental health crisis. Although Walter was holding a knife, less lethal methods could have been deployed.

Due to the whiteness mindset, Black people and other people of the global majority's mental health crises are seen as more dangerous. A whiteness mindset renders these people as different from white and less-melanated people who are often met with empathy when experiencing mental health problems. In fact, Dr. John Paul Wilson[12] and his colleagues found that, in a series of seven research studies, non-Black US residents perceived Black men as larger and more threatening than white men of the same size.

Similarly, Dr. Jennifer Eberhardt[13] found that white people, whether consciously or unconsciously, are more likely to perceive the image of a gun or knife when they see Black faces faster than when they see white faces. Being Black or highly melanated from the global majority, you can't trust that seeking mental health services won't end up with you involuntarily confined or dead. No police officers, regardless of race, should be called when Black people are suffering from mental health challenges, due to the ways in which whiteness impairs officers' ability to see human beings in need of care and not deserving of punishment or neutralization. Operating outside of the whiteness mindset, we might be able to develop caring, effective ways to respond to mental health crises that do not involve detainment or force. One method may look like convening a community of elders, mothers, and fathers who are trained in mental health first aid. These groups could be activated during crises to aid families so that intervention leads to de-escalation and not death.

However, such strategies are likely to never be actualized as long as people ruled by the whiteness mindset are allowed to determine and enforce standards of legitimate mental health care. Whiteness in mental health protects itself from being challenged by eliminating would-be psychologists (who reject the assumptions and values of the whiteness mindset) from becoming credentialed and "legitimate" professionals in the first place. Black and other people from the global majority are systematically kept out of the mental health profession at every step of the way, including the internship process, just like I was.

✦✦

"I mean, did I drink the Kool-Aid?" I asked the Black man across the room from me.

Dr. Baptiste was a professor and therapist who appeared to be less than a decade older than me. We were in his office in the West

Village. The pale yellow walls were sparsely dotted with decorative pictures. Bookshelves filled with texts by Sigmund Freud, Melanie Klein, and Nancy McWilliams, pioneers and experts in psychoanalytic therapy, flanked each side of a window that looked out onto Bleecker Street. The sounds of New York City crept in, providing a background to my anxious thoughts. I sat forward in the leather chair across from the therapist so that my feet touched the ground.

Dr. Baptiste was dressed in a collared white shirt under a charcoal V-neck sweater. His khaki chinos and brown loafers completed the look of a young New York City therapist. A small table with a glass carafe filled with water was between us. He picked up one of the glasses on the table and poured, offering some to me as well. I declined. He took a few sips and put the glass down. This was my second session, and I already felt comfortable.

I had found Dr. Baptiste using the *Psychology Today* therapist directory. He was one of the few Black male faces that appeared in my search. I was intentional in my desire to work with a Black, male, PhD-level therapist, someone who would understand what it was like to be a Black boy navigating a white world.

"What do you mean?" Dr. Baptiste asked.

"I mean, my whole life I've received praise for being smart. My teachers always loved me. I've always made good grades and excelled in school. I *was* the best candidate. Plus, I'm Black. That's supposed to be a bonus, right? That's what they always saying on their websites. 'We value diversity. We strongly encourage diverse applicants to apply.' And then when we do, they reject us. They ain't got no Black people over there. They need me."

He pondered my response, resting his hands on his lap.

"Am I not that bitch?" I half joked. Dr. Baptiste smiled.

"Oh my god, what if I'm delusional? What if I'm really *not* that bitch and I have just been thinking I am?" I panicked.

Dr. Baptiste raised his hand to slow my spiraling. "Just pause right there. You're getting yourself all distressed."

I took a breath and tried to calm down.

He continued: "Let's just say that you really *are* highly intelligent. That you *are* an excellent student and would make an outstanding intern. Let's say you are the *best* candidate. You think because you are the best you will get the best?" He asked the way a Black man who has walked a little farther down the road asks a more naïve one.

"Umm..." I stammered. "We know that when you're Black it doesn't mean that you get what you earn or deserve. But I was really hoping it would be different this time. What else could I have done?"

I had approached internship the way I had approached every academic and professional goal in my life, with my Black excellence. I had accrued 995 hours doing direct therapy intervention with clients in a professional setting. I had received 326 hours of supervision from a licensed clinical psychologist to help me refine my therapeutic skills. And I had spent 84 hours administering psychological tests to children and adults who needed mental health assessment. According to the APPIC 2012 Survey of Internship Applicants, I had more therapy intervention and supervision hours than most of the applicants that year.[14] In two of the three categories, I had excelled, and I was still in the fifty-fifth percentile in the third. But that was not enough.

I had spent my life believing that although racism and heterosexism existed, if I just worked harder than everyone else, I should still have a pretty good chance at accomplishing my goals. That was the first time that strategy had not worked. That was the first time I had failed at something important to me. I learned that academic and clinical excellence were not enough to conquer the whiteness mindset.

"I guess at the core, I always knew that I couldn't outwork racism or homophobia, but I wanted it to be true," I said as I plopped on the seat cushion in Dr. Baptiste's office at the start of my third session.

He peered at me in silence.

"It just sucks that you can work this hard and it still not be enough."

Dr. Baptiste raised his eyebrows.

"But it's true. I worked this hard and it was not enough," I said, resigning to the fact. "I guess what I'm trying to figure out is, what do I do now?"

"What do you do now?" Dr. Baptiste reflected.

"Of course, I will have to apply again. I can't not graduate. I've sacrificed too much. I only have this one thing left to do." My eyes started to water.

"Help me understand the emotion," Dr. Baptiste said.

"It's just that it isn't fair. And I know life isn't fair. But damn, it should be. And I know that shoulds are signs of illogical thinking, but I'm not a therapist right now, I'm a patient, and this is how I feel."

My internal therapist-in-training was sparring with my emotional self out loud. A soft smile went across Dr. Baptiste's face.

I continued, "I guess I will have to do what I was trying to avoid doing, apply all over and potentially move out of New York and take my life into my own hands. Tone down my Blackness and my gayness so that I can avoid racism and anti-gay violence and discrimination."

"Do you think it will require all of that?"

"Obviously it does. The way I did it before didn't work. So I have to try something different."

"You just shifted all the way to the other side of the pendulum. At first you came in here talking about how you were the best candidate and how you should have matched. Now you sound defeated and willing to suppress who you are to get an internship." He looked at me with empathy.

"Then what am I supposed to do?"

"You have to keep drinking the Kool-Aid."

I looked at him with a question mark on my face.

"You said that you thought maybe you had drunk the Kool-Aid, that you had started to believe that you are really smart and gifted. You are those things." He paused. "Look at yourself. You are a Black, same-gender-loving man. Not only did you get into a clinical psychology PhD program, you have done well in it, finished your master's thesis, successfully working on your dissertation, and now you've run into a snag. There is an internship shortage, man. This could have happened to anyone. It *has* happened to many."

"Maybe you're right and I'm not wrong about my intelligence and hard work. But it is harder being a Black, same-gender-loving man trying to get the training I need to help my people."

Was being unmatched an outcome of whiteness, some inadequacy with me, or a fluke? Part of the effect of the whiteness mindset is that it causes people to question themselves. Two of the core values of whiteness are materialism and individualism. In a world structured by the whiteness mindset, the cure for feelings of inadequacy is to look outside of oneself and pursue achievements.

Individualism persuades people that the center of the world is them. This means that no matter what happens, they are the ones who are responsible for the triumph or hardship. This mindset had convinced me that my worth hinged on this internship, that without it I was not valuable, and that I was somehow completely individually responsible for the situation. In reality, my value was inherent. And while my work and excellence mattered, the system I was working in was far larger than my individual effort. The whiteness mindset had me questioning myself, my credentials, and my role in not matching. Was I to blame? Had I not worked hard enough? Was I not good enough? Maybe I wasn't fit to be a mental health professional?

Now I know that the whiteness mindset was and is the problem. The barriers I experienced were in place before I started on my path to becoming a psychologist. Those barriers are intentional and systemic, keeping white people in power in the mental health field and the whiteness mindset predominate in our minds.

## CHAPTER 6

# How I Know White People Are Crazy

I failed the diversity project.

My Black, same-gender-loving, born-poor, nonapparent-disability-having ass failed the diversity project.

I sat in a conference room surrounded by four white women—Dr. Westwood-Court, Dr. Bleekman, Maddie, and Bella. Blue and green eyes watched me with measured expressions, all communicating concern.

I shuffled in my seat. My eyes fixed on the glittering light dancing across the melting snow in the parking lot outside my internship site in downtown Indianapolis. I tried to steady myself, anchor myself to the space. I took a deep breath, but I felt disoriented. The drop ceiling in the dank room seemed as if it was coming down. Although I was on the fifth floor, I might as well have been in a stuffy, dark basement. The muted beige on the walls warped into gray. Everything seemed to be rejecting me. The pale faces seemed to be commanding me to *get out*.

My emotions bounced like a tossed tennis ball, ricocheting from confusion to rage to helplessness. My body was stiff, straining to hold up my collapsed spirit in the office chair. I dug my fingers into the seat as words swirled in my head:

"Are you fucking kidding me? Dumb, white women! What just happened? You muthafuckas is sick. Oh no. What am I going to do? Will I flunk the internship? You can't take my dreams from me. I have to be a doctor. God, please."

My inner voices, a vortex.

My outer voice, silent.

✦✦

I had arrived at this place innocently enough, in pursuit of a better life—for myself and my people. My seven-year-old self's desire to be a doctor was one step away from being a reality. Study hard and get good grades so you can get into college. Check. Make A's in college. Check. Volunteer at mental health clinics. Check. Apply and get into graduate school. Do well in graduate school. Make your white professors and supervisors like you. Check. Check. Check. I had pursued the plan to the letter. I was now at my final hurdle: completing the yearlong doctoral internship at the Indianapolis Midway Academic Medical Center.

I learned so much that year. I sharpened my skills providing psychotherapy for veterans who suffered from post-traumatic stress disorder. I learned how to administer and interpret tests to determine the effects of traumatic brain injury. I was even trained to help people manage chronic pain using psychology.

The internship year is notorious for being one of the most strenuous experiences of the training process. You learn so much, so fast. It was like trying to drink from a fire hose. I expected to be challenged by the work. Thanks to my father's lessons, I also expected my white supervisors and clients to make me work twice as hard to get half as far. I expected their skepticism of my skills. I expected their rejection of my legitimacy. I anticipated they would smile while enacting their carnage. I was not disappointed.

Black psychologist role models were lacking at the Indianapolis Midway Academic Medical Center. Dr. Cydnee Waycross-Brown, the only Black psychologist on staff, seemed to operate on the margins of the Psychology Department. The gray streaks in her hair and wrinkles on her cheeks suggested she was in her fifties. She was a sturdy, conservatively dressed woman who often wore a look that said: "I'm ready for retirement." Her practiced smile seemed to push back weariness, likely fatigue from the isolation and microaggressions she must have experienced year in and year out. I remember her giving just one training for my intern group. It was about bipolar disorder. The only Black psychologist at the medical center felt small to me. I only ever saw her at the Psychology Department meetings, never leading hospital-wide initiatives or research projects. In the department meetings, she rarely shared her opinions. Maybe she was tired and worn out from being the only Black woman in her department for decades. I don't know. Maybe I was projecting my unease in the space onto her. Was her smallness only in my head or was it a fact?

All my other supervisors were white, cisgender, heterosexual psychologists. The whiteness of the place felt large. Good intentions and 1970s white pop-culture references filled the air. There was no shortage of allusions to ABBA or the Doobie Brothers. The sameness in sexuality was striking, too. Everyone seemed to be heterosexual and married with children. They shared pictures of their progeny playing with watercolors and Batman capes.

"Isn't he cute?" they exclaimed expectantly.

I was obliged to agree.

Although there was little evidence in the Psychology Department, the all-white, all-heterosexual diversity committee agreed that diversity was indeed a priority. They had codified it in their trainee handbook as one of the five domains in which we interns needed to demonstrate competency.

"All of our clients are diverse. They bring with them diverse backgrounds and experiences. As psychologists, it is very important that we understand how to respect and treat clients from backgrounds different from our own. To facilitate getting outside our comfort zones and understanding what it's like to be a minority, you will complete a diversity project." Dr. Westwood-Court, the training director, beamed with enthusiasm as she began to describe a required assignment to my intern cohort during one of our clinical group supervision meetings.

She was a psychologist in her late thirties. Her specialty was trauma and personality disorders. She looked as if she could have been part of a Wiccan community, kin with Cher's character in *The Witches of Eastwick*. She often engaged us in discussions about "meeting patients where they are," and seemed open-minded concerning all things cultural. She communicated a genuine respect for her clients, sharing stories of her efforts to help them in their process of healing. I respected her clinical expertise but questioned her cultural humility when it came to people from the global majority.

Dr. Jillian Bleekman, a staff psychologist who specialized in sexual trauma and spirituality concerns, continued the explanation.

"You will put yourself in a situation where you are a minority for at least two hours. We want you to experience what it is like to be the odd person out. You will then come back to group supervision and share with us what you learned from your experience." Dr. Bleekman moved her blue eyes from Maddie to Bella to me. Her heavy words and frame struck me still. I stared back.

I was shocked.

The voices in my head protested: "Excuse me? Wait... what? What did you say? Are you telling us to go be a minority for two hours? Ma'am, that's called my life. How is this assignment at all appropriate for someone who is already a minority? This is fucked up."

My Southern Black father's warning fired off in my head: "Never tell white people the truth. They can't handle it. Even when they are wrong, they will find a way to make it your fault."

Heeding his internalized advice, I did not give voice to my thoughts. I was offended and hurt by how they trivialized diversity with this weird project that clearly only had white, heterosexual, cisgender, able-bodied interns in mind.

Although I was fuming, I kept my face smooth and used a tactic I knew would work. I feigned confusion and hesitantly raised my hand.

"You have a question, Jonathan?" Dr. Westwood-Court asked.

"What should I do? This is my life. I'm always a minority." I tried to sound as meek as possible.

Dr. Westwood-Court smiled warmly and said, "Well, put yourself in a situation where you are a different type of minority. What ways are you not usually a minority?"

"Ma'am, I am a Southern, Black, same-gender-loving man who grew up in a working-class home in Augusta, Georgia. And I have sickle cell anemia. When am I not the minority?"

Of course, I didn't say this. I knew my whites. I tried to cultivate a look of openness so as to not seem annoyed or averse to learning. I guess she interpreted this look as more confusion and offered, "So you are usually a minority because of your race and sexual orientation, right? What other identities do you have that might make you a minority but you don't usually experience a minority status because of them?"

Again, I was sat there silently. The training director attempted to console me, saying, "Don't worry. No one has ever failed this assignment. We just want you to have an experience of being a minority and come back and tell us about it and what you learned."

I sensed she did not want to engage with my questions any longer. So I put a piece of gum in my mouth and concentrated on the flood of delicate, sweet mint flavor. I exhaled through my nose and sent up a prayer for serenity.

Dr. Westwood-Court went on to describe a *gold-star* diversity project. "Bella, you remember Caroline? She was an intern here last year?"

Bella nodded yes.

"Caroline was one of our best interns that trained with us last year. For her diversity project, she attended a service at an all-Black Protestant church." She paused and looked at each of us. "This was a significant shift for her. She had grown up in predominately white environments where everyone looked like her."

I sat there willing myself not to roll my eyes. Dr. Westwood-Court articulated each syllable with care as she described how all of Caroline's classmates, teachers, and clergy were just like her in skin color and values. Caroline's childhood place of worship had been the Catholic church where Father Doyle doled out the body of Christ and the blood of Jesus. Parishioners kneeled in silence and crossed their chests as they listened to scripture. The rituals were precise, polite.

"Given this rearing, it made sense that Caroline was apprehensive. She told us that she was unsure of whether she would be accepted by the Black congregants. But she challenged herself to move beyond her anxiety. And she learned a lot. After completing the project, she shared with us that the congregants made her feel so welcomed. She felt at home." Dr. Westwood-Court's pride for Caroline radiated into the room. I rejected it, refused to beam it back. My face, a stagnant lake.

Dr. Westwood-Court continued, "Caroline learned that their worship experiences were not so different from hers, except they were much more lively and the music was so rhythmic. She was impressed by the big, colorful hats that many of the women wore and the way people danced in the aisles. She really put herself out there and came back with a better understanding of what it was like to be a minority."

Dr. Westwood-Court finished her story and looked intently at each of us. First Maddie, then Bella. Her gaze finally landed on me. I put on a happy face; my torn and raging heart was not her business.

But my internal world was frenzied. I . . . was . . . appalled. I wanted to jump on the table and scream.

My inner voice raged, "What did she expect them to do? Rob and rape her in the church? This is how I know white people crazy!" I felt as if I had just been assaulted physically, mentally, and spiritually.

Before listening to that story, I sensed that I was separated from my white supervisors and peers due to culture and professional training. After listening to that story, I felt separated from them due to humanity. Could they not recognize the innate humanity in others?

Caroline's diversity project was voyeuristic and dehumanizing. It was as if she was visiting a foreign land that was rumored to be dangerous. To her surprise, she left with the stunning revelation that the inhabitants were civilized.

For me, and apparently only for me in that space, the story and its telling represented the sickness of the whiteness mindset. The project fragmented the *regular* white people from the *diverse* Black people. Clearly Caroline and the diversity committee carried the whiteness mindset within them. They set themselves as the default. As the default, the way they saw the world was always most important.

Caroline had achieved the goal of putting herself in a situation where she was a statistical minority. But was that good enough? Did she not still carry unspoken power in that space?

Caroline creeped into the church and soaked up the artistic, spiritual gifts. But there was no evidence that she had confronted what she represented as a white woman in that place. Had she reckoned with the legacy she carried on her skin? Did she realize she represented the scores of white women whose deceptive words incited murder? Did she know that she evoked the well-meaning white women social workers who ripped children from their families?

For several congregants in that church, the combination of Caroline's gender and race was likely triggering, insidious. But their love of the Lord instructed them to pray for those who persecuted them. It had probably never occurred to Caroline that the congregants could welcome their enemy, offer her peppermint, and wish her a blessed day.

The assignment did not require Caroline to reflect on herself as a person with a heritage of destruction. It only requested that she put herself in a situation where she was a minority for two hours.

The whiteness mindset rendered a diversity project into an exercise of egotism and a display of cultural psychopathy. Putting ourselves in a situation where we were a minority for two hours was not only offensive to actual minoritized people, but it also encouraged us to center ourselves. It placed us, consciously or otherwise, in conflict with the people who would be in the majority. It was an us-versus-them paradigm, minority versus majority. This positioning is consistent with a primary assumption of whiteness, fragmentation, and a value of whiteness, competition.

The assignment did not encourage cultural exploration of the environment before engagement. It did not require reverence for the people before reaching out to them. There was no reckoning with how our presence in the environment would impact a community, only what we would take from it. It was a one-sided scene, defined by individualism.

I looked around the faux-wood-grain table and tried to determine if my fellow interns were buying the story. The two white women who sat next to me seemed fully engrossed. They showed no signs of distress at Dr. Westwood-Court's storytelling.

Maddie, a frail white woman whom I often felt empathy for given her health struggles, raised her hand.

"I'm uneasy around old people. They often have a lot of illnesses that make me anxious, given my own health. Could I visit a nursing home and do my project on that? I would be a minority among them as a young person."

"Sure," Dr. Bleekman replied. "That sounds like a good idea."

Bella, the other intern in my cohort, was a very smart and friendly white woman in her late twenties. She had previously completed a clinical placement at the Indianapolis Midway Academic Medical Center as part of her doctoral program. She knew the hospital and city very well. I often texted her with questions about navigating the medical center and finding good restaurants in Indianapolis.

Exuding confidence, Bella ran her fingers through her auburn hair and said, "I think I'm going to volunteer for the homeless count this year. Would it be okay for me to do my project about the homeless?"

"I think that's a great idea!" Drs. Bleekman and Westwood-Court responded in unison.

I sat there puzzled. Did they not understand the inherent whiteness and othering that Caroline's story had perpetuated? Did they not see how fucked up this assignment was?

As perplexed as I was by this situation, I wanted to pass my internship and graduate with my doctorate, so I silenced my inner voices…again.

Later that day, Dr. Linwood and Dr. Shulman, my direct supervisors, were very attentive when I shared my confusion about the project with them. I reported to them daily, and their role was to guide me in my psychotherapy and neuropsychological testing. They approved all my notes and signed off on them. Both doctors were white, heterosexual, and cisgender. But they had sense. They seemed to be able to recognize the innate humanity in people, even those who were not white. Dr. Linwood and Dr. Shulman recognized and respected my humanity. They encouraged my growth and didn't try to fit me into their boxes.

My eyes shifted between my advisors as I recounted my experience. Dr. Linwood had a pained expression on her face as she listened to me describe the diversity group supervision meeting. Her shoulder-length brown hair was tucked behind her ears. Her red lips closed and her eyes widened as I talked. Dr. Shulman stood by the closed door of the office. His blond balding head looked as if it might touch the ceiling. His strapping frame, outfitted in beige khaki pants and a plaid button-down short-sleeve shirt, loomed next to me. He gave it to me straight.

"Jonathan," he said in his heartland accent. "I don't even know why they are having you do a diversity project. You could probably teach a course on it, man. But it's one of those American Psychological Association things that's required. So let's just figure this out."

"I want you to know that it's not like I think I'm too good for the assignment. I just think it's wrong for me. I know I have privilege in some ways: being a man, for example. But I'm always a minority. And I just don't know..." My voice trailed off as I pleaded my case.

"We know that. You don't need to explain. We really should have thought about this some more as full committee. We're in this with you," Dr. Linwood assured me.

✦✦

Both my supervisors acquiesced to the stipulations of the American Psychological Association (APA), which accredited doctoral psychology programs and internships. The APA sets regulatory and ethical guidelines for psychologists' and psychology trainees' professional conduct. At the time, I had no choice but to accept my fate. But now I understand just how ill-equipped the APA and the so-called diversity committee at my internship were to "teach" me about diversity. The APA was the same organization that had perpetuated racist stereotypes and provided scientific support to justify Black intellectual inferiority, mental illness, and harm for over a century.[1]

The same APA that issued an apology in 2021 for its "role in promoting, perpetuating, and failing to challenge racism, racial discrimination, and human hierarchy" and still failed to implement crosscutting, financially backed policies that directly impacted Black and other people of the global majority. I have not heard of any national or global work to address Black and other people's mental health, bringing them into the psychology field and empowering those already in the mental health profession to do healing work beyond the whiteness mindset.

The APA was in existence for 110 years before it finally published *Guidelines on Multicultural Education, Training, Research, Practice, and Organizational Change for Psychologists.* This document attempted to provide recommendations on how to understand one's own culture and the culture of others while practicing psychology. In reality, it suggested how a group of overwhelmingly white mental health professionals should conduct themselves.

These guidelines seemed well-intentioned. However, in the nearly all-white, all-cisgender, and all-heterosexual space at the medical center, their impact was minimal. I was hard-pressed to find Black physicians or psychologists. The only cultural connection I shared was in the form of smiles and nods from administrative assistants, nurses, patient transporters, housekeeping staff, and cafeteria workers. They were so proud to see one of their own training to become a doctor. I looked forward to their smiling faces every time I entered that space. Those knowing looks and nods were grounding and gave me a split-second feeling of home in an otherwise isolating environment.

It was not just the lack of people of the global majority at my internship but also the fact that the diversity committee seemed to be clueless about what it actually meant to support a Black, same-gender-loving man like myself. I did not feel welcomed or supported to learn and grow beyond the confines of a whiteness-centered understanding of mental health.

It was in this space—with a clear divide in staff and ideology—that I was told to increase my awareness and appreciation for diversity by putting myself in a situation where I was a minority for at least two hours.

We decided that I would visit a sports bar and try to understand sports culture because I was not at all familiar with or interested in sports. My direct supervisors and I reasoned that I would be a *different* type of minority in such an environment. Although this did not totally make sense to me, Dr. Westwood-Court accepted this plan. So, with much trepidation, I committed to completing the assignment.

One cold November night I ventured to a sports bar in downtown Indianapolis. That night there was supposed to be a basketball game playing on television. The plan was to go watch the game with sports enthusiasts in the bar and soak up sports culture.

It was hard to leave the house that night. The weather was already dipping to the forties at night. It all seemed dumb. I did not understand why people—mostly men—would dress up, sometimes even paint themselves, and holler and hoot about someone shooting an alley-oop.

Despite my reservations, I picked an outfit that wasn't too gay or too nerdy. A pair of regular-fit jeans. A long-sleeve T-shirt as opposed to one of my regular button-downs. A warm charcoal jacket, sneakers, a hat, and a scarf.

I gave myself a pep talk in the mirror.

"You can do this! You'll sit at the bar, order a Shirley Temple."

"Wait, that's so gay. Maybe you should get a beer?" a stern voice in my head interrupted.

"But I don't like beer."

"Order a Coke. That's more manly," the stern voice suggested.

The pep talk continued: "You'll watch the game, drink your Coke, spot someone or a group, and strike up a conversation about sports."

"But what if they think I'm trying to hit on them? What if they beat me up? You've seen *The Matthew Shepard Story*." My mind was racing with all the what-if, worst-case scenarios.

"You have to do this."

"Use your man-voice when you talk to them."

"Ugh, I don't want to do this. This is so unfair and stupid!" I whined to myself.

After about thirty minutes of internal debate, I made it out of my apartment.

When I arrived at the sports bar, barely anyone was there. The floor felt sticky. The smell of liquor made me think of poverty and bad decisions. Announcers' voices and the screams of fans bounced from the TVs and off the walls. The sounds took me back to the excruciatingly long and boring Sundays of my childhood. I remembered my father sucking his thumbs watching football from sunup to sundown. The whistles signifying penalties pierced my ears.

As a child, I wanted to watch *Breakfast with the Arts* on A&E and *In Living Color* on Fox. I was fascinated with the stories of artists and amused by Homey D. Clown. But Joshua didn't play that. He hogged the TV in the living room, not seeming to care that my brother and I did not have one of our own. I suffered in silence and hoped he would fall asleep so I could switch the channel. The ache of powerlessness pulsed in my chest as I stepped into that bar and back into those memories.

I hopped up onto a barstool. My eyes timidly beckoned the bartender.

"A Coke, please. With a straw," I managed to eke out. I prayed I didn't sound too gay. The bartender put the drink in front of me. I paid. The condensation cooled my hands but did nothing as the rest of me burned with intimidation. Butterflies tickled my insides as the smell of cigarette smoke blew into my nose. I turned to my right. Another stool separated me and a blond, burly man in a yellow-and-blue Pacers hat. He ordered a Budweiser and reached into his blue jeans for his wallet.

"It's now or never," a stern voice said in my head.

"But I'm scared," my inner voice whined.

"Man up." The stern voice was unsympathetic. "You've got to do this to graduate."

I made eye contact with the man. "I'm Jonathan," I said in my best *man*-voice. "Who's your favorite team?"

The guy looked at me with skepticism. "Bill." He nodded.

"Hi," I responded.

"I'm rooting for the Pacers, of course." He looked at me like I was a Black gay man in a place he didn't belong. I knew that look and took a deep breath.

I powered through and rattled off my questions: "How long have you been following them? What do you like most about basketball?"

Honestly, I had no clue what I was doing. I hoped he did not call me the f-word or the n-word. Would he call me both? I guess God was with me. Bill obliged in answering my questions hastily. After he finished, he did not query me. He took another sip of his beer and quickly moved away. I was embarrassed. Feelings of inadequacy flooded me as his curt responses triggered memories of laughter and ridicule and, alternatively, disregard from my peers due to my lack of knowledge of sports. The shame my father made me feel all those years during my youth for not being the right kind of boy resurfaced. My body tightened with twinges of inferiority.

On the drive home, I listened to Kirk Franklin's "More Than I Can Bear." I felt like I had gone through the fire that Kirk sang about and been broken down. But I tried to remember my dignity. I tried to remember the end goal of the exercise. At home, in the shower, I tried to wash away the humiliation.

✦✦

If I could go back in time, I would suggest to Drs. Linwood and Shulman that they advocate for a diversity project that challenges the whiteness mindset. Diversity can't be addressed with one singular project at all. To understand, appreciate, and promote multiculturalism requires a lifelong process. I would de-emphasize diversity and center cultural humility.

*Cultural humility* is the active engagement in an ongoing process of self-reflection to better understand ourselves and others with the goal of establishing and maintaining honest, mutually beneficial, and healing-oriented relationships.[2] In contrast, diversity emphasizes welcoming and indoctrinating people into the whiteness mindset or "the norm." The mindset and the systems behind it are rarely examined.

Cultural humility opens up the space to, first, recognize the whiteness mindset in ourselves and the world around us. Second, cultural humility invites us to examine our own culture and our relationship with the whiteness mindset and the systems of oppression reinforced by it. Third, cultural humility requires that we take responsibility for shifting away from the whiteness mindset and instead embrace a mindset that centers working to ensure equity for all, interconnectedness, and harmony.

Using the lens of cultural humility, I would have the interns practice daily self-reflection for the entire year. Reflections would include noting when they noticed the whiteness mindset at play in themselves and their environments, when they noticed cultural clashes between themselves and their clients, and when they felt uncomfortable in their professional roles. Each week interns would gather to discuss their reflections, sharing what they'd observed. Together, they would be able to interrogate the whiteness mindset and explore alternative, culturally expansive ways to respond in those moments. We would focus on processing the emotions and bodily sensations that accompanied the events that we explored.

This type of ongoing, collective self-reflection would move us away from the individualistic and comparative paradigm of the whiteness mindset. It would also allow us to reject the whiteness-based assumption of fragmentation that only focuses on how one thinks about an event. Instead, interns would be encouraged to gather their thoughts, actions, emotions, and bodily sensations into an integrated whole. Healing would be communal and holistic, fostering an expansive way of being human and in relationship with others.

But time machines don't yet exist, and I did not have a comprehensive knowledge of the whiteness mindset at that time, nor the power to make such suggestions. So I did the project as assigned, swallowing my suffering.

The following week, I reported back to Maddie, Bella, Dr. Bleekman, and Dr. Westwood-Court. I tried to pretend that it was enlightening to be surrounded by team spirit and pride.

"I really felt like a minority in a different way I didn't know I could. The experience opened my eyes to the world of sports."

"Okay…" Dr. Bleekman offered doubtfully.

"I was a little scared at first. But the people in the bar embraced me. They told me all about the history of the team. I felt included even though I was a minority," I embellished, echoing

Caroline's revelations. Truthfully, I had not learned anything. It was traumatizing.

My performance was not convincing. Dr. Westwood-Court and Dr. Bleekman excused themselves and left the room. On the other side of the glass door, I could see them discussing. Dr. Bleekman shook her head no. Dr. Westwood-Court shrugged her shoulders. They bounced back into the room with smiles on their faces.

"Jonathan, we appreciate how you tried to experience being a minority in a different way. But to be honest, we think you should redo the assignment," the training director and diversity committee director announced. "It sounds like you experienced more bar culture than sports culture. We want you to try it again. Maybe pick something where you will be more immersed? How does that sound?"

I could barely hear anything they said after the words "redo the assignment." In response to the threat, the muscles in my face automatically morphed into a meek mask.

My internal voices erupted: "Well, whose fault is that? I told you what I was going to do. I don't know shit about sports. How am I supposed to know how to experience sports culture?"

These furious thoughts momentarily shielded me from the crushing blow of an unjust failure.

Failing the diversity project fucked with my health. My mental and physical health was already in flux from the sheer pressure of excelling as a doctoral psychology intern. I carried hefty hopes of becoming a doctor. Trying to materialize those hopes tested my spirit. I had sacrificed so much to get to the Indianapolis Midway Academic Medical Center. I had left my family and my boyfriend to move to a homogenous urban center surrounded by farmlands. I was living in a modest one-bedroom apartment with no furniture in the living room. My bed was from IKEA and uncomfortable as fuck. The table and single chair I owned were fold-ups. I carried this load for the education that would allow me to serve my community and escape poverty. Now I had to deal with this!

I had been carrying that load since I was in the first grade, when I decided to become a doctor. I wanted to be like those smart professionals in white coats who took care of me when I was a child suffering from pain. The adults told me I had to make good grades and love helping people. So I devoted hours to studying and reading. I went to college and then graduate school to learn how to heal the mind. I bypassed proms, frivolous sex, and wild nights of drug experimentation, essentially my youth, to bear the weight of becoming a doctor. That weight accompanied by the brutality of whiteness, and my silence about it, took its toll during my internship.

That year I was back and forth to the hospital thinking I might have cancer—my platelet count was abnormally high. The doctors never made a diagnosis even after I had a painful bone marrow biopsy. I also thought something was wrong with my heart. I suffered from episodes of extreme pressure on the left side of my chest. It felt like an anvil was pressing on it.

"This is what a heart attack feels like, right?" I panicked. "Maybe, I have heart cancer?" I jumped to unlikely conclusions. An echocardiogram and a two-day heart monitor did not find anything out of the ordinary.

Then there were the tingling and vibrating pulses in my hands and feet. A series of increasingly focused WebMD searches convinced me I had multiple sclerosis. Again, doctors could not determine an underlying medical cause.

It wasn't until after I completed the internship that I realized all those alarming symptoms were due to stress. Once I was safely back in New York City with my boyfriend, the symptoms magically disappeared.

After being notified that I had failed the diversity project, my direct clinical supervisors, Drs. Linwood and Shulman, and I were frustrated and confounded.

Dr. Shulman told me, "Jonathan, we could fight this. Dr. Linwood and I will have your back. But it might be a process. The other choice is to redo it and graduate without delays."

This was unfair. But the most important thing to me was becoming a doctor. So I redid the project. It was decided that I would attend the Indy 500 qualifying trials. Again, this made no sense to me, but Dr. Westwood-Court accepted the proposal.

The day of the race, I suited up. I chose a not-too-gay-or-too-nerdy pale yellow Oxford long-sleeved shirt and straight-legged blue jeans. I blared music and danced my distraction.

Jay Electronica's "better in tune with the infinite" provided the soundtrack for my pre-exposure pep talk. The lyrics helped me to remind myself that I was connected to something greater than Dr. Westwood-Court, Dr. Bleekman, and the distressing diversity project. Those women could make me do the project as much as they wanted but they would not defeat me. I sulked out the door into the chilly sunny day.

At the races, cars whizzed around the circular track. Children munched on morsels of kettle corn and KitKats. Adults chomped on fried chicken tenders and fairground-sized turkey legs. The smell of hot grease and burned rubber nearly made me nauseous. I stayed for two hours and hastily departed.

The following Monday, I reported my new experience to Drs. Bleekman and Westwood-Court and my colleagues. Performing the role of the enlightened intern, I recounted my exposition of the history of the Indy 500. The race car culture and the people there had charmed me, I fibbed.

"I really felt like a different type of minority," I said, giving them my best Sidney Poitier.

The grateful, vulnerable negro was on display. I divulged my emotional evolution that started as apprehension but ended with enjoyment of the Indy 500. My eyes were wide and my hands flew about.

I punctuated my presentation with a warm smile, hoping it hid my venom. Drs. Westwood-Court and Bleekman excused themselves from the room. They were back in seconds.

They smiled as they deemed me competent.

I had taken their diversity test twice.

By the end of my internship, my morale had been halved. I was more competent in my psychotherapy and diagnostic skills, and I finished my program as Dr. Jonathan Mathias Lassiter. But that achievement came with a devastating cost. Many Black and other students from the global majority must do more than just put in long nights of studying. We have to not only effectively regulate the intense emotions that arise when working with suffering clients, we must also suppress our pain when our culture is ignored and our intelligence and skills are challenged because of our supervisors' and professors' subtle and overt bias. We must do more than sacrifice time with family and friends. We are also required to choose isolation in predominately white institutions and cities so that we can hope to graduate on time. The predominately white field of psychology that is structured by the whiteness mindset demands that people from the global majority pay with our peace, mold our professional passion to its will by pursuing goals whiteness deems worthy, and forgo our cultural values and ways of being to master its methods. To succeed, we must adopt the values of individualism, competition, and materialism as our own or be barred from participation. We must center whiteness or fail.

## CHAPTER 7

# Shiny Object Syndrome

It was a *Graduation* type of morning. Kanye West's third studio album was the soundtrack as I navigated the slippery sidewalks of New York City. After I completed my internship, I gleefully moved back to New York City, this time in Harlem, to be with Benjamin. We had been dating long-distance for most of our relationship since 2008. Having earned my PhD, I was pursuing additional training in research and psychotherapy so that I could become licensed to practice independently. Living with Benjamin in his townhome in Upper Manhattan provided a comfortable foundation to pursue the next step in my career.

That fall morning, I was feeling myself. I was emotionally charged, channeling my feelings into a defense. Hurt into anger. Anger into arrogance. Arrogance into a shield. A lengthy email from my supervisor, a white guy named Tyrone, had ignited a firestorm of frustration inside of me.

From: Tyrone Sturgess

To: Dr. Jonathan Mathias Lassiter

Subject: supervisory issues

First, Jonathan, I want to say that I am glad you are here. I need to give you some supervisor-ly thoughts.

At our last meeting about you helping me with a research project, you mentioned that I would be "seeing something from you soon." I noticed that in your paper ideals and proposal you seem to be looking at active projects and trying to take the "lead" on things. This is dangerous. I suggest you take a step back.

Sincerely,

Tyrone

When I received this email from Tyrone, I was baffled. What was he talking about? He had asked me to work with him on the research project. I hadn't approached him. My area of research was spirituality and mental health. I was trying to be helpful by working with him on his project, after *he* asked me to. But I was the problem in his eyes. As soon as Black people show initiative and promise, we become threats.

On the train to work, my agitation was fueled by Kanye West's and Lil Wayne's bravado on the song "Barry Bonds." My internal voice went wild: "I'm a fucking genius. I have visionary, groundbreaking intellect. I get shit done. My solo dolo Black PhD ass might be the underdog at this place, but my purpose is bigger than a postdoc. What does he know? Fuck that nigga."

I walked into my favorite bagel shop. The narrow, packed shop in Midtown was crowded as usual. Some people sat at the few tables, devouring pastries. Most folks were in a single-file line waiting to place their order. The remainder stood in a clump by the cash register counting the minutes until their order was up. When it was my turn, I approached the counter and requested my usual.

"Turkey sausage and eggs scrambled hard on a toasted blueberry bagel with cheddar cheese, please."

The guy behind the counter repeated my order. I confirmed. He printed, ripped, and handed a ticket to me. On shuffle, "I Wonder" played. Kanye rapped about divine inspiration and the inevitability of his success.

Same, I thought. All my research ideas were divinely inspired. I was doing God's work. What was Tyrone doing? Cowering and riding the coattails of his boss. My supervisor was a coward.

Breakfast in hand, I walked the block and a half to my job. The sun had yet to come out on the dreary morning in New York City. The doorman of the building opened the tall glass door and pushed the elevator button for me. My anger subsided long enough for me to smile and thank him.

On the sixth floor, I signed in and walked to my desk. I put down my bag, took a deep breath, and walked toward the cold, sterile conference room for the biweekly staff meeting.

I saw Tyrone was sitting in the room staring off into the distance, looking at nothing in particular through his Coke-bottle lenses. He was a five-foot-seven white guy, bald and heavy built. My blood bubbled. My thoughts were disrespectful. I remembered those paragraphs he had typed. He had framed his email as an attempt to guide me, but I interpreted the email as "know your place, nigger."

Truthfully, I was both livid and scared after reading his note. I was livid that he would condescend to me in such a way and that he had misunderstood my intentions. My goal was not to step over him, it was to be proactive and productive. But he labeled these characteristics as hazardous enthusiasm. That was the first time that had happened to me. Usually, my supervisors praised my independence and proactivity. Traits seen as signs of excellence by others were marks of arrogance to him.

I was scared because he seemed to be categorizing me as a troublemaker. He assured me that his email was without malice. But how could that be? He, my supervisor, was admonishing me. I was a problem that he had to correct with "supervisor-ly thoughts."

He had all the power in his hands, and I needed him. He was the one who had to sign off on my postdoctoral clinical hours. His signature would render me free, professionally independent to practice as an autonomous psychologist serving the communities I cared about.

I was once again in a position where I would have to silence my voice to achieve a greater goal. To survive, I had to subdue my drive. The wages of the whiteness mindset were weighing on me yet again.

The road to becoming a licensed professional clinical psychologist is a long one with many hurdles to jump. There are four years of college, four to five years of a doctoral program, and the one-year full-time clinical internship. Then you are awarded your

PhD. But before you can set up shop and practice on your own, you must get licensed.

Licensing requirements differ in each state. My goal was to get licensed in New York, which required that I pass the licensing exam. The New York licensing board also mandated the completion of a one-year (defined as 1,750 clock hours) postdoctoral fellowship. Only after I met these obligations would I obtain autonomy in my professional life.

At the encouragement of my therapist, Dr. Baptiste, and the advice of my grad school mentors, I decided to complete a postdoc that combined research and therapy. They reasoned this would set me up to pursue a variety of careers.

Based on the recommendations of one of my research advisors, I decided to do my postdoc at the Center for HIV InVestigational Studies (CHIVES). CHIVES was a renowned research center associated with one of the largest public universities in New York City. The mission of the center was to research and promote strategies for HIV prevention and treatment. The center was founded in 1993 by Tyrone's boss: Dr. George Patton.

Dr. Patton seemed to be a combination of genius and narcissist. He was a pioneer in HIV prevention research at a time when psychological research about gay and bisexual men was taboo. He brought scientific inquiry to such topics as hypersexuality and medication adherence. Across his career, he was awarded over $55 million in federal grants to fund his research. To me, he seemed to be a certified narcissist given how he exploited the admiration of students and younger scientists to make himself feel better. He was preoccupied with getting as many grants as possible, regardless of whether the topics of the research were meaningful to him. And his utter disregard of the vulnerable communities he claimed to serve with his research was appalling.

According to the *New York Post*, three years after I left CHIVES, Dr. Patton resigned after being accused of drug use and misuse of government funds. My experience of Dr. Patton was of someone who had no use for me. He was concerned about getting grants, publishing research articles, and collecting praise. This was the environment in which Tyrone supervised me.

Tyrone was my primary clinical supervisor; he had received his PhD in counseling psychology, with a specialty in family psychology, about five years before I did. He specialized in white, gay, male couples and HIV testing. I thought he was brilliant at statistics and thoughtful when it came to most psychotherapy issues. There were moments when he said something so insightful that I thought to myself: "Dang, Tyrone, that was deep." He was even nice sometimes. But mostly, he was condescending, dismissive, and defensive.

At the time, I believed Tyrone was threatened by my drive and ability to get things done quickly with a high level of quality. Now I also understand that Tyrone was a product of his environment. Dr. Patton perpetuated the whiteness mindset in the research center by fostering an environment of limitation and scarcity where his employees had to vie for money, authorship on research papers, and attention. This contributed to individualism and competition in the workplace. He overworked and underappreciated those closest to him, like Tyrone. Tyrone was trying to find his own path forward but seemed thwarted by his boss. Infected by the whiteness mindset in the space, he probably suffered from depression and anxiety. He tried to pass the effects of the whiteness mindset on to me.

Walking into the room with my breakfast bagel and Earl Grey tea, I noticed the anxiety on Tyrone's face, a familiar expression. He often seemed nervous, preoccupied with pleasing Dr. Patton.

That morning I heard a voice. It was God's, I'm sure. In a low, calm, and assertive manner, it said: *He's miserable. Don't let miserable people make you miserable.*

From the outside, he looked like he was reaping all the benefits of whiteness: money, favor, and status. Sure, I could see the drawbacks: high stress, panic, and lack of sleep. But before that moment, I had dismissed those as minimal side effects of success. Yet, that morning, I understood that the benefits of whiteness did not necessarily outweigh its wages, even for white people.

With that revelation, it was as if a floodgate opened. The weight of the dread I was carrying swooshed away. I felt relieved, light. My buoyancy was renewed.

✦✦

"You have shiny object syndrome," Dr. Baptiste, my therapist, said.

"What?" I was in my second year of seeing Dr. Baptiste. Having worked through my disappointment, shame, and despair over not matching to an internship, I continued to see him after returning to New York from Indianapolis. He helped me deepen my understanding of who I was and better navigate the world as a Black, same-gender-loving man and psychologist.

"You see these shiny things from far away and you go after them with all your gusto. When you get close to them, you see that they are actually dull and you are unsatisfied." Dr. Baptiste sat back in his leather chair and looked into my eyes.

I met his gaze and took a deep breath. I turned away and considered his words.

"I really thought working at this postdoc would be great. I remember reading the research coming out of the center when I was in grad school. I wanted to be a part of that. And now I am, and it's toxic as fuck."

"You're seeing how the sausage is made."

"Huh?"

"It's like sausage looks nice on the outside, but in order to make it, you have to grind up meat, fat, and who knows what else. It can be unappetizing."

"Working at CHIVES *is* unappetizing. From the outside, they seemed to be doing great work. But they just recreate the wheel with a few minor edits each time. They don't care about the people. They only care about what will get their research funded. And they dismiss me because they think my research is stupid. They don't care about looking at the spiritual aspects of health. They just care about sex and drugs. And they want me to do that, too."

"The experience is dull. It lacks luster. You're disillusioned."

"I'm disillusioned," I repeated in astonishment. "Damn, I hate disillusionment."

Dr. Baptiste smiled.

"It seems like life just keeps disillusioning me. First with my internship, now with my postdoc. Is anything actually the way it seems?" I asked, not expecting an answer.

Dr. Baptiste tilted his head to the side, still grinning but projecting empathy.

"I guess the answer is no. I'm just trying to get my licensing hours so I can create my own spaces and serve my people. But Tyrone is talking about me like I'm dangerous. They just can't let a Black man be great. His insecurity is fucking with me."

"People often do what's safe, proven," Dr. Baptiste emphasized. "They want you to do that, too. If you don't, it scares them. You threaten their comfort. You thought you were pursuing the height of success. Now you realize they just want you to fit into their box. You see how dull the object is now. But you couldn't have known that before you got up close to the object."

The statement took shape in my mind as I breathed slowly. Dr. Baptiste's words helped me have empathy for myself, my struggles, and my limitations.

The rewards from the systems structured by the whiteness mindset can be so pretty and shiny from afar. They can distract you from your connection with yourself and something greater than yourself, leading you to chase after accolades and success, regardless of what it takes to achieve it. The environment shaped by Dr. Patton's whiteness mindset, which was reinforced by the whiteness of the psychology profession, lured me in. I was enamored by CHIVES's prestige. Although I was initially drawn to what I thought was their groundbreaking community-centering work, I stayed at the center even after having my heal-the-world bubble burst. I truly believed that it would open doors for me in my career. Dr. Patton may have been a toxic person but his power made others respect him. In a world shaped by the whiteness mindset, how one treats others is not nearly as important as products and profit. I hated this. But I believed I had to play the game to win the rewards.

CHIVES was an environment rotting from whiteness. As my Black elders often said, “A fish rots from the head.” To me, Dr. Patton evidenced several symptoms of the whiteness mindset, including psychopathic thoughts, negative emotions, and alternatively lack of emotion and engagement in harmful, oppressive behaviors. One of my psychotherapy supervisors, Dr. Donovan Mase, once revealed to me that Dr. Patton had invited him to be a collaborator on a grant. However, as soon the grant was secured, Dr. Patton stopped consulting him about research decisions and disregarded his rights as a scientist on the project, essentially cutting him out.

Dr. Patton was a white gay man whose priorities seemed to be gaining and consolidating his power in the HIV research and federal grant world. He seemed to cultivate hierarchy and conflict at CHIVES. People were swept away in pursuing their selfish goals, as modeled by Dr. Patton. I, too, was persuaded by the whiteness mindset and began to perpetuate it.

As the highest-ranking Black scientist at the organization during my postdoc, I was consulted by many of the younger Black, Latine, and Asian American students and employees for advice about how to navigate the noxious environment.

“He don’t even listen to us,” Imani, a Black trans woman, exclaimed in frustration.

“Who doesn’t listen to you?” I asked.

“George. When we got this job, they said they wanted to know how we thought about things. They said they valued our opinion,”

Cynthia, another Black trans woman said. She pointed toward his office with her bedazzled pink fingernail, her mouth twisted in disdain.

"Naw, I see what it is now. He just wanted us to be the face of his little tranny project, but he don't want us to have a voice," Evelyn, a Puerto Rican trans woman, added in her heavy Nuyorican accent.

"What you think we should do, Jonathan?" The three women looked at me hungry for a response.

"Follow me." I did not want to have the conversation out in the open cubicle space. I led them to an empty conference room. I closed the door and continued.

"Listen, George is like that. He is brilliant at getting grants because he knows just what to write and then does what he wants after getting the money. I'm sorry you were brought onto this project under false pretenses. You feel unheard. But you've seen how he responds. You will only receive his wrath and dismissal. So you can either stay on and do what you can, or you can leave and put your energy elsewhere. That's what this field of HIV prevention is: white gay men controlling the narrative for all LGBTQ+ people. And it's not just him. That's the NIH research world."

"That's fucked up," Evelyn countered.

"I wish I had something better to offer you. But people have been complaining about him forever and nothing happens because he gets the grants. Don't y'all know the saying that 'cash rules everything around me'?" I shrugged.

One by one, all the trans women hired for the research project resigned, all within three months. They exercised their power to do something different, rejecting the whiteness mindset they had encountered. I decided to stay in hopes of harnessing the position into a promising career. I was a victim of whiteness, but I had also become complicit in it.

Tyrone, my trans women colleagues, and I were not the only ones who seemed to be miserable at CHIVES. In environments shaped by the whiteness mindset, everyone suffers. The suffering often looks different depending on one's identities, but it is suffering nonetheless. The rewards of whiteness can look like a shiny object, but the whiteness mindset is deadly. The whiteness mindset that harmed the mental health of the people at CHIVES is the same whiteness mindset that constrains the well-being of people both inside and outside of the psychology and mental health fields. Pursuing prestige over purpose, and profit over people has tragic consequences.

Shiny object syndrome exists outside the professional sphere as well. Consider how the whiteness mindset harms Black students who choose the prestige of Ivy League institutions over an education at historically Black colleges and universities (HBCUs) that are more often grounded in their heritage and can provide self- and cultural esteem. During college and university admission season it's common to see social media and sometimes TV news reports lauding Black students who gained admission into Ivy League and so-called elite schools.

Headlines such as "Black Teen Accepted into All 8 Ivy League Colleges" splash across the screen. These students and their loved ones are understandably ecstatic about higher education. However, admission to an Ivy League school is somehow pursued as the supreme achievement. This perception is fundamentally tied to whiteness that identifies these institutions steeped in segregation and exploitation as the bastions of intellectual pursuit and professional networking. These institutions are categorized as prizes to be pursued due to the privileges of whiteness found there among faculty, staff, and students.

Ivy League institutions benefit from financial power, receiving 178 times more money from philanthropic foundation donations than HBCUs.[1] In fact, in 2019, the eight Ivy League universities received $5.5 billion from the largest one thousand US foundations; in contrast the ninety-nine American HBCUs received just $45 million. This funneling of wealth allows for institutions with predominately white faculties and student bodies, whose single largest racial group is white, to build better facilities and offer more financial aid to their students than HBCUs.[2] These financial benefits attract low-income students who wish to avoid educational debt.

The privilege and prestige of Ivy League institutions also entices the children of wealthy people who are more likely to associate with students from similar class backgrounds. These students gain professional opportunities through networking and nepotism. This type of power makes some Black students and the children of people from other global majority groups believe that attendance at such institutions imbues their lives with purpose and will create opportunities for them. Just as I chased the institutional prestige of CHIVES, fully aware that it would be a boon to my resume, so too are countless students lured toward prestigious schools only to find the environments are ultimately toxic, shaped by the whiteness mindset. Several scholars, including Dr. Jennifer M. Johnson and her colleagues, have found that Ivy League Black students often report being a minority on campus. In their paper, "Ivy Issues: An Exploration of Black

Students' Racialized Interactions on Ivy League Campuses," Dr. Johnson and coauthors reported that Black students disclosed being hyper-surveilled and surrounded by statues and buildings named for racists on campus.[3] Yet, the whiteness mindset is too strong in many Black students and parents.

For some Black parents, having their children attend an Ivy League institution is a badge of honor. This is especially meaningful because many people suffer from racist socialization based on stereotypes that convince them that Blackness is associated with being illiterate, dumb, and criminal. Paraphrasing Toni Morrison, such racist socialization has Black people believing that they need to go to Harvard Business School to open a grocery store or read Descartes to be smart.[4] The whiteness mindset convinces these Black students that an education from predominately white institutions will protect them from stereotyping. They will be shielded from the savagery of poverty. They will be spared from attacks on their self-esteem. This is a false, distorted belief based in the whiteness mindset.

Research about Black students in so-called elite educational spaces clearly characterizes the repercussions of being in spaces structured by the whiteness mindset. The detrimental effects include lack of a culturally relevant education, social support, and connection to cultural heritage.[5] Black students are tokenized, objectified, and marginalized.[6] They rarely are assigned readings by authors who share their backgrounds. Black professors are scarce. They are also subjected to racist incidents on campus, such as hanging nooses and security guards pointing guns at Black students.[7] In essence Black students are deculturalized.

*Deculturalization* has been defined by Black education expert Dr. Felix Boateng as a process through which a person is deprived of their culture and then conditioned to live by the cultural values of others.[8] In this way, pursuing the shiny object of a whiteness-shaped Ivy League education, Black students are deprived of their indigenous cultural values and rewarded for living and perpetuating the very whiteness-based culture that marginalizes them and the communities they may come from. This sort of deculturalization plagues not only Black students but all students of the global majority when they seek education from predominately white institutions—"elite" or otherwise. This type of deculturalization is now being rapidly codified in US educational systems with DEI book bans that bar students from learning about any stories that do not center white people, culture, and norms.

For me, becoming a clinical psychologist was a process of simultaneously chasing shiny objects while also attempting to resist deculturalization. The institutions in which I trained, like the Indianapolis Midway Academic Medical Center and CHIVES, reinforced the whiteness mindset. At times, I tried on the mindset and let it guide me. But it always guided me to a place of despair and poor health.

Chasing the shiny objects of white spaces and the perceived benefits of the whiteness mindset puts Black and other people from the global majority at risk of mental and medical problems. Dr. Ebony O. McGee, a Black woman professor of diversity and STEM education at Vanderbilt University, and her colleagues found that the harms of whiteness come with hefty ailments. These conditions include depression, anxiety, hair loss, diabetes, heart disease, and suicide.[9] Some students also have reported suffering from racial violence. The benefits of the whiteness mindset have a high cost.[10]

I was chasing prestige in the image of whiteness when I chose my postdoctoral fellowship. I knew the risks but ignored the voice that told me to prioritize my well-being for the reward of having the big name on my curriculum vitae. My sacrifice did open doors for my career. It also sent me running from one predominately white toxic environment to another. Out of the buttermilk, into the mayo.

# Part 3

# Whiteness Is a Mental Health Problem

## CHAPTER 8

# "I Feel Like They Don't Want Me Here"

It was a Tuesday around 12:30 p.m., halfway through my office hours. Twice a week, Mossberger Mountain College required that faculty make ourselves available for students to walk up and ask questions about class or "get to know us." I hated office hours.

Although I liked my third-floor office, which was well sized with a large window that overlooked the lush west lawn, I did not feel completely comfortable in it. It did not feel like mine yet.

My first job after completing my postdoctoral internship was as an assistant professor at Mossberger Mountain College, a predominately white institution in eastern Pennsylvania. After my horrible experience at CHIVES, I was convinced that I did not want a career where my livelihood depended on getting grants, exploiting marginalized communities, being miserable like Tyrone, or treating others miserably like Dr. Patton. Although I loved doing therapy with clients, I was not yet fully licensed to practice independently. I still needed to take the licensing exam. So I could not open my own private practice just yet.

After talking with my therapist, it seemed that an academic career could provide me with a steady paycheck and health insurance while I studied for the exam that would grant me full professional freedom. So I decided to pursue academic jobs that focused on teaching with research being secondary. I hoped that a teaching position would allow me to mentor Black students in a culturally attuned way that decentered the whiteness mindset. I wanted to be a light that guided them into the mental health field to become future professionals. Plus, the job allowed me to indulge in my nerdiness and conduct research in my own way that fully celebrated Black and same-gender-loving people. Even better, my paycheck was not dependent on how many grants I got. I just had to teach my classes. Being a professor had a lot of perks, but it was far from perfect.

As an assistant professor, fresh and enthusiastic, I was at the bottom of the food chain. The all-white faculty of eleven professors welcomed me with wide smiles. They seemed happy to have me as one of them.

Yet, I did not feel like one of them. I was on the tenure track, but not yet tenured. Tenure guarantees you a job for life and academic freedom. With it, you can write or say whatever you want. You can't curse out colleagues, sleep with your students, embezzle money, or anything like that. That will get you fired immediately whether you have tenure or not. But barring that kind of extreme behavior, tenure ensures you have a job. One day six years from my arrival, it would be those eleven white professors who'd vote on whether I should be granted tenure and promotion or not. Although they were nice, they would be my judges. This meant that I had to constantly watch my p's and q's to ensure their comfort if I wanted a chance at being let into the tenured club.

In my head, my father's voice warned, "You have to know what white people want before they do." I felt I wouldn't be able to be my full self until I had the job security of tenure. I would not be able to relax until I was sure of my permanent position on the faculty. My office looked the way I felt inside: unsettled.

It did not have comfy plush chairs or couches for students and colleagues to sit and chat with me. There was no mini refrigerator for Rubbermaid-encased lunches. No Keurig machine for tea during late evenings at work. There were no pictures of my mother, father, siblings, or boyfriend on my desk. I had barely decorated my office. Why put so much effort into design if I would just eventually be denied tenure or even resign? I thumbtacked Amazon-bought posters on the wall.

The flimsy posters had quotes from Alice Walker and Audre Lorde like: "The most common way people give up their power is by thinking they don't have any" and "There is no such thing as a single-issue struggle because we do not live single-issue lives."

There were six floating bookshelves on the wall behind my desk. At five foot two, I could not reach the top shelves, so those remained bare while I found a few books to populate the bottom racks. These were mostly my old grad school books with titles like *The Handbook of Emotions*, *The Construction of Homosexuality*, and *Statistics: The Easy Way*. I kept most of my books at home. There are few things I love as much as a home library. I did not want to raid it for books to seed shelves in a place I was not sure I would be allowed to plant roots.

This concern was not unfounded. I was not just being the paranoid Black man. But when you are Black, *cultural paranoia*—also known as a distrust of white people in predominately non-Black spaces as a defense against racism—is a healthy thing. Drs. William H. Grier and Price M. Cobbs coined the concept of *cultural paranoia* in their 1968 book *Black Rage*. These two pioneering Black psychiatrists explained that Black people's distrust of white people, mindsets, and systems is not a sign of psychosis but indicative of healthy adaptation in an anti-Black world. This cultural paranoia was passed down to me from my dad. I knew that just because my white colleagues smiled in my face did not mean that they would want my full empowered Black self as a permanent fixture in the space that could challenge their power—which is exactly who I would be if I got tenure.

Black professors, once they are in the door and have worked as many as six to ten years for a university, are often denied tenure. They are unceremoniously not invited into the tenured club. A review of data from the National Center for Education's 2022 statistics revealed that Black male professors make up 6 percent of professors in tenure-*track* positions and 4 percent in tenured positions.[1] For Black women, the pattern is similar, with 8 percent as tenure-track professors and 6 percent as tenured professors. We are losing Black professors along the promotion path. Meanwhile white professors increase in numbers as they advance in the profession, going from 59 percent of tenure-track professors to 72 percent of tenured professors. So although I technically had six years to prove my worth before going up for tenure, I had no confidence that Mossberger Mountain College would not find some reason to get rid of me despite my achievements. Based on the statistics alone, there was a good chance that I would not make it over the tenure hurdle.

A report published in 2022 by The Education Trust used aggregate data across five years (2016–2020) from analysis of the Integrated Postsecondary Education Data System to calculate tenure equity at public institutions in the United States.[2] Across 542 US colleges and universities, 34.7 percent had a C grade or lower in their rate of promoting Black professors. Additionally, 4.2 percent of the institutions surveyed had no tenured Black faculty at all.

These statistics are crucial because the higher your rank in the academy, the more power you have to advocate for yourself and your students. Tenure evolved to protect the intellectual freedom and risk-taking of professors; knowing that their jobs were secure, they were free to explore controversial topics and do research that might defy the power structures of the university. Black professors are arguably the most in need of such protection, and yet they remain less likely to secure it. Lack of tenure makes it hard to stand up to racism, and other systems structured by the whiteness mindset, without risking your job.

Countless Black faculty grin and bear it. But instead of directly pushing back against the brutality and isolation of the whiteness mindset at the college, I avoided campus as much as possible. Most of the time my classes were scheduled for Tuesday or Thursday afternoons. So on those days I would come in, teach my classes, and host office hours. My research lab meeting was on Wednesday nights. Other than that, I was off campus.

Although my colleagues were not overtly racist, heterosexist, or otherwise discriminatory, the very fact that I was the only faculty member in my department with a speck of melanin was evidence that they had not committed to increasing racial and ethnic inclusion among the faculty. Despite their verbal sentiments and written policies, their actions revealed the cultivation of a place where whiteness predominated. I was not interested in my colleagues' faux wokeness, their professed "commitment to diversity, equity, and inclusion." Their actions—or lack thereof—and narrow whiteness mindsets forced me to have to choose between isolation and deculturalization or financial well-being and professional opportunity in academia. I resented this predicament.

But despite my reluctance to be on campus, I still held office hours twice a week. I was happy to talk with students who had questions about material from our previous lectures. It was students trying to get to know me that I did not care for. For the most part, students at this elite—well, actually it wasn't elite, it was just expensive—small liberal arts college were from wealthy white families that reeked of racial, financial, and social privilege. They were not especially gifted, just entitled. They were more focused on knowing what they needed to do to get an A than using knowledge to liberate their minds and souls. So when students came to me to ask about how my research was going or if I had any suggestions for readings on intersectionality, it all felt phony. The neoliberal superficial wokeness that they performed turned me off.

My feelings about Tai were different. Tai, a twenty-year-old Black man from South Side Chicago, was the first student to stop by my office on my first day at the job.

"I saw your picture on the website of new faculty and wanted to stop by to meet you," he said, trying to contain his excitement. The look in his eyes revealed his silent thought: *Oh good, finally a Black psychology professor.*

It was the same thought I had whenever there were Black professors on the predominately white college campus I had attended some twelve years before. Having a Black professor, you were thankful that finally there would be someone in front of your class who looked like you. You were confident that they would get you, have your back.

About ten minutes into our first conversation, I was asking him what he wanted to do after obtaining his college degree. He shared that he wanted to become a teacher or school psychologist to help Black youth from the neighborhood where he grew up.

He added, "I want to write about Black men and love."

A broad smile lit up my face and my heart opened. I had never heard a *heterosexual* Black man articulate such a pure emotion-laden desire to me outside of the psychotherapy room. He shared his emotional vulnerability freely with me. That was Tai. I immediately developed a respect for him. I saw myself in him. From that moment on, I was invested in his academic success and overall well-being.

A few months later, Tai peeked his head in the open doorway of my office. I smiled and waved him in. He sat in the hard office chair next to my desk, wearing his signature blue baseball cap.

"I feel like they don't want me here," Tai said, huffing out a sigh and a little of his hope.

"Who doesn't want you here?" I asked.

"The professors, none of them."

"What happened?"

"I was in Adolescent Psychology class and the professor is going on and on about Erikson's psychosocial stages of development. Trust versus mistrust, autonomy versus shame, you know. And I'm like: How does this apply to me or the kids on the South Side of Chicago where I'm from? It's like they don't even think about us in class."

He was not wrong. Erik Erikson is a renowned white German American psychologist and psychoanalyst in mainstream Western white psychology. His career in American psychology ranged from the 1930s to the 1970s, with him becoming popular in the 1950s after publishing his book *Childhood and Society*. In it, he proposed "eight stages of man," or psychosocial stages that characterize human identity development across the lifespan. His theory is still taught in psychology classrooms around the world. But Erikson posited three additional identity stages that are seldom, if ever, taught in psychology classrooms.

Erikson wrote of three stages that applied specifically to Black people, whom he saw as being thwarted by racism and doomed to suffer a "permanent loss of identity." These identities were as follows:

1. Mammy's oral-sexual "honey-child," who is characterized as tender, expressive, and rhythmical;
2. The evil identity of the "nigger," who is characterized as dirty, anal-sadistic, and phallic-rapist; and
3. The clean anal-compulsive or "white man's Negro," who is characterized as restrained, friendly, but always sad.

In Erikson's imagination, the effects of the whiteness mindset—and one of its results, racism—on Black people contributed to them being either hypersexual, violent, or neurotically depressed. Yet, the whiteness mindset for white "American" people could lead to developing hope, willpower, purpose, competence, fidelity, love, care, and wisdom. The whiteness mindset—and its assumptions of fragmentation and value of competition—convinced too many people that the wellness of white people often coincided with the oppression of others. Tai was marginalized in the mind of his professor and the theorists she taught.

My heart ached for Tai. He was not the first Black student to feel as if the Western Eurocentric psychology curriculum left him out. Hell, it left pretty much everyone out that wasn't a white, middle-class, heterosexual, cisgender person. The truth is Black people are made to feel as if they are not welcome in the psychology field at all levels, regardless of their role. This often leaves Black psychology students feeling disconnected from their coursework and disengaged in their classrooms.

Tai's confession highlighted what Dr. Amos N. Wilson, a Black psychologist, wrote in his 1978 book *The Developmental Psychology of the Black Child*. In this important under-read and under-referenced text, Dr. Wilson argued that a psychology built on theories and clinical practice with white children cannot adequately address the types of mental health concerns that Black children may face due to the oppressive educational, economic, and other cultural systems that they navigate.

It wasn't just Tai; many of my Black students were disheartened and tired of psychology and the mental health field not taking them seriously and only viewing them as deviations from the norm or problems to be fixed. It's natural that they would be reluctant to study psychology, work in the field, or take mental health seriously. Psychology as it is taught to many Black students has very little to offer them.

Psychology in the form it is presented in Western schools and universities is based on ideas and scientific studies developed predominately by highly educated, middle-class, old, heterosexual, white men who worked mostly with middle-class, heterosexual, white women. Most psychology departments are filled with similar white men and women who pass those Eurocentric ideas along to students.

If you are Black or from the global majority, you have to look outside of the traditional psychology textbooks to find yourself.

Whitewashed psychology represents an erasure of psychological ideas that originated in ancient African societies. The African roots of psychology predate all others. The oldest thinking and ritual behaviors related to humans' inner lives can be found in the philosophical, scientific, and mystical practices of the Ethiopian, Nubian, and Kemetic societies. According to Dr. Molefi Asante's *The History of Africa*, these societies originate as far back as 11,000 BCE. These societies conceived psychology as the study of the human spirit. It is the study of how people understand and define their humanness within the context of a community.

Anunian and Kemetic philosophies consider the self a spiritual entity projected into the physical realm. Dr. Linda James Myers, who developed the theory of optimal psychology, proclaimed that the African worldview encompasses viewing the spiritual, mental, and physical aspects of being as one, knowing one's self through words and pictures as well as vibrations and rhythms.[3] The values of an African-centered psychology lie in interpersonal harmony and interconnectedness; embracing self-worth as an intrinsic fact that derives from one's very being; and viewing life as unlimited.

Life is thought to be expansive, operating on three planes of existence: the before-life, earth-life, and after-life. The human spirit is thought to be eternal. Even if the body dies, the spirit continues to live. These African-centered assumptions are not based in limitation, scarcity, or annihilation. From an African-centered psychological perspective, we are always connected with the divine and the divine, life-giving energy in others. Because of this connection, the way we engage with others impacts us. Competition, individualism, and materialism do not make sense in this worldview.

The earliest conceptualizations of psychology were not limited by whiteness. An African-centered psychology is a more complete assessment of the human experience that acknowledges the knowable and unknowable. This way of thinking predates any other recorded thought on the study of humanness, challenging the white-supremacy myth propagated in Eurocentric psychology.

This African-centered perspective of psychology is echoed in the similar ideas of Jain philosophy, Buddhist understandings of the human psyche, and Kabbalistic mysticism. These approaches to understanding what it means to be human and harnessing the power of healing all acknowledged the essential role of the sacred spiritual worlds. They did not reject them or narrow them to what could be counted or measured. Instead, the seen and unseen, the known, unknown, and unknowable, were all embraced.

The psychology of today, the theories and science that shape the mental health services created and used around the world, are based on the white supremacist belief that white people and the way they understand the mind is the beginning and default of psychology.

Psychology students from the global majority report experiencing stereotyping, alienation and isolation, cultural bias, prejudice, and challenges to their academic qualifications and merit at school. Psychology students from the global majority do not see themselves or the communities they represent reflected in the mainstream images of psychology. Researchers found that Black Americans were 12.6 times more likely, and Asian American and Latine Americans 5.1 times more likely to report stereotypical representations in their educational coursework compared to white American students. In turn, Asian Americans were 49 times more likely, Black Americans 23.7 times more likely, and Latine Americans 19.9 times more likely to report that their group was not represented at all than to report fair and accurate representation as compared to white American students.[4] Students from the global majority are overwhelmingly presented a curriculum that paints white people and their norms as humanness, deprived of an image of humanity that includes them, and ultimately dehumanized while trying to earn a degree.

This is obvious when you look at the psychologists and "classic" research studies that psychology students are expected to learn in American psychology classes. In any introductory psychology textbooks you will see chapters on social psychology, behaviorism, personality, abnormal psychology, and so on. These chapters are filled with studies that are deemed to be foundational to the understanding of psychology. Yet, the participants in those psychological studies are overwhelmingly or entirely white.

Lists of classic psychological studies often include the Milgram experiment, the Stanford Prison Experiment, the Bobo doll study, and Ivan Pavlov's classical conditioning study. Stanley Milgram was a white American psychologist who worked at Yale University. He was curious to determine if ordinary people could be influenced to violate the human rights of others such as the Nazis had done in World War II.

Forty men were recruited to participate in Milgram's study in New Haven, Connecticut.[5] The participants were paired with a second individual who, unbeknownst to them, was an actor. The participants were assigned to a "teacher" role, while the actor was assigned to be the "learner." Learners had to learn, memorize, and recite a list of word pairs. They were strapped to a chair with electrodes stuck to their wrists in a room that was separate from the teacher and the "experimenter"—another actor who pretended to be running the study.

The teacher was told by the experimenter to administer an electric shock if the learner got any word pairs incorrect (each time moving higher in voltage). Switches on the shock generator administered from 15 volts (slight) to 450 volts (extreme). The shocks weren't real, but the teacher was unaware of this as the actor playing the learner behaved as if they were being harmed.

Also unknown to the teacher, the learner was instructed to get the word pairs wrong on purpose so that the teacher would have a reason to administer the fake shocks. The learner was instructed to bang on the wall of the room (so that the teacher could hear them) after the teacher clicked the 300-volt switch. Milgram found that most participants turned to the experimenter at this point and asked if he should continue or not. The experimenter told the teacher that he should continue.

Milgram found all participants continued to administer shocks up to 300 volts and that out of forty subjects, twenty-six of them (more than half) continued to administer shocks up to the (extreme) 450-volt level. Milgram concluded that people's moral principles to not harm others could be compromised in the presence of a legitimate authority figure—in this case the "experimenter"—that instructed immoral behavior. These results were somewhat confirmed in 2009 by a white American psychologist, Jerry M. Burger, at Santa Clara University when he conducted a similar experience with eighty men and women.[6]

Such findings are often presented to college students as universal. Professors argue implicitly, and sometimes explicitly, that these findings would be seen among anyone put in that situation. I am not convinced. The demographics—race, ethnicity, socioeconomic status—of the people included in those studies do not represent the majority of the people on the globe. If we examine race and ethnicity alone, we see that many people are not included in these researchers' views of universal psychology findings.

In Milgram's report, he does not even report the races and ethnicities of his subjects. He only reports that they are from New Haven, they range in age from twenty to fifty, and that 62 percent of the subjects were white-collar (e.g., salespeople) and professionals (e.g., engineers). Most participants (82.9 percent) in Burger's study had at least some college education and were either white (54.3 percent) or Asian (18.6 percent) people. These predominately white and middle-class participants hardly represent most Americans or students, let alone the global majority of people who are melanated and live in non-Western countries.

So Milgram's question remains unanswered. The reason people violate others' human rights when instructed to do so may be one thing for white people and it may be something completely different for Black people, or for people from different nations. It may be completely different for people across sexual orientations, gender identities, and for those who hold two or more marginalized identities. It could be that the internalization of the whiteness mindset causes people to view authority as infallible even if the authority is morally questionable or blatantly harmful. What is called universal is actually culturally specific. How can anyone responsibly use those findings to describe "human nature" when the study participants were not *just* humans but "white humans"?

Even more demoralizing, the theorists whom students are exposed to are almost never Black or from any other group of the global majority. A Google search on May 14, 2024, for the "most influential psychologists in history" yielded a pantheon of white male faces and names. The American Psychological Association's 2002 list of the "Eminent Psychologists of the 20th Century" is overwhelmed by white male theorists. And a more recent list published by TheBestSchools in 2022 of "The 50 Most Influential Psychologists in the World" included no visibly Black people.[7] It is as if no notable Black psychologists exist in the world that is "mainstream psychology." Yet, many Black students are expected to learn and memorize studies, theories, and theorists who do not consider them.

When people from the global majority are discussed in the psychology field, it's often in negative terms. Dr. Robert V. Guthrie points out in his book *Even the Rat Was White* that some of the earliest research studies of racial differences related to psychological abilities attempted to define white people as separate, members of a "higher" form of human being than people from the global majority. For example, a series of psychological studies from as early as 1881 and 1895 reportedly proved that people from the global majority, namely Japanese, American Indigenous, and Black American people, had quicker reaction times to sensory stimuli and thus were more impulsive, while white people were more reflective.

The interpretations of these studies' results were blatantly biased, designed to imbue white people with a presumed desirable quality of reflectivity and people from the global majority with the ostensibly undesirable quality of impulsivity. Other early studies conducted by white psychologists also allegedly found evidence of Black Americans' lack of ability for abstract thought but prowess in sensory and motor skills. All of these "studies" simply supported the racist lies of the time and justified treating Black people like workhorses.

This type of psychological mythmaking has defined white people as mentally adept and physically underdeveloped, implicitly, and sometimes overtly, suggesting that white people's intellectual skill should be valued over the physical capacities of people from the global majority. This defines white people as the standard in the realm of intelligence. These interpretations highlight how scientific findings can be used to uplift and humanize or, conversely, to pathologize, fragment, and dehumanize.

There are those who would protest that the findings of those early psychological studies are outdated and do not reflect contemporary mainstream psychology. I agree that such blatantly racist interpretations of research findings are almost nonexistent in today's world. However, this kind of overt racism has been replaced with a colorblind mentality that does not address race directly. Much psychological research still implicitly positions white people as the default against which all others are measured. You don't have to look far to find evidence of this exact assumption.

It is common practice for editors of peer-reviewed psychological journals to publish articles with titles such as "Millennials, Narcissism, and Social Networking: What Narcissists Do on Social Networking Sites and Why," "Finding Female Fulfillment: Intersecting Role-Based and Morality-Based Identities of Motherhood, Feminism, and Generativity as Predictors of Women's Self Satisfaction and Life Satisfaction," and "Friendships Between Men Across Sexual Orientation: The Importance of (Others) Being Intolerant."[8]

The broad language in the titles—"millennials," "female," "women," "men"—suggests that surely the authors of these studies have recruited and conducted research with a sample of diverse participants who represent a microcosm of the diverse human species. These research articles' titles suggest that the findings of the studies are, within a margin of error, of course, applicable to all men, women, and millennials. A glance at the methods sections proves otherwise. The samples are virtually racially homogenous. These studies included 6.8 percent, 8.8 percent, and .08 percent of people from the global majority. This is a gross underrepresentation of the approximately 25 percent of US citizens, and 85 percent of people worldwide, who are from the global majority.

While findings from these studies are an addition to the understanding of psychology, they should be clearly understood as an examination of psychological concepts among white people in America, not as universal concepts or even American concepts. However, no journal editors required that the authors change their titles to reflect the predominately white culture of their participants. The absence of reference to white people is commonplace and this small sample of studies is unfortunately representative of the widespread assertion that the psychology of *white* people is the psychology of *all* people. This type of erasure obscures the culture of white people and the influence of the whiteness mindset on psychology. It makes it hard to understand the essence of the whiteness mindset by obscuring it and elevating the psychological experiences of white people to be those of the entire human race.

Dr. Richard Dyer, a professor of film studies, wrote in his book *White: Essays on Race and Culture* that "there is no more powerful position than that of being 'just' human. The claim to power is the claim to speak for the commonality of humanity.... Whites are people whereas other colours are something else." In this way, white people implicitly set themselves as the arbiters of humanity and maybe even the only true embodiment of it.

Experiences of dehumanization and disempowerment in a system structured by the whiteness mindset leave Black students, like Tai, and other students from the global majority insecure in their academic abilities, unsure of their sense of belonging in higher education, emotionally battered by racial insensitivity, and feeling powerless to address these issues. In response, students engage in self-censorship, assimilate to whiteness-centered academic program norms, and abandon scholarly pursuits of interest and use to Black people.

Overall, the low numbers of Black students who persevere in psychology lead to few Black people receiving degrees in psychology. And because of the whiteness mindset that structures psychology, even those students who do get degrees will most likely end up replicating the values of the whiteness mindset. Still without degrees, Black people don't enter the mental health profession as therapists providing psychotherapy, scientists designing culturally aligned treatments, professors opening the door for other Black students, or administrators shaping mental health policy. It's a vicious cycle of exclusion. Without Black people in these positions, Black patients remain underserved, harmed by racially biased providers, and abused in predominately white spaces. These circumstances ensure that health disparities persist. At this point, I'm convinced that the marginalization of Black and other people of the global majority in the field of psychology is intentional.

Many of my Black colleagues and I are intimately familiar with the endless obstacles placed in front of Black students. We went through it ourselves. Different decades, same shit.

✦✦

Dr. Yu had just finished lecturing about logic models in my Advanced Research Methodology course during my doctoral studies at the California Professional Psychology University. Nerdy me, I had taken copious notes. All through class, my mind was percolating, pondering how I might use that knowledge in the future. It was around noon, and after my three-hour class, my stomach was shrieking for sustenance. I was fantasizing about the turkey sandwich I would order from Boudin Bakery across the street at Fisherman's Wharf.

Along with the other students, I filtered into the common area on the second floor. I saw Francesca by the classroom door, and I waved and smiled as I kept walking. That sandwich was on my mind, and I wasn't planning to stop. Before I could turn and take the stairs, I saw Francesca start in my direction. I paused.

"Hey, Jonathan."

"Hi, Francesca. How are you doing today?"

It was as if Moses had put down his rod in the middle of the Red Sea. Waves of tears suddenly flooded Francesca's face.

Francesca was two years junior to me in my doctoral program. I had met Francesca at her new student orientation. As one of the few Black students in my cohort, I wanted incoming Black students to know they had an ally who could help them navigate the program. I wanted them to know that I could be an additional resource for them. Francesca accepted my offer. We bonded over being Black, same-sex attracted, and first-generation soon-to-be-doctors. We were breaking family curses and centuries of oppressive chains.

"Oh no." I was alarmed by her emotional eruption. "What happened?"

"I don't feel like I belong here. These students say some of the most offensive, racist shit and the professors don't say nothing. Then when I speak up and call them out, I'm told that I should respect everyone's opinion. It feels like they don't want me to have a voice."

Listening to Francesca, who was a first-year student, I remembered my own experience of feeling racially assaulted in academic and clinical training settings. I felt her pain and the confusion that accompanied it.

Boiling with empathy for her and rage at the academic psychology machine, I said, "It's because they *don't* want you here."

Francesca looked at me with astonishment. Honestly, I didn't know where those words had come from. But in that moment, I was not thinking. I was feeling. My higher power, flowing.

"Look around," I continued. "How many Black professors do you see here? Don't you know that when they created the first psychology programs, you and I were not the students they had in mind? In their imaginations, we are not meant to be here. But we are. And it is up to you to make sure that you stay here, against all odds. The world needs your brilliance. The world needs your intelligence and the perspective that only you can offer. So cry, get mad. But use that to push you forward, to the top."

I was preaching although I hadn't planned to. The words coming out of my mouth were designed to console her, but I was being comforted by them, too. I guess both of us needed this message. It was like we were in a bubble. The students around us were on the outside. We were safe, surrounded by a soothing divine energy. Francesca concentrated on me. I focused on her. Her dark skin glowed and her Black cornrows shined. At five foot nine she smiled down upon me. God shined down on us, and we shared a harmonious breath. She thanked me for my words.

"Anytime," I replied. She went to class. I went to get my sandwich.

The message I shared with Francesca was one of resilience. Scholarly research on the history of psychology supports the statement I made to Francesca. History illuminates the struggles of the Black students like Francis Cecil Sumner and Inez Beverly Prosser who were pioneers in American psychology.

Drs. Sumner and Prosser were the first Black man and woman, respectively, to graduate from psychology PhD programs in the United States, earning the title of psychologist. There were no Black psychology faculty to mentor them. In fact, Dr. Sumner's academic advisor, Dr. G. Stanley Hall, a white American psychologist born and reared during the antebellum period, believed that Black people were intellectually inferior and members of adolescent races.

What was true for the very first Black psychology students remained true for me, and is still a reality for my students: In an academic system structured by the whiteness mindset, Black students and others from the global majority have had to generate their own power from within and use adversity to propel them forward. It is an uneasy and unjust position to be in. Resilience is the cornerstone of the foundation that Black students, like Tai, Francesca, and myself, had to build upon to survive the assaults of whiteness at school.

To protect their power, many white-minded people pretend to welcome a few non-white people in their spaces while ensuring these *others* never gain actual autonomy. Multicultural sensitivity and diversity are popular topics in psychology training programs. While the American Psychological Association and many APA-accredited schools and internship training programs tout diversity on paper, many Black students find that is not the reality.

As a graduate student, I often heard my clinical supervisors comment, "There are several different forms of diversity and too often people get hung up on race."

The first part of that statement is true, of course. The second part often comes off as an attempt to silence complaints about the very real lack of racial diversity among psychology students and professionals. The tone of that statement and the number of times it was made in response to questions about diversity or race highlighted an unsettling thought for me. Was this comment an excuse to not discuss race? Was it their get-out-of-the-race-question-free card? Deflecting to the various definitions of diversity obscures white people's complicity in the lack of training psychology students receive related to working with Black communities.

Discussions about race and ethnicity were rarely undertaken in any sustained or formal manner at most of the clinics in which I trained. Over the course of my entire internship year at Indianapolis Midway Academic Medical Center, only two psychologists from the global majority ever presented. There was only one formal discussion of race throughout the whole year. A Black American psychologist who was unaffiliated with the organization was brought in from four hours away to conduct it. There was so little diversity in the organization that it had to reach beyond its walls to find a qualified speaker on the topic.

At this site, race and ethnicity were boiled down to one presentation and not discussed in any formal manner during the rest of the year. And that presentation was limited to Black Americans, without focusing on other people from the global majority. I am not opposed to Black people's unique and similar experiences as human beings being highlighted in the study of psychology. It should be a foundational component of psychology education. However, the manner in which the spotlight was shone on Black people was troublesome.

Black people are often discussed in psychology as if they are outside of society and in some cases outside of the species. Black people are presumed to diverge from the default of whiteness-defined humanity and thus are the special cases. They are often examined and presented in a consumable manner to onlookers who, with scientific and objective perspectives, try to understand them. If Black people are the special cases, then who is the standard? Whom does this type of racial and ethnic diversity training serve and whom does it not serve? White people and their race and ethnicities are rarely included in conversations about race and ethnicity. Their racial and ethnic heritages are erased by whiteness. They are placed outside of the paradigm of diversity and once again become the default. Even when attempting to discuss race and ethnicity, psychology training often only reinforces the dominance of the whiteness mindset.

✦✦

Looking into Tai's face, I felt needed and appreciated. Tai and I found community in each other. In my sparsely decorated campus office, we became mentor and mentee. We were older and younger brother. We were uncle and nephew. We were balm for the wounds whiteness inflicted upon us on that campus.

I poured my energy into that young Black man. Not only because I doubted anyone else would, but because I wanted him to have an educational experience beyond whiteness. I wanted Tai to experience—at least moments of—a world where he was at the center. There was space for him to exist in his wholeness, without the burden of stereotypes conjured by the whiteness mindset.

I worked to give him opportunities that I did not have along my own educational and professional path. I shared my time and insights. I advocated for him. I bought him textbooks. It gave me joy to see his growth. I wanted to show him love—pure, familial, unconditional, gracious, and restorative. I wanted him to feel in his flesh the type of love that he revealed he wanted to write about.

Tai went from peering into my door on my first day to being my star psychology student. He took several classes with me: Multicultural Psychology, Abnormal Psychology, and African American Psychology. Where his grades coasted in other classes, they soared in mine. He joined my lab where I taught him how to design research studies. I took him to New York City with me to participate in the United Nations' annual Psychology Day. I wanted him exposed to a larger, grander world than the one he grew up in. We traveled to Boston for conferences where he developed his public speaking skills. We published book chapters together where he flexed his writing abilities. We spent hours together imagining a world where he, I, and other Black people flourished and were adored. It has been my experience that in spaces ruled by the whiteness mindset, it is only the community of other Black people that centers and frees us.

When Tai graduated, I told him I wanted to take him and his friends out to celebrate. He requested that I take him to an escape room. He, I, and two other Mossberger Mountain graduates, Ahmad and Nelson, entered the Pirate's Chamber to recover treasure and escape before our time ran out. Four Black men collaborated, strategized, joked, laughed, and persisted in that space. We were triumphant in our liberation.

## CHAPTER 9

# "Dr. Lassiter Is Intimidating"

An educated Black man is considered a dangerous person. That's a fact, even in the second millennium. Dr. W. E. B. Du Bois wrote as much in 1903 in his groundbreaking book *The Souls of Black Folk*. Generations of Black people before Du Bois had paid with their lives for pursuing education and using that education to liberate themselves and others. In the United States, education is considered both a noble pursuit and dangerous ammunition, depending on who has it and what they do with it. The students at Mossberger Mountain College seemed to view my highly educated, Black, same-gender-loving male self as a threat.

I had just swallowed a handful of dried wasabi edamame when I opened the mid-semester evaluation that my Health Psychology class had completed the previous week. I always liked to do a mid-semester evaluation to understand how students perceived their progress in the class and my teaching efforts. These evaluations helped me make changes to my tactics to assist students' learning as needed. Such evaluations were recommended by my senior colleagues to demonstrate that I prioritized students' learning needs and preferences. One of the comments read:

> I would say that the class has an intimidating way about it. It's challenging and that's expected. But maybe a more easy-going way about the class would help. I like Dr. Lassiter a lot. But I know that some of the other students in the class are intimidated by him. They are somewhat nervous to speak up in class.

I felt a sudden heat in my mouth that was traveling up into my nose. "Are these muthafuckas serious?" my inner voice retorted. I walked out of my office and knocked on my colleague's open door. Dr. Elisa Barron was a counseling psychologist who specialized in teenagers' development. I knew that some of the students from my Health Psychology class often hung out in her office chatting and working on class assignments.

"Hi, Elisa, got a sec?" I asked. Elisa smiled with a full mouth and welcomed me into her office. I had caught her in the middle of an afternoon snack as well. I felt bad for interrupting.

"This won't take long," I said apologetically. I explained the feedback I had received and asked her if any of the students in my class had mentioned it to her. She informed me that some students had confided in her that they found me intimidating because I "expected them to know the right answer." I was confused.

"Are other professors in the department not expecting students to have the right answers? Am I doing something wrong?"

"No, we expect them to have the right answers or at least thoughtful answers. I think they just aren't used to someone like you. You're new. And they are just used to having us white professors," she shared matter-of-factly. "They'll get used to you and warm up to you soon."

Thankful for her candor, I went back to my office.

So, was this a racist thing? A homophobic thing? A gender thing? Was it a combination of me being Black, same-gender-loving, and male? Statistically, I was a unicorn. But damn. Yet another strike against me.

Black professors often get poor reviews from students at predominately white institutions.[1] In fact, researchers have found that students perceive Black professors to be significantly less competent and legitimate than white and Asian faculty.[2] In addition, students have also reported perceiving Black faculty as less honest and honorable than white professors. There is even some research that suggested that students paid less attention to their Black professors during class than white ones.[3] Other studies' findings have indicated that students use their course evaluations to express anger and disapproval at having to discuss topics in a scholarly way, especially when those topics address racism and other types of oppression.[4]

Was I being penalized because I integrated discussions of class, ableism, and patriarchy into my Health Psychology course? Another comment from a student during that time hinted that might be the case:

> I thought this was supposed to be health psychology. It's like multicultural psychology with a few health disorder slides

> thrown in. There is too much discussion about identity, racism, and sexism. I just want to know how to counsel a potential patient about coping with cancer.

Moving against the whiteness-supported fragmentation of scientific rigor and social justice, my classes seemed to annoy some students. This is also true in general US society. Many people complain about discourses and initiatives that seek to integrate both justice and innovation. Black people are often accused of talking about race too much. There seems to be an insistence that if Black people focused on doing good work, they would not have to worry about discrimination because the work would speak for itself. For example, the Fearless Fund—a program to give Black women in tech grants to fund their work—was recently deemed to be reverse racist and discriminating against non-Black people. Anytime there is an attempt to lessen the impact of racism and the whiteness mindset in a profession—psychology, health care, tech—these attempts are perceived as negative and as hindrance to excellence. The people who draw attention to issues of social injustice are often perceived as divisive and, in my case, intimidating.

Did those students perceive me as more intimidating because I refused to be the Sambo stereotype found in historical racist literature? Were they upset because I was not a submissive, funny, subservient version of a Black man that the whiteness mindset implicitly and explicitly made them expect? Black professors are often advised by non-Black colleagues to smile more and be more entertaining.[5] Dr. John Paul Wilson, a white male social psychologist at Montclair State University, conducted a series of studies with his colleagues assessing how race and sexual orientation might influence US residents' perceptions of leadership qualities. They found that for Black men, the warmer their faces were perceived, the more favorably they were rated as leaders.[6] Perhaps if I had acted in ways that made my students feel warm and fuzzy inside, they would have responded better to my authority.

As a Black, same-gender-loving man, I was bound by the judgments of my students that were based more on their perceptions than my actions.[7] Dr. Justin Preddie, a Black, bisexual social psychologist, and his colleague Dr. Monica Biernat reported that Black gay men are perceived as significantly different from both Black men and gay men.[8] They found that among mostly white and heterosexual groups, Black gay men are uniquely perceived as loud, nice, friendly, funny, dramatic, and outgoing.

With my orderly, straitlaced, nerdly demeanor, I was transgressing these expectations. To the students, I was not warm. By requiring rigor, I ripped away Black-gay-male-specific stereotypes that may have benefited me.[9] I was not the sassy, loud, comical, and histrionic best friend Black-gay-man that my students hoped for. I was not the professor they wanted me to be. And because of that, I was judged as intimidating. I was a threat.

After much soul searching, taking my students' perspectives, and discussing this with some of my Black colleagues who were also professors, I came to a realization. For many of my students I was the first Black male figure they had ever personally known. My position of power was unfamiliar to many of my white students who grew up attending predominately white institutions and living in predominately white neighborhoods.

As a Black, same-gender-loving male authority figure, they were required to meet my standards. I was not in service to them. They needed to demonstrate their academic acumen to me. The very nature of who I was and my role in that classroom turned all their stereotypes about Black men upside down. In their minds, there was the angry Black man, the thug, or the servant. The Black gay man was the *RuPaul's Drag Race* queen with the right mix of reading for filth and friendly recommendations. I made the students reconsider these definitions of Black gay men. I made them think twice about their power in the presence of a Black gay man. My Black, same-gender-loving embodiment of intellectual excellence and authority was hard for them to cope with. It fucked them up!

Black excellence is more of a threat than Black disorderliness or thuggery. In his book *We Were Eight Years in Power*, Ta-Nehisi Coates asserts that Black people who demonstrate intellectual and functional competence over and above that of non-Black people are the ones who really strike fear in the hearts of those infected by the whiteness mindset. It is these excellent Black people who incite anti-Blackness from non-Black people. It is these Black people who must be put in their place, lest they prove the pathology of the whiteness mindset. It is these outstanding Black people who highlight the absurdity of the myth of white superiority and the lie of Black inferiority. It is these Black people who are denied promotions, tenure, and election to the highest positions in the country despite their distinguished qualifications.

✦✦

That white girl straight up disrespected me.

It was December in the Northeast and the sun had set at 4:36 p.m. I was grading quizzes and papers in my office. I heard doors creaking and shoes clomping as many of my colleagues left for the night. With one earbud in, I was feeling myself listening to my Bad Bitch playlist. "I'm Dat Chick" by Kelly Rowland, "Lost Ones" by Lauryn Hill, and "Labels or Love" by Fergie played in succession. The braggadocious energy helped me breeze through evaluating the assignments.

The hi-hat of Cardi B's "Bodak Yellow" tick-tick-ticked as Piper tap-tap-tapped on my open door. It was the final week of the semester and Piper had emailed requesting to meet to discuss her grade in the Introductory Psychology course I taught. I had an inkling that she wanted to try to convince me to change her final grade. Although her grade on her final paper was a C–, she had earned a B+ in the class overall. I paused my music and waved her in.

"You need to change this grade on my paper or it's going to be a problem." Piper sat in the chair next to my desk.

"Excuse me, ma'am!" My inner voice just knew that this young twentysomething, white woman had not just or-else'd me. "Who the fuck do you think you are?"

I closed my eyes and took a deep breath. It was no more than a split second but it was enough to stop me from exploding, keeping me employed.

"Piper, this is the grade you earned. Unless you can give me an extenuating circumstance, it's not changing."

"I don't have an extenuating circumstance."

"Were the instructions unclear? They were outlined in the syllabus and we discussed them in class. You did not come to me expressing confusion."

"No, they were clear."

"So what's the issue?"

"But do you really think this is intro-level work?" she said, questioning my pedagogy.

"Yes. If it wasn't, you would be doing much more student-led work and projects instead of lectures and exams. We went through all the information in class. Additionally, the syllabus states that you are responsible for material discussed in the class and material in the textbook, even if it is not discussed in class."

"I know what the syllabus says."

"Okay, then you are aware of the requirements. This is the grade you earned. That is the grade that I will submit to the registrar's office," I said evenly.

"Well, a lot of people are going to be mad at you," she said with exasperation.

"Lucky for me I am a clinical psychologist. I am well trained to handle strong emotion."

"Well, I'm going to your boss. I'm going to tell the chair." She twisted her face in disgust.

"I support you doing what you think you need to do." My inner voice blasted off: "You gon do what to who? Let's find out and see. Uh-uh. Not today, Satan."

Piper got up in a huff. Her brown, flat hair whipped as she stormed out of my office.

"Bye," I whispered. I got up and closed the door behind her. I was hype as I paced in my office. My neck was rolling and my hands were waving embodying my full Cardi B and the stern Black women of my youth.

"I don't know what she thinks this is but it ain't that," I snapped. "I ain't the one, the two, or the three. She got me fucked up. She got the right one today. I'm Joshua Lassiter's son. She think she about to chump me? Not on my watch!" I talked my shit to the empty room.

✦✦

The whiteness mindset with its assumption of scarcity and values of materialism and competition have transformed education into a market.[10] In recent generations, many public colleges and universities have continued to raise their tuition and fees to supplement the decreased funding they receive from their governments. Schools spar for "top" students who can pay full tuition. More accurately, schools compete for cash. Students are treated as customers and teachers as customer service representatives.

In response to market conditions, many universities work to make students believe they are in control of their education. This includes initiatives like promoting greater student choice, the ability to evaluate their instructors, and increased transparency in school performance criteria, like faculty-to-student ratios and graduate employment rates. More insidiously, these responses structure knowledge as a commodity that can be purchased and exchanged. Education, shaped by the whiteness mindset, has become more about product and profit than a process of enlightenment and illumination.[11]

✦✦

Madison, a white female student enrolled in my Abnormal Psychology course, wanted to speak to my manager.

"If you can't do it, I will just go to the department chair. And if he won't do it, I will go to the dean."

Madison was upset because I would not create another assignment for her. That semester I had developed an assignment where students read a book, *YoungGiftedandFat* by Dr. Sharrell Luckett, and worked as a group to develop a theory-based way of understanding the main character's mental health problems. They then had to share their work with the class in a formal presentation.

"Dr. Lassiter, is there a way I can read another book or do a different assignment than the Conceptualizing Sharrell assignment?" Madison asked one afternoon after class.

Students were dispersing out of the large lecture hall. I was packing up my textbook and lecture notes, preparing to head home.

"I'm sorry. Repeat what you just said." I was not sure I had fully heard her.

"The Conceptualizing Sharrell project. I can't read that book. Can I do another assignment?"

"What's wrong with the assignment? Why can't you read the book? Are you unable to find it in the bookstore?" I figured she was having difficulty acquiring the text. I was ready to brainstorm more ways for her to get a copy when she shook her head no. She sighed and gripped the straps of her backpack.

"The book has sex and cursing in it. I can't read that book. It's against my beliefs."

I paused and contemplated my response. Was this a religious thing? I quickly scanned the mental image of the faculty handbook for mention of altering courses to accommodate a student's religious beliefs. I knew that I could not discriminate on a student based on religion. I was not doing that. But I was not sure if refusing to change the assignment might constitute discrimination. I didn't want to do anything to jeopardize my job.

"Madison, this has not come up before. I would have to come up with a completely different assignment. It is a group assignment. You would be the only one reading a different book. That would mean that it would become an independent assignment for you. You would be working alone. Part of what I was hoping to do was to have you work with your peers to discuss and figure these things out together."

"I understand. But I can't read things like that. It would be harmful to me. I don't want to go into it, but I have my own sexual-abuse past."

"I completely understand. You don't have to tell me anything you don't feel comfortable telling me." I took a breath. "Let me talk with the department chair for suggestions about how to proceed and I will get back to you."

"Thank you, Dr. Lassiter." Madison turned and exited the room.

I stayed behind with my mind buzzing and my nervous system knotted. Although I had kept my composure with the student, I was concerned. Could this student's discomfort lead to poor evaluations and negative professional repercussions for me? In the now empty room, I put my hand on my heart and intentionally identified five things I could see, four things I could touch, three things I could hear, two things I could smell, and one thing I could taste. I tried to ground myself in the space. My mind rebelled and ran in multiple directions.

## DIRECTION 1

I want to be helpful. And I don't want to trigger her into having an emotional breakdown. But this is Abnormal Psychology. The class is all about *abnormal* behavior. The ways in which people's behavior is dangerous, deviant, dysfunctional, and distressing. Is it reasonable for her to expect me to drop everything and come up with a whole different assignment custom-made just for her? How will she learn and grow if she never pushes pass her comfort zone?

## DIRECTION 2

Who does Becky with the good hair think she is? So she just gon dictate how I run my class. I can't read this book because it might trigger me. Well, girl, what you think you gonna do if one of your future clients brings up sexual assault in a session? Are you just going to be like, "Sorry, client, I can't talk about that with you. It's too triggering." As an ethical professional, you have to learn how to be there for your clients and then take care of yourself on the back end. Or better yet, avoid the field. Choose something else for yourself. This class is optional. You don't have to take my course. But no, instead of dropping the course, I'm going to ask this Black man to change the course so that I don't have to deal with painful feelings. The nerve. The privilege. This ain't Burger King. You can't have it your way.

## DIRECTION 3

Calm down. You don't know what her request is about. Just go talk to your chair and let him do his job to help you figure this out. He's definitely dealt with this before. You don't have to do it alone.

"Alek." I peeked my head into Dr. Tolman's open door.

He looked up from his computer. The sun set on the sprawling lawn outside of the windows in his office, and I could hear the slight chirping of crickets. He ran his hand through his shaggy salt-and-pepper hair. He wore a red plaid shirt and the beige pants that seemed to be his uniform. I admired his book-filled office. As a book nerd, being surrounded by tomes always made me feel tranquil.

"Hi, Jonathan. I'm just getting ready to call it a day. How can I help you?"

"This will be quick. At least, I hope. I'm ready to go home, too." I grinned.

"Okay, fire away."

I shared the situation with him.

"I don't recommend that you change the assignment. It's been on the syllabus since the beginning of the semester. She has the right to drop the course if she truly believes she can't get through the assignment. But I think she would be doing herself a disservice. It's Abnormal Psychology. If she continues to study psychology and work with clients, she is going to hear these types of things a lot. This could be an opportunity for her to practice using her coping and self-care skills in the face of upsetting stimuli."

I left Alek's office feeling better. I wasn't being unreasonable. As it turns out, this student was acting in accordance with a consumer model, an outgrowth of the whiteness mindset. I resisted. The student eventually dropped the class.

One of my favorite stories that I've heard Toni Morrison share is how she told her creative writing students that they "don't know anything."[12] I always chuckle because her assertiveness and dismissal of the young, know-it-all, self-obsessed student reminds me of my Black ancestors. Although I do believe that, in general, students come with a lot of lived experience that can be enlightening and facilitate the learning process, too few students seem to actually value the learning process. Said another way, I found that many of my students only cared about their grade, not the material they were learning for its own liberatory value. They approached education as a tool, not as a process. Thus, many of them treated me as someone to give them access to that tool and not as a guide or co-learner in a community of scholarship. They did not seem to respect my lived experience and expertise. This went against everything I learned from my parents and teachers.

I was raised in a tradition where—as a child, apprentice, or other role as a pupil—you sat down and shut up. You listened to the adults in the room and learned something. You didn't have to agree but you knew enough not to "push back" against the elders. Sitting down and shutting up is not the end point, but the starting point. The goal is to listen, see, learn, and practice enough so that you become equipped to contribute responsibly to the goals of the community. Not pushing back is not about curtailing people's right to speak up about injustice. It is about helping people realize that what they think they know continues to evolve the more they live and learn. What a student thinks they know at the beginning of the semester will shift by the end the of the semester. By going through that educational process and paying attention to their emotional reactions, students can figure out how to use information—whether it is affirming or painful—to speak truth to power. That's some Black shit. In fact, that's some African-centered-values-based living.

African-centered values are often closely related to the seven cardinal virtues of Ma'at.[13] Ma'at is an ancient Kemetic goddess and considered the spirit of all creation. Maatian virtues are truth, justice, harmony, balance, order, reciprocity, and propriety. Ways of teaching that center these values seek to help students develop their whole selves: mind, body, and spirit. Students are viewed as physically incarnated spiritual beings who bring with them gifts and talents from their creator and ancestors. These gifts are most appropriately used in service to one's community and family, striving to be divine and excellent. To harness these gifts and talents, students must undergo a perpetual process of learning, unlearning, and relearning.

Students cannot do that if they are preoccupied with the superficial achievement of high grades, proving that they are smart through mastery and advancement instead of furthering their responsibility to their communities and the greater divine.[14] Liberatory education is about meaning-making that fosters the values of Ma'at, not just knowledge acquisition and regurgitation. In the whiteness-shaped institutions of higher education where professors led students in acquiring facts and skills, my African-centered notions of agitating students' comfort and getting them to think about their responsibilities to disempowered communities got me labeled as everything from "inappropriate," "mean," and "intimidating" to "biased," "too focused on social justice," and someone who "doesn't know what he's talking about."

The education system shaped by the whiteness mindset is antithetical to the true purpose of education. In ancient civilizations, students learned from elders. Students and elders were not considered equals. This has changed, and now the people who are the least qualified to do so are put into a position of evaluating and challenging experts. Students are taught to believe that their opinions hold equal weight to the years of study and experience that their teachers and professors have undertaken. This is a false equivalency that is perpetuated in an education system based on a market mentality and rooted in materialism where students are customers who must be kept happy. This system is disordered.

In general, order in communal spaces helps a system function for the good of all. Sometimes order is conflated with hierarchies, and so some well-meaning people reject the concept. Hierarchies are often used to justify one group holding power and another group being subjected to that power. A hierarchy is fixed. In a hierarchy, a thing maintains its position regardless of the needs of others. In contrast, order emphasizes maintaining stability and balance in the natural flow of the universe. Order is not fixed. There is an order to all things, but that order is contextual and can change from moment to moment to ensure the well-being of the entire system. As one of the principles of Ma'at, order is believed to be necessary for healthy functioning. It can be used to empower and protect as well as to provide guidance to novices. For example, in a hierarchy, power flows vertically with power concentrated at the top. Order shares power horizontally and circularly, with power flowing among the group. Leaders emerge based on the goals of the group. The goals are ever evolving and thus leaders shift as needed.

Order was exemplified in my classroom when students led discussions and facilitated learning activities such as the Conceptualizing Sharrell project. I possessed the most knowledge and experience with the subject matter. However, to encourage the growth of the entire classroom it was essential that students experienced themselves as thought leaders presenting information, sharing ideas, as well as asking and answering questions from their classmates. Their power was in their voice and how they showed up for their classmates. Observing and conversing with them, I deepened my understanding of their needs, what they liked, and how to better facilitate their learning.

In a place of order, all members have an essential role. I cannot effectively teach if I don't understand and care about my students. And the students can't learn without openness and trust. However, in an educational system structured by the whiteness mindset, a teacher-student relationship based on order, trust, and open engagement is corrupted. I often found my students not trusting my expertise. They disregarded my attempts to establish order and instead tried to overpower me, challenging me to change assignments and threatening to "get me in trouble" with my department chair. For order to function as it is intended, all parties must be aligned in their goals. Many of my students were not and neither was the educational system.

"Dr. Lassiter, I have a question for you," Amy, another white woman student, said as she approached me after class. It was another semester at Mossberger Mountain College, and I was teaching a new section of Abnormal Psychology.

"Yes, Amy." I smiled on the outside, even though this was my last class of the day and I was ready to go home. But it was my job to be available for students, so I put my impatience aside and welcomed the question. "How may I help you?"

"Well, I had a question about the Conceptualizing Kanye assignment."

That semester I had instructed the students to conceptualize the mental health of Kanye West. It was 2018 and Kanye had recently made another splash in the news, declaring, "When you hear about slavery for 400 years. For 400 years?! That sounds like a choice."[15]

Students were assigned to listen to his music and watch interview videos. They were then asked to pretend they were his therapist and come up with a mental health diagnosis for him and suggest treatment recommendations based on their understanding from the class. They would then write up their findings and turn in a paper. Finally, they would give a group presentation to their classmates.

"Okay," I said. "What's your question?"

"We're not therapists but you want us to diagnose Kanye West. Isn't that unethical?" she asked with sincerity.

"Of course you're not therapists. This is an assignment for the sole purpose of learning. You are pretending as if you were a therapist. It's a learning exercise, not an official record."

"Yeah, but the American Psychological Association's ethics code says that we shouldn't make statements about someone's mental health in public. So I think the assignment is unethical because we will be talking about someone in public and we aren't qualified to diagnose him."

Now I was annoyed. Although the student was seemingly genuinely concerned about behaving ethically, why would she assume that I would assign her an unethical assignment? Why would she assume that I am not aware of the APA's ethics code? There I was, her professor: a licensed clinical psychologist with a full PhD. I was considered qualified enough by the other, white psychology professors she trusted to stand in front of the room and instruct this class. But when it came to this assignment, I must have made some mistake. She knew better than me. I was acting unethically. For my sake, the sake of all the students in the class, and Kanye's rights, she needed to bring this to my attention. These are the types of subtle indignities that Black professors face all the time from students who implicitly question their intelligence and authority.

My inner voice: "So you know the APA ethics code better than me? The one with the clinical license? The one with the degree? The one who had to take coursework and pass multiple exams devoted to ethics?"

I tilted my head up and then locked eyes with the student. I nodded with a warm smile on my face.

"I think I know what the issue is." I invited the student to take a seat in one of the desks in the empty classroom. "Amy, have you taken ethics yet? It sounds like you've taken an ethics course here."

"Yeah. Dr. Mosci's class. I'm taking it this semester."

"That makes sense." I smiled again to keep from seething. "You're probably thinking about the guidelines around making public statements and the ones related to psychological testing. But I think you're a little confused."

My inner voice said, "You loud and wrong. Obviously, you not paying attention in that class either."

I continued smoothly, "First, let's discuss the ones related to public statements. Those guidelines apply to licensed professionals. They prohibit us from making false or deceptive statements in a public space. So that does not apply in the case of this assignment. First, you and the other students are not licensed professionals. Second, you are not making false or deceptive statements. You will be presenting your well-reasoned hypotheses about Kanye based on your understanding of abnormal psychology and his work that he has made available to the public. Third, the classroom is not a public space. It is a closed learning environment. The presentations will not be recorded and they will not leave the class."

"Oh," Amy responded.

"And regarding psychological testing, first, this isn't a psychological evaluation. The reports you do in here will not be a part of Kanye's official health record. So the psychological testing guidelines don't apply here. You might also be wondering about guidelines prohibiting psychological testing being done by unqualified persons. But again, this is not an official evaluation. Plus, even if it was, you're a student. Students are allowed to do testing for training purposes as long as they are supervised by a licensed professional. The assignment is completely ethical. You have nothing to worry about." I nodded again this time with an open-mouthed grin.

"I see now," Amy said. "I guess I was worried for nothing. Thank you for explaining this to me."

My inner voice: "You were worried because my Black ass couldn't possibly know what I was doing. It's unfathomable that a Black person can be so qualified. Your white sensibilities make it hard to believe."

"Of course," I said, standing. "That's what I'm here for." I smiled again.

## CHAPTER 10

# Nice White Women

Psychology—as an American academic discipline and profession—is a field where white women represent the majority of the workforce. As the majority, they have a large influence on how the field operates, shaping people's experiences within the profession. Margaret Floy Washburn was the first white woman to earn her PhD in American psychology, in 1894. She was an independent career woman—a prolific writer, productive researcher, and gracious professor. Twenty-seven years after earning her doctorate, Dr. Washburn became the second woman to rise to the highest height of professional psychology and was elected president of the American Psychological Association. She was also the second woman to be named a fellow of the National Academy of Sciences. Dr. Washburn was a hardworking person who adeptly navigated the rampant sexism of her time to excel in her profession.

Although psychology was initially a white-male-dominated profession, after the passage of Title IX of the Education Amendments of 1972, the number of women earning doctorates in psychology grew steadily. In 1984, women reached parity with men. Since then, women have surpassed men in the field. Based on the latest data from 2021, white American women made up approximately 55 percent of the professional psychologists in the country.[1] The clear beneficiaries of affirmative action, in forty-nine years white women went from the margins to representing the single largest group in psychology. White women benefited from the whiteness mindset in the mental health field and academic psychology, allowing them to shape the discipline in their image. These "nice white women" have created a harmful environment, and I have personally felt the sting of the forcefulness of their whiteness mindsets in psychology. White women in psychology have more power than they may think. It will take their numbers to move the discipline away from the whiteness mindset. However, instead of being allies or accomplices, they are often preoccupied with centering their own emotions to the detriment of everyone else.

✦✦

Another Tuesday, another block of office hours. I was at my desk focused on the large computer screen in front of me, working on a research study about Black, same-gender-loving men, their spirituality and health. Specifically, I was interested in how spirituality influenced health attitudes and responses to intersecting racism and heterosexism in their lives. No students had come by that day to ask questions about class. However, in the last twenty minutes three colleagues had already stopped by to chitchat and make small talk. I'd finally gotten back to work and sat typing as I listened to my Concert

Dance Soundtracks playlist. "In the Middle, Somewhat Elevated" by Thom Willems was whipping, hissing, and banging in my ear when Dr. Joyce Rice appeared in my doorway.

Dr. Rice was one of my senior colleagues who specialized in cognitive psychology—the science of how people think and process information. She was a full professor—the highest rank a professor can reach—and had been working at Mossberger Mountain College since the 1990s. A woman at least in her mid-fifties, she was thin and had an absentminded-professor vibe about her.

She was always *nice* to me. She frequently stopped by my office to engage me in conversation about myself, my background, my family life, trying to get to know me. She always let me know when there was food in the faculty kitchen. Frequently she would notify me when my copies were ready in the printer room. Many times, she brought them to me or slid them under my door if I was not in my office. She often complimented the posters in my office and sometimes commented on the "interesting" books on the shelves. She seemed to enjoy chatting with me.

I hate niceness. Kindness, I love. Kindness is expressed through behaviors that demonstrate giving, boundaries, caring, nurturance, responsibility, and reliability. Niceness tends to be a hollow expression of words that communicate politeness, decorum, and collegiality. Kindness takes risks for the greater good. Niceness prioritizes individual comfort at the expense of growth and healing. Nice people pretend to care about others but will choose themselves in moments of consequence. Nice people are fake. They lack follow-through. I have no use for them. Yet, the psychology profession is full of them. Dr. Rice was nice. Many white women have mastered nice while being silent about injustice. For example, my white female colleagues cried about the election results in 2016 (and would do the same in 2024) and talked about how committed they were to multiculturalism. Yet, statistics suggested that they and their sisters overwhelmingly voted to uphold white values, culture, and norms. I heard their cries to me but not to each other.

If Dr. Rice wanted to be kind to me, it would have begun before I even started working at Mossberger. Being kind would have looked like her actively and consistently working to create an environment where I would not be the only Black person on the psychology faculty. It would have looked like her rallying her colleagues to cultivate a space where I was not bombarded by Black and other students from the global majority because they felt overlooked by Dr. Rice and the other psychology professors. Kindness would look like her nominating students from the global majority for departmental awards instead of the typical list of students (mostly white women) who showed academic acumen but low connection to marginalized communities.

Kindness for me, and for people who are marginalized by society, looks like people with power not needing us to educate them on how to be decent human beings. It looks like them prioritizing genuine connection, growth, and peace over power, protection, and imbuing themselves with purpose while simultaneously devaluing others' culture. I couldn't care less about Dr. Rice asking me about my weekend when my Monday started with me having to justify to college representatives why Black students should have their own psychology club and how these students having their own, safe space is not divisive. Dr. Rice, in her decades of employment at Mossberger, and my other white female colleagues, should have already done the work so that such a justification from the only Black professor in the psychology department would not be necessary. White women, like Dr. Rice, need to keep their small talk and focus their energy on making it unnecessary for marginalized people to justify themselves to systems structured by the whiteness mindset.

A particular version of niceness, the *nice counselor syndrome*, was rampant at Mossberger. Drs. Fred Bemak and Rita Chi-Ying Chung[2] defined and explained nice counselor syndrome in one of their seminal articles published in the *Journal of Counseling & Development*. The husband-and-wife team wrote that nice counselor syndrome entails trying to present oneself as a nice person by promoting cooperation with others via avoiding and deflecting conflict, thereby upholding the status quo. These people do not rock the boat and may appear to be playing both sides of an issue, again to avoid conflict. This niceness has negative effects in the classroom and the psychotherapy clinic. Mental health professionals who avoid conflict in the face of injustice often encourage their clients to do so as well. They often recommend individual strategies for problems that can only be solved with collective action.

Nice counselor syndrome is often reinforced by the person's fear of being disliked and subjected to negative peer pressure. They also often fear professional backlash and isolation, refusing to agitate the status quo so that they won't be labeled a troublemaker. In response to conflict, people with nice counselor syndrome often experience anger, anxiety, guilt, apprehension in acting, and uneasiness around strong emotion. All of which makes them even more reluctant to work for equity and justice.

Nice people often feel powerless and thus fail to use the power they do actually have. They are so eager to please and afraid to engage in conflict that their "niceness" prevents them from meaningful action. After all, these nice white women make up 55 percent of the psychologist profession. When it comes to psychology professors, it is estimated that women make up 53 percent of faculty, 49 percent of tenured faculty, and 56 percent of people in leadership positions. If they don't have the power, who does? Certainly not my Black ass or my colleagues from the global majority.

✦✦

"I have a question for you," Dr. Rice said, smiling.

"Sure thing. What is it?" I asked with feigned enthusiasm.

"You know Tanya?"

I nodded yes with wide eyes.

"Well, I just wanted your take on something."

Yikes! My body tensed. Tanya was a bright and anxious young Black woman who had enrolled in my African American Psychology course the previous fall semester but eventually withdrew from the class due to mental health reasons. What did Dr. Rice want to discuss with me? It was giving racial content.

"Okay," I said, inviting her to take a seat in the chair next to my desk.

My inner voice protested, "Why she here, Ike? Why she here?"

Dr. Rice closed the door slightly and sat down.

"I just don't know how to handle this situation with Tanya. I thought maybe since you know her, you might be able to help."

That was a lie. By her own admission, she wasn't even sure that I knew Tanya until a moment prior. She probably just assumed I did, given that we were both Black.

Translation—I thought maybe since you're Black, you can help me figure out how to deal with my Black student in a way where I don't seem racist.

There, Dr. Rice was in my office requesting my help, my labor. She approached me, wrapped in her niceness, hoping to avoid conflict with her Black woman student.

Tanya was in her fourth and final year as an undergraduate. I found her to be an intelligent woman who seemed to be very committed to Black communities on campus and around the country. In my African American Psychology course, she was engaged in class discussions, sharing insightful comments and thoughts. However, I also learned that Tanya had a tendency to turn in assignments late. Super late, two or three weeks late.

When queried about tardy assignments, she disclosed that she had been diagnosed with an anxiety disorder. She shared that anxiety often caused her to feel paralyzed when trying to complete work. Tanya also mentioned to me that part of her anxiety was due to being at a predominately white college. She described feeling isolated and that many of her professors did not understand her. I empathized with her, having been in that same situation myself several years before when I was a college student.

We came to an agreement. She would let me know when she felt overwhelmed and, if needed, we would adjust deadlines. However, those deadlines could not be more than two weeks after the assignment was originally due. Furthermore, she had to turn in the assignment on the new deadline or receive a zero for the grade.

I was trying to communicate the sincere empathy I had for a young Black woman trying to navigate a world structured by the whiteness mindset. At the same time, I explicitly informed her that even in a world of rampant injustice, she must meet the responsibilities of her chosen path or choose a new path. We could be flexible, but at the end of the day we have to show up for our responsibilities. Unfortunately, Tanya was unable to keep the agreement and she eventually withdrew from my course. I was concerned about her, and Dr. Rice *seemed* to be worried, too.

As the statistical majority in the discipline, white women perpetuate much of this whiteness mindset, but the burden of navigating these symptoms often falls on Black faculty's shoulders. Black faculty are often treated as the in-house diversity experts, maids of academia, comforting mammies, and the negro whisperers among our colleagues. Dr. Anthea Butler, the Geraldine R. Segal Professor in American Social Thought at the University of Pennsylvania, expressed to *Inside Higher Ed*, "You have an issue, you bring it to a nontenured faculty member who is a person of color, or a woman, and they have to do all the heavy lifting because they teach race or some related issue. Everyone's calling them all the time, they can't get enough work done and you've already set that person up for failure."[3]

This was exactly what Dr. Rice was doing. Due to my disempowered position as an untenured faculty member, I was forced to listen to her woes. I needed her goodwill when it was time for my departmental colleagues to vote for whether I should receive tenure, and so I was a captive audience for her troubles.

Looking out the window behind me, Dr. Rice wrung her hands. The skin on her thin fingers was red as she rested them on her lap and refocused on me.

"Well, she was in my class last semester and she had some trouble getting the assignments in. She said it was because of all the racial unrest going on." Dr. Rice paused and looked sympathetic.

I mimicked the concern on her face.

Dr. Rice continued, "I, of course, tried to be understanding and ended up negotiating for her to receive an Incomplete in my class. She was supposed to have turned in her missed assignments three weeks after this semester started. That was two weeks ago." She sighed. "I'm wondering what your take on it is."

My inner voice screamed: "Bitch, get out my office with this shit. If y'all hired more Black professors, you wouldn't have to come to me, the one resident negro. Better yet, if you educated yourself outside of your myopic whiteness and learned a little more about racial and social justice issues you could figure this shit out yourself!"

Here my white female colleague was in the office of the only Black faculty member, seeking his counsel about how to conduct herself with a student. She was the veteran educator, not me. She had more experience working with students than I did. It seemed to me that her lack of cultural humility rendered her an incompetent educator. Even worse, it felt as if she wanted me to remedy *her* remarkable ineptitude.

Regardless of the obvious limitations of a whiteness-oriented education, many white psychologists believe that they are competent in their ability to address racial issues when they arise with clients and feel comfortable discussing race in their work.[4] Some research suggests that white women perceive themselves as even more culturally humble than their white male counterparts.[5] These white psychologists' perceptions are indicative of their delusions and overconfidence. White women are no more allies to Black and other people from the global majority than white men.

Black and other people from the global majority have consistently reported experiencing high levels of microaggressions—such as the denial or questioning of their experiences of racism or stereotyping—with white psychologists working in the therapy room, classroom, and research lab.[6] Furthermore, there is conflicting evidence that white psychologists can learn to effectively serve clients from the global majority even after receiving training to increase cultural humility. The research suggested that although cultural knowledge is generally increased, changes in attitudes, awareness, and skills were mixed.[7] Some people who underwent cultural humility training evidenced positive change, some reported no change, and others reported stronger culturally biased attitudes.[8] The whiteness mindset does not require white psychologists, mental health providers, or physicians to have the required skills to effectively work with Black and other clients from the global majority or anyone who is not a cisgender, heterosexual, neurotypical, able-bodied, middle-class, and housed white person.

The overwhelming whiteness of the mental health space has made it possible for white professionals to get degrees, get hired, and work in bubbles where they believe the way they think about the world is universal. They have the privilege of ignorance and delusion. Society shaped by the whiteness mindset bestows another benefit: power. It gives them the power to shape their classrooms, research labs, and clinical offices based on their ignorance and delusions. Dr. Rice's interactions with me and Tanya reeked of this ignorance.

Part of the power of the whiteness mindset is its influence on Black and other mental health professionals from the global majority. Because all mental health professionals are trained to master mental health treatments shaped by the whiteness mindset, Black and other providers from the global majority also dole out treatments that perpetuate whiteness within their clients. Knowingly and unknowingly, they counsel their clients into living lives consistent with white norms.

According to Dr. Wade Nobles, mental health care in Western countries has been developed out of white people's understanding of the world that prioritizes being self-sufficient, perceiving one's environment as being something to control, respecting the individual rights of others, and independence. Through their use of psychotherapeutic approaches such as cognitive behavioral therapy, solution-focused therapy, and other methodologies that reinforce white people's understanding of the world, Black and other therapists from the global majority encourage their clients to further internalize the whiteness mindset and become well-adjusted to injustice. Too often what therapy looks like in Western countries is teaching people who are suffering from the whiteness mindset how to put on a mask of wellness. This mask of wellness encourages white women like Dr. Rice to "care about Black students" but do very little to dismantle the oppressive systems that harm these students, lest they risk their power and proximity to it. Too many white women in psychology smile while perpetuating the whiteness mindset. They encourage Black professors, like myself, to collude in their carnage.

The mask that Paul Laurence Dunbar wrote about in his groundbreaking poem "We Wear the Mask" was working overtime during my meeting with Dr. Rice. My authentic facial response would have included eye-rolling and mean-mugging. Instead, I wore a calm countenance.

"Dr. Rice, I had Tanya a semester back and she had a lot of trouble in my class, too. There is only so much we can do for students. They are adults after all. We can only work with them as much as they work with us. It sounds like she's not holding up her end of the bargain after being given a lot of leeway."

Dr. Rice's face opened up. "I just feel bad giving her a failing grade," she replied.

"I'm sure you do, nice white woman like yourself," my inner voice said sarcastically.

My outer voice offered, "We all have to meet the expectations required of us if we want to accomplish our goals. Otherwise, we have to bow out."

Dr. Rice smiled. "Thank you. I feel better now. You really helped me."

"My pleasure," I responded and returned her smile.

"Ain't that a bitch," my inner voice said. "So that's what this was about. You were asking me for permission. You wanted me to help you feel better. You come in here and disturb my peace because you wanted the Black guy to cosign you failing the Black girl."

In overt and subtle ways, Black professors are often asked to help their white colleagues reduce their white guilt. Dr. Lisa Spanierman, a white woman professor of counseling and counseling psychology, and her colleagues have conducted work on the psychosocial costs of racism for white people. Since 2004, they have identified several consequences that white people experience due to their conscious and unconscious embrace of the whiteness mindset and racism. These consequences affect their emotional experiences, how they think, and their behaviors.[9] One of these consequences is white guilt or remorse about race-based advantage.

Dr. Janet Swim, a white woman professor of psychology, and Deborah Miller explored the topic of white guilt. In their research, they found that white people with moderate to high levels of white guilt reported having lower levels of personal prejudice against Black people. They also endorsed holding stronger beliefs in the existence of white privilege compared to white people with low levels of white guilt.[10] Spanierman and her collaborators found that white people with higher levels of white guilt were more receptive to pro-minority attitudes such as the belief that "being white gives [white people] a responsibility toward minorities."[11] Those with more white guilt also tended to feel less comfortable with their own racial identity. Said another way, some white people who feel guilty about being white sometimes feel uneasy about their own racial identity and believe that they have a responsibility to be *nice* to marginalized people.

Dr. Rice exhibited all these characteristics. She knew that racism existed and that there was a racially tense environment on campus. She genuinely wanted to give Tanya a fair chance. Unfortunately, Dr. Rice's white guilt overshadowed her ability to respond to Tanya's academic difficulties in a helpful way. She was too overwhelmed in her white guilt to approach Tanya as a Black woman student who was having a hard time coping and thus failing to meet course requirements. Instead, she was only able to see Black. Not woman, not student. That myopic focus on race hindered a presumably intelligent professor's problem-solving abilities. She became absorbed with her own guilt from benefiting from whiteness. This self-absorption kept her from realizing that going to the only Black professor in her department to reduce her white guilt was in itself an act of centering her whiteness. It became a way for her to center her own emotions, her lived experience.

This centering of her white guilt was more powerful than an actual shared experience with Tanya or myself. Her whiteness in that moment was aggressively taking up space. There was no room for anyone else's reactions that did not treat her whiteness with gentleness. I intuitively suppressed my emotions in that moment and allowed whiteness to flourish so that I could survive another day at the office.

The interaction between Dr. Rice and me was an example of what Dr. Irene H. Yoon, an Asian American professor of educational leadership and policy, has described as whiteness-at-work. *Whiteness-at-work* is when a person appears to address issues of whiteness but is actually perpetuating it.[12] Actors and social media personalities Nicole Daniels and Lisa Beasley hilariously depict whiteness-at-work with their characters "the nonprofit boss" and "Corporate Erin." Their videos are presented in POV-style where the characters are often talking directly into the camera, as if in a meeting with the viewer. In one video, the nonprofit boss expresses her support for an affinity space "for other workers of color" but then wonders if it would leave out white employees. She goes on to share that the "whole organization is a safe space" and encouraged the employee to "reach outside [their] comfort zone and connect with some white" employees. Corporate Erin also "bumped up" Black History Month to meet "key client deliverables" in the first quarter of the year. While their characters' comments are absurd, they are not far from reality. Whiteness-at-work prioritizes the status quo while pretending to care about a person's well-being. The nonprofit boss and Corporate Erin characters feigned care for their employees' well-being and ability to connect with their communities and culture. However, at the end of the day, they put an emphasis on ensuring that white people's comfort and capitalistic goals were prioritized. This is the whiteness mindset working at its finest.

Both Dr. Rice and I participated in perpetuating a whiteness mindset in our dealings with Tanya. Tanya was suffering from *racism-related stress*—psychological and emotional distress due to experiencing race-based discrimination or being in an environment shaped by racism.[13] The small liberal arts college where I was on faculty and where Tanya was a student had experienced two anti-Black events. One of them was the photoshopping of a noose around the neck of a Black nonbinary Black Lives Matter activist who had previously come to campus to speak about racial equality. The photoshopped picture was copied onto a flyer that was posted around campus. The other event involved a white male police officer pulling a gun on a group of Black male students in a student common area for allegedly being "too loud." These events, understandably, induced high levels of racism-related stress in Tanya and other Black people on campus.

The racism-related stress negatively impacted her mental health, causing anxiety, fear, and hopelessness. It also contributed to poor academic performance that played out in her lack of academic motivation and eventual withdrawal from classes. How could she concentrate on schoolwork in an environment that she perceived as racially charged, physically unsafe, and threatening to her well-being?

Dr. Rice and I knew about the racist events that had taken place on campus. I, especially, knew about the effects of racism-related stress. But I did nothing but effectively tell Tanya to push through it. That was what I knew to do. That *was* what I was doing. I, too, felt uneasy on campus. Angry, frustrated, always watching my back for danger. I was powerless in a department of white people who would determine my professional advancement and financial well-being. But as her professor, I did hold influence in Tanya's academic life. Instead of advocating for change, I leaned into whiteness-at-work. I addressed the effects of racism with Tanya without addressing the racism itself.

In an alternative universe not controlled by people guided by a whiteness mindset, Tanya may have been able to attend an affordable or free, well-resourced university where she was not a minority on campus. No racist events or anti-Black security guards would exist on the grounds. She would have the opportunity to choose a university where she did not have only one Black psychology professor. She would be able to learn in an environment that centered cultivation of the whole student, not just academic knowledge. In a world that is not structured by the whiteness mindset, learning is centered on one's knowledge of themselves in the context of their community and culture, as well as the experience of one's whole self. And all that knowledge is channeled into one's liberation, growth, and oneness with spirit and all living things. But in the Western world, these opportunities rarely exist. Even historically Black colleges and universities and other minority-serving institutions teach Eurocentric curriculums. Even in some African countries, faculties of all Black professors shun their own cultures and disseminate white-supremacy myths. The whiteness mindset coerces us all despite our race, ethnicity, nationality, sexual orientation, gender identity, class, profession, and training.

Dr. Rice used her nice-white-woman-ness to distance herself from her feelings of white guilt. She did not use her position of power to intentionally and consistently advocate for change on the campus before or in the aftermath of the events. She seemed more concerned about academic policy. What was she to do with a student not meeting academic standards, and how was she to do it without seeming racist?

She prioritized her emotions and in doing so she coerced me to collude in her whiteness-at-work through the subtle wielding of her power. As she was a senior colleague with evaluative influence on my career progress, I was afraid of her possible retaliation. She and her nice-white-woman-ness defined the parameters of the department culture as one that prioritizes comfort and politeness over engagement and change. In this circumstantial bind, I gave in to affirming my colleague's whiteness mindset rather than critiquing it. Under the reign of nice white women in the psychology field and in my department, I allowed myself to be turned into an instrument of the whiteness mindset.

## CHAPTER 11

# Killing Me Softly with Diversity

I woke up with a sonic boom in my back. It pounded me out of slumber and into panic. What was happening? The shock waves of pain spread from my back to the center of my chest. Was I having a heart attack? Grabbing the tufted ivory fabric behind me, I sat upright on the couch. I tried to focus on my breathing. It was sporadic like ellipses, coming in insufficient, shallow puffs. I got up to look at myself in the mirror, hoping to ground myself in the image, but my face looked back bewildered in the large bathroom vanity as if to say: "Jonathan, you in danger, boy."

Danger! My memories assembled and finally locked into place: You are having a sickle cell crisis.

Really? It had been nineteen years since I had a sickle cell crisis. And it hadn't felt like this. Instead, it felt like a thousand knives stabbing me all at once. Yet, standing in my living room, the agony slammed into me, threatening to overtake me.

My brain bounced: What should I do?

This was my first medical emergency while living alone. My mother was 710 miles away in Georgia. My boyfriend was 107 miles away in his apartment in New York City. My best friend was 7 miles away presiding over a rehearsal for the Mossberger Mountain College theater kids. I could not rely on anyone. I had to get to the hospital.

My body raw with agony, I eased on a jacket, my shoes, and a skullcap. With painful steps, I made my way from my third-floor apartment out into the winter air. I sat in my car, willing the pain to lessen just a little so I could drive myself to the emergency room. I managed to make it to the stop sign right outside of my apartment complex. That's just what I did: stopped. I realized that I was not going to be able to get to the hospital on my own. My anguish was too great. I turned around and drove back into the parking lot of my building. I sat in my car as I pressed 9-1-1 and told the dispatcher that I was having chest, back, leg, and arm pains due to a sickle cell crisis.

"Please, send someone. I'm in a silver Ford Focus in front of Building I."

About ten minutes later, I heard a siren and saw flashing lights. I grunted gratitude to god and my ancestors. I almost fell out of my car wheezing, trying to wave down the emergency medical technicians.

"I'm the one that called. I have sickle cell anemia and I think I am having a pain crisis." I strained out the words. The three thin white men in blue uniforms ushered me into the back of the ambulance, took my vitals, and administered pain medicine. Finally, relief. My head ballooned into a cloud and nothing else mattered. My body melted on the mattress.

I spent ten days in the hospital recovering from the breakdown of my blood cells. After discharge, my boyfriend cried telling me that I almost died. My best friend whispered her worry of losing yet another loved one. How had I gotten there?

✦✦

Believing people with a whiteness mindset when they say they value diversity and multiculturalism can lead to health risks and in some cases death. Sometimes people want to believe in the goodness of others so much that they overlook whiteness in the environment and in their colleagues. People who are of the global majority often have experiences in predominately white organizations that are detrimental to their emotional and physical health. Too many of us work hard and swallow the poison forced down our throats by people operating according to the assumptions and values of the whiteness mindset. We suppress our anger, our sadness, or despair. Emotional suppression kills. How many times will we let the whiteness mindset and its outcomes—racism and other forms of bias—overtake us?

Dr. Roy L. Brooks, a Black professor of law at the University of San Diego, described the *Clyde Ferguson syndrome* in depth in one of his most searing papers examining whiteness.[1]

The Clyde Ferguson syndrome is named after Clarence Clyde Ferguson Jr. He was a former dean of the Howard University School of Law, former distinguished professor of law at Rutgers University Law School, and the Henry L. Stimson Professor of Law at

Harvard Law School. As evidenced by these white-people-defined prestigious professional posts, Ferguson was a very hardworking, high-achieving person. Despite his pioneering career and perseverance, he prematurely died of a heart attack at age fifty-nine. The syndrome Dr. Brooks named after him describes exactly that scenario—when a high-achieving minoritized person is recognized for their success, but suffers crushing health implications as they work themselves to death to keep up with the mounting requests and demands without receiving proper support.

For example, an Afro-Latina professor may be promoted and awarded tenure for her research. However, now she has several requests from community organizations to collaborate with them, Latine students seeking her out for mentorship, the dean of her school expecting her to bring in more grant money and chair committees, and her white peers trying to invalidate her research. Simultaneously, she does not receive any additional support from her university or community members. Success and recognition become toxic and costly to her health as she tries to balance all of these demands. The whiteness mindset convinces her that through sheer individualistic effort she can amass more material markers of success and prove her worth in a system that was not created for her or does not see her as inherently valuable. The mindset induces fear of losing her position and prestige. The primary goal becomes acquisition of achievements, which she convinces herself will lead to justice and empowerment for her community. The whiteness mindset causes her to devalue her relationships and deprioritize her connection to something greater than herself and the material world around her. She puts her energy into trying to meet the standards of those who do not value her. She ends up isolated, burned out, and spiritually depleted.

The whiteness mindset is a major source of stress in many Black professors' lives. Many Black professors and other professors from the global majority end up losing their way and the passion that brought them to their work in the first place. Some Black professors go in the opposite direction and try to be everything to everyone in a system that deprives them of basic support and care. According to Brooks, stress for these professionals may look like having to navigate disrespect from white students and the pressure (and privilege) of showing up for students who are from the global majority. Black professors must also deal with the lack of support from school administrators. Additionally, many Black professors carry the guilt of being middle-class while knowing that many of their family members are still financially struggling due to capitalism that hoards resources for a very small few. This stress kills.

According to ABC News and *The Guardian*, Dr. Antoinette "Bonnie" Candia-Bailey, the former vice president of student affairs at Lincoln University, died by suicide after alleging that she was harassed and bullied by a white male administrator.[2] This Black woman administrator suffered from anxiety and depression. A friend who spoke at Dr. Candia-Bailey's funeral described the conditions this Black woman faced as "inhumane, disingenuous, cruel and heartless." Dr. Candia-Bailey's story is just one example of the extreme impact the whiteness mindset has on Black professionals.

Far too often the whiteness mindset, and the unjust systems it perpetuates, wreaks havoc on Black minds, bodies, and spirits. Although we don't have statistics on how many faculty from the global majority have died due to the stress of the whiteness mindset that they must face while trying to do their jobs, we do know that ongoing stress shortens life expectancy. This is true of Black professors and other professionals who navigate predominately white fields or who work in environments shaped by the whiteness mindset. Unfortunately, there are few mental health resources to help Black people navigate the whiteness mindset in professional settings.

✦✦

Diversity almost killed me. Well, my attempts to cope with white people's lies about valuing diversity almost killed me. Almost losing my life once and for all taught me the lesson: White people do not value diversity, they value power, keeping their world ordered by the whiteness mindset.

About a month prior to being hospitalized, I had a two-day, on-campus interview at the Massachusetts Research University (MRU) for a multicultural clinical psychology assistant professor position. Tired of the whiteness-at-work I was experiencing at Mossberger, I decided to apply for another position that I hoped would offer better conditions. I came across the job ad in an email from the Society for the Psychological Study of Culture, Ethnicity and Race's listserv. The ad read:

> We plan to hire a top scientist with expertise in multicultural clinical psychology. In particular, we seek candidates whose research contributes to understanding and fostering mental health of individuals from diverse racial and ethnic

> backgrounds. Candidates who focus on African American or Latino populations are particularly encouraged to apply.

After reading the job ad, I was motivated to apply. I had ample experience teaching multicultural psychology and African American psychology. My research focused on Black American, same-gender-loving people's health inequities. Plus, I had co-edited a book on the subject. I was definitely a top scientist in the area, having received federal and institutional funding for my projects. As requested, I compiled my cover letter, curriculum vitae, statement of research interests and teaching philosophy, three samples of representative research papers, and the names and contact information of three references.

I submitted my application via the online job portal on November 1, 2017. On November 20, I received an email inviting me to participate in a Zoom interview. I was elated. On December 1, I met four pale smiling faces for a videoconference. They asked me questions about my professional background and why I wanted the job. After answering the standard questions with warmth, humor, and passion, I ended the call feeling confident that I would advance to the next round of interviews.

About three days later, I received an email from the search committee chairperson.

> From: Dr. Lonora Hains
>
> To: Dr. Jonathan Mathias Lassiter
>
> Subject: Letters of Recommendation

Dear Dr. Lassiter,

Thanks for interviewing with us via Zoom. We only have two letters of recommendation for you—one from Dr. Wexler and one from Dr. Braun. We had requested a letter from Dr. Clarke but have not received it yet. We will need three letters of recommendation to move forward.

Is it possible to get a letter from either your graduate school mentor or post-doc supervisor? Additionally, although we only require three letters, two additional letters would be ideal. Finally, your letter from Dr. Braun, your former English professor as an undergraduate, is not suitable. We would like a letter from someone more familiar with your work.

Thank you.

Although this email was straightforward, it did set off my whiteness radar.

Okay, fair, you want to be sure that my third letter of recommendation was submitted before moving me forward. That's standard. However, the search committee now wanted two additional letters—although only three were required?

...And there it was: changing the rules, requiring more of Black people.

I heard my father: "As a Black man, Slim, you are going to have to work twice as hard to get half as far."

I thought of Jay-Z's rhymes on "99 Problems" about the racism of the legal system that gives Black men longer sentences. There was always a Black tax.

My situation was not unique. Black people across several professions experience whiteness-based racism when on the job hunt.[3] First, applicants with "Black-sounding names" are about half as likely to be contacted for job interviews compared to applicants with "white-sounding names." Black job applicants' resumes are often given less consideration, as resume screeners spend less time reading them. Researchers have found that compared to white employees, Black people are assumed to be less skilled and efficient workers and are scrutinized more. This hyper-scrutiny means that supervisors are more likely to notice a mistake if one is made by a Black person, compared to a white one. This sets up an environment where Black workers are then fired at higher rates than their white counterparts because they are being monitored more. Basically, the whiteness mindset assumes Black inferiority, analyzes Black employees looking for evidence of that inferiority, and then fires Black employees for making minor mistakes that confirm supervisors' preconceived belief about Black inferiority. In psychology, we call this confirmation bias.

MRU's search committee chair's email hinted at an environment where—if I were let in—my Black ass would, once again, be the only one on faculty and would probably often be asked to do more than others. I paused.

I knew the words of my father and Shawn Carter in my head were right. Yet, I had a hard decision to make. As a young professor I was tired of being harassed by the white people at my current job at Mossberger Mountain College. I hoped that maybe the white people at MRU would be a little better. And if not, at least it would be a higher-paying position at a more prestigious school, attributes that the inexorable mindset of whiteness had taught me to value. I propelled myself forward. I swallowed, secured the additional letters from two of my dissertation committee members, and awaited acknowledgment.

The search committee chairperson promptly responded, writing, "Thanks for these. Your post-doc supervisor is George Patton, right? Can you get a letter from him?"

With those words, the situation went from bad to worse. First, I was asked for two more additional letters than required. Now I was being instructed to have one *particular* white man write a letter legitimizing me. My zeal morphed into exasperation. The two Black elders' words echoed again in my head like a warning. Again, I ignored them. My ambition pushed me forward and I scrambled to get that specially requested letter. Dr. Patton wrote it. Ten days later I was invited for a two-day, on-campus interview to meet with the faculty members in the clinical division of the Psychological and Brain Science Department. My heart hopped with hope.

The night before my interview, I kissed my boyfriend and left his apartment in Inwood. As I drove north on I-95, I left the city lights and tall brick buildings behind. Ahead of me were narrow highways, quiet New England towns, and possibly my future.

I was tranquil and slightly melancholic as I pressed pause on Gregory Porter's "Be Good (Lion's Song)" and turned off the car as I stopped at the Campus Center Hotel.

The next morning, after an agitated sleep, I dressed in my best navy blue cotton suit with a black-gray-and-white-checkered shirt.

My black shoes and gray knit tie completed the look. I examined myself in the mirror and then headed out to commence the grueling marathon of smiling, nodding, being charming and intelligent. My schedule was packed for the next two days, as was customary for academic job interviews. They made you jump through so many hoops. In addition to a forty-five-minute job talk where I had to explain my research, I was scheduled for sixteen thirty-minute interviews, three breakfast meetings, and daily lunch and dinner meetings.

When I stepped outside of the hotel into the ascending sun, I got a glimpse of the frostbitten campus that was littered with soaring buildings, squat squares, and rolling greens. A few shivering students shuffled to classes. I said a prayer for prosperity and put on the face all Black people—who have been raised right—know to wear in front of white people. It's a face of warm neutrality—not scary and not too happy, lest I come off as unhinged or, worse, arrogant. The face held just the right mix of enthusiasm, sincerity, and affability.

Along with this demeanor came head tilting, to communicate serious consideration of what was being said to me. As a Black, same-gender-loving man, I had learned to play up my sexual orientation in these spaces. Highlighting my femininity just a little tended to help white women relax their shoulders. They seemed to act as if they believed that a same-gender-loving man was more similar to them, not as aggressive as a heterosexual one. White men seemed to consider me less of a threat, possibly believing that my masculinity was inferior. If needed, they could easily intimidate me with their brute forcefulness. I used their stereotypes to my advantage. I was in full-on "get this job" mode.

On day one of the interview, I was pumped with caffeine, hoping to keep my neurons firing fast. In the Psychological and Brain

Science building, I walked down a long corridor. I felt pressure in my gut. I had to pee, maybe something more. Whatever it was, I had to hold it as I made my way to my next meeting. My guide's heels clicked, surrounding us in echoes as we hurried along. The Psychology Department's administrative assistant, Marisol, a short, Latina woman—one of the few people from the global majority I had met thus far—smiled and pushed her auburn bob out of her eyes as she waved her hand to announce we had arrived at our destination.

If I were to ask any of the white people in the Psychology Department at MRU if centering whiteness was their intention, they would have denied it. Yet, with the exception of the administrative assistant, only three faculty members out of forty-five were people from the global majority. Only one of those people was Black. I'm sure my interviewers would tout how much they valued diversity, equity, and inclusion. People with a whiteness mindset believe the lies they tell themselves. At least, they desperately want to believe them. Some might consider these well-meaning people to be aversive racists. Drs. Samuel Gaertner and John Dovidio published the seminal paper defining *aversive racism* in 1986.[4] According to Dovidio and Gaertner:

> Aversive racists sympathize with the victims of *past* injustice, support the principle of racial equality, and regard themselves as nonprejudiced, but, at the same time, possess negative feelings and beliefs about *Blacks*. (Emphasis added by this author.)

Drs. Dovidio and Gaertner highlighted in their work that aversive racism is common among well-educated and liberal white people in the United States. This racism usually shows up in countless ways that I and other Black people have witnessed. Some people infected by the whiteness mindset feel their racism as discomfort, disgust, and fear.

Regardless of the predominately white faculty's feelings about their whiteness and aversive racism, I was committed to landing the job. Marisol wished me good luck and walked back to her desk. I looked into the small square space, barely adorned, and met the smile of a dark-haired white man with bushy eyebrows and Homer Simpson stubble sitting at his desk. He stood to shake my hand.

"Good morning, nice to meet you," he said in a nasally deep voice.

"Good morning. I'm Jonathan."

"Adrian."

"Thank you for taking the time to meet with me."

"Oh, no problem." He smiled. "Last year, I was in the position you are in now." Dr. Adrian Gordon was the most recent hire in the clinical division of the department.

"Any advice?" I joked.

"Honestly, I don't know how I got this job. I guess I'm just lucky," the thirtysomething white heterosexual male professor revealed.

"You're being modest." I smiled and changed the subject. "Well, tell me about your transition to the department. How has that been?"

Dr. Gordon continued to talk with enthusiasm. He had a calm friendliness to him. The way he sat in his office chair and smiled widely communicated confidence.

As he talked, my mind lingered on his candid comment. I didn't know how he had gotten that job either. At least not based on merit. I had reviewed his resume—and those of the other people I was scheduled to meet with on campus—before arriving to MRU. He was not impressive even by white people's standards. He had only seven peer-reviewed publications in scholarly journals, no major grants, and no teaching experience when he interviewed for the position.

Was what he was calling *luck* really just white able-bodied heterosexual male privilege? On the other hand, I had ten peer-reviewed publications in scholarly journals, an award-winning book, and almost two years of college teaching experience. I should be a shoo-in, right?

My last interview day was January 27. By February 20, I felt like the girl in "Doo Wop (That Thing)." It had been three weeks and I was wondering if they would call. I emailed a follow-up and was directed to the department chair. The chair replied to my inquiry.

> From: Dr. Carly Rollins
> To: Dr. Jonathan Mathias Lassiter
> Subject: Search Update
>
> Dear Dr. Lassiter,
>
> All I can tell you at this time is that we are waiting for the Dean's approval before moving ahead.
>
> Best,
> Carly

I should have taken that email to mean they had chosen someone else. But I was hoping against hope. I was desperate to leave my current job. I was tired of the entitled, barbaric white students who equated my Blackness with servitude and my colleagues' subtly racist comments. I couldn't take much more. I had to escape.

I know I had done an amazing job with my interviews. One faculty member who attended my research talk commented, "That was a captivating talk. You've set the bar really high for the other candidates."

But being directed to the department chair set off a firestorm of frenzy inside me. I was feeling anxious, wondering, "Damn, these other candidates that much better than me?"

After being directed to speak to the department chair, I was sure that my Black ass was not going to get the job.

But a part of me was refusing to let the dream deteriorate. Back on Mossberger's campus, I had just finished my day of meetings with colleagues and students. My nerves were jangled. Sheryl, my best friend, suggested we get some alcohol. Over drinks at a Mexican restaurant, I vented my anxiety. I was both drained and agitated.

In between looking at the menu, she beamed compassion at me. Her long jet-black braids framing her tawny cheeks made her look like she could be Poetic Justice-Janet's cousin.

Sheryl and I took turns using our warm salted tortilla chips to scoop out the guacamole. After about three sugary boozy drinks, I was talking my shit.

"But seriously, I know they didn't get anyone else better than me. They can't! I mean that person doesn't exist. Not doing what I'm doing."

"I know," Sheryl joined in. "Man, fuck 'em. They make us jump through all those hoops and then hire the white person."

Sheryl was not wrong. A few prominent white professors have publicly stated the unspoken: that search committees may be intentional in centering whiteness in their hiring processes. Dr. Marybeth Gasman, a Distinguished Professor at Rutgers University, made it plain when she wrote in *The Hechinger Report* in 2016: "The reason [universities] don't have more faculty of color among college faculty is that we don't want them. We simply don't want them."[5]

Dr. Gasman, a white woman and proclaimed leading scholar on historically Black colleges and universities, presented five reasons she had personally witnessed in her—at the time—sixteen years of being a faculty member at "elite institutions" such as the University of Pennsylvania. She penned:

1. The word "quality" is used to dismiss people of color who are otherwise competitive for faculty positions. . . . "Quality" means that the person didn't go to an elite institution for their Ph.D. or wasn't mentored by a prominent person in the field.
2. The most common excuse I hear is "there aren't enough people of color in the faculty pipeline." . . . When I hear someone say people of color aren't in the pipeline, I respond with "Why don't you create the pipeline?" "Why don't you grow your own?"
3. I have learned that faculty will bend rules, knock down walls, and build bridges to hire those they really want (often white colleagues) but when it comes to hiring faculty of color, they have to "play by the rules" and get angry when any exceptions are made. Let me tell you a secret—

exceptions are made for white people constantly in the academy; exceptions are the rule in academe.

4. Faculty search committees are part of the problem. They are not trained in recruitment, are rarely diverse in makeup, and are often more interested in hiring people just like them rather than expanding the diversity of their department.
5. If majority colleges and universities are truly serious about increasing faculty diversity, why don't they visit Minority Serving Institutions—institutions with great student and faculty diversity—and ask them how they recruit a diverse faculty. This isn't hard. The answers are right in front of us. We need the will.

None of this is news to the highly qualified Black people like myself who have had stellar interviews for employment positions and then did not get the job. It does not take a rocket scientist or a PhD in psychology to count. If your workforce is *all* white, or all white with the exception of one or two melanated faces, then there is a problem. And there is no need for an implicit-bias training workshop to figure that out. There is no need for an investigation.

But regardless of how obvious the centering of the whiteness mindset is in the hiring process, Black and other people from the global majority have little recourse. We are often not in the position to push back.

"It's just not fair. I know I'm better than the other candidates. As a Black, same-gender-loving man, I had to be to even get in the room."

"You right. They don't let us in the door without having already done two, three times more than them just to prove we know what we doing."

"And what were all of those letters for if they weren't going to give me the fucking job!"

"I know…" Sheryl sighed.

"They wanted the white man they knew to vouch for the nigga. Can this nigga read? Is he a good negro?" I mocked.

Sheryl smiled. "But you never know. They haven't said no yet. For all you know, you could still be in the running. They just might be slow."

"I hope you're right. I really do." I felt my eyes watering.

"Naw, you have to get that job."

As Sheryl finished her hopeful declaration, a waiter came over with a tres leches cake with a single burning candle and a glass of champagne.

"Someone told us it's your birthday," he said, looking at me. I looked at Sheryl shocked. She looked back bewildered.

"Umm, okay. It's not my birthday," I said to the waiter. "It must be a mistake."

"Well, it's here now. Why don't you just enjoy it?" he replied.

"Okay." I shrugged. "Thank you." The waiter set the items down and walked away. Sheryl and I shared a puzzled look.

"You think it's poison?" I halfway joked.

"Naw," Sheryl laughed. "It's a sign. See, god already wants you to celebrate. That job at MRU is yours."

"Listen, from your lips to god manifesting it into the universe." I drank the sparkling liquid while sharing the dessert with Sheryl.

I was trying to be in the moment. Take the cake and champagne as a sign of good fortune. But it was a struggle. My shoulders were sunken. The stress of the situation and circulation of alcohol in my bloodstream left me feeling depressed. I went home that evening and collapsed on my couch. An hour later, I woke up fighting for my life. I spent ten days in the hospital getting blood transfusions and being pumped with pain meds.

About a week after being discharged from the hospital, I got the official email.

> From: Dr. Lonora Hains
>
> To: Dr. Jonathan Mathias Lassiter
>
> Subject: Search Committee Results
>
> Dear Dr. Lassiter,
>
> Thank you for interviewing with us. We had a very strong applicant pool. However, you have not been selected for the position. We wish you the best of luck.
>
> Sincerely,
>
> Dr. Lonora Hains

These four sentences unceremoniously nailed the coffin shut on the MRU job. Yet, the oxycodone I was taking to manage my pain buffered me from an emotional crash.

A few months later, I checked MRU's departmental website to see who they had hired. Although there was no sure way of knowing,

I assumed the new face on the website was the new hire. That face belonged to a fair-skinned Latina who studied trauma and intimate partner violence primarily among Latine people. She was fresh out of graduate school and, according to her publicly available resume at the time, seemed to have done even less than the white guy they hired before her. Neither of them had the resume that I had. However, I was happy for her and hoped she would excel despite the obstacles she would surely face.

The whiteness mindset is often looking to protect itself. One of the ways it does that is by only allowing in people who will not threaten it. I was already an accomplished professor. My research was blatantly pro-Black. I have no doubt they did not want to have to deal with potential challenges to their status quo. A Black, highly qualified person is a threat, dangerous. Dr. Carl Hart—a world-renowned Black neuroscientist and author, and one of my personal heroes—wrote about his difficulty getting Black faculty hired in the Psychology Department he chaired at Columbia University. In *Drug Use for Grown-Ups*, Dr. Hart wrote:

> Black candidates, it seemed, not only had to have an extraordinary academic record but also had to be deemed non-threatening. If a current faculty member felt threatened by the candidate's independence, intellect, popularity, success, whatever, it was a wrap.... Instead of focusing on the applicant's record, [hiring discussions] too often descended into innuendo and whispering campaigns based on rumors from anonymous third-party sources. The anonymous

> information is usually disclosed by faculty members who are the biggest proponents of "diversity."[6]

Black people who hope to become psychology professors are faced with an impossible task that often leads to more mediocre white men and women being hired over "highly qualified" Black applicants. The Black applicant may have more experience and impressive achievements—usually accomplished with less access to academic resources, social capital, and economic assets. But they are not white. Being white is the known. It is comfortable. And most people prioritize their comfort over their well-being and the well-being of society. Institutionally desirable diversity typically amounts to hiring melanated versions of white subordinates. Deans and department members want melanated people who will not complain or challenge their whiteness mindsets and the systems of power they have put in place. Preference is given to people who study traditional mental health problems (e.g., depression, trauma) using statistical methods *but* with samples composed of melanated people. These faculty are expected to have graduated from PhD programs that their colleagues recognize and publish in academic journals their colleagues respect. And, maybe most importantly, they cannot be too forceful about diversity and social justice. These candidates should talk about race and justice, but not push the point beyond the standards of *niceness* in the institution. After all, the institution highly values diversity and recognizes it needs to do better. The Black faculty member needs to remember this and have patience. The path to becoming a Black psychologist who works in predominately white institutions is a minefield of navigating being *diverse enough* while also being nonthreatening.

Centering whiteness in the hiring process keeps Black professors out of the halls of academia, but this does not equate to only interviewing white candidates. Due to "diversity mandates," many job searches for professors must have a certain number of job candidates who are women or "people of color" at each stage of the hiring process. At least that was true when I was interviewing. Now with the recent whitelash against "DEI," racists are emboldened in their push opposing the consideration of race and other markers of difference among potential employees.

In 2018, you often saw jobs ads stating: "We encourage members of historically underrepresented groups to apply."

Sometimes the ads are even less committal and more obligatory: "The New Woods University is committed to a policy of equal opportunity in all its activities and programs, including employment and promotion. The New Woods University does not discriminate on the basis of age, race, color, creed, sex or gender (including gender identity and expression), pregnancy, sexual orientation, religion, religious practices, mental or physical disability, national or ethnic origin, citizenship status, veteran status, marital or partnership status, or any other legally protected status."

All candidates expect to be seriously vetted during the application process. It is common to ask for research statements, teaching philosophies, sample publications, and letters of recommendation. However, psychology departments over-scrutinize Black candidates before even offering them an interview, and their materials are often not good enough on their own. Just as Frederick Douglass's narrative had to be verified by William Lloyd Garrison's astute white intellect, today's Black scholars, too, find that their work and credentials need to be verified by white ones. This vetting is not just through letters of recommendation, as I experienced at MRU. White people also personally reach out to each other about candidates from the global majority.

One of my former professors shared with me an email he received from one of the faculty members, whom he knew personally, on the search committee at another school I had applied to for employment after the whole MRU disaster.

> From: Dr. Chester Arlington
> To: Dr. Dustin Lightfoot
> Subject: Search Committee Results
>
> Dustin,
>
> I'm writing to get some more information about Dr. Jonathan Mathias Lassiter who has applied for a faculty position with us. There's a couple of things we like about him. First, he seems highly qualified and his interests meet our department needs. Second, as you might expect, to fulfill our diversity hire mandate. The search committee asked me to reach out to you as I'm the diversity and social justice guy in our department. We wanted to get more information about him before actually inviting him for an interview. Can we talk this week? There's a lot to discuss.

Best,

Chester

The email shocked me. What on earth could he want to ask my former professor before he even talked to me? Were my cover letter, research statement, teaching philosophy, and curriculum vitae not enough? My former professor informed me that search committees sometimes contact the writers of letters of recommendation before offering an interview. Apparently, it was a convention. And yet, the email unsettled me. Whiteness lingered between the lines, making me question their coded meaning. My understanding of American history shaped my interpretation of the words I read.

First, the committee member—Dr. Chester Arlington—seemed to doubt my credentials with his reservation: "he *seems* highly qualified." It's reasonable for someone to want to verify one's academic record. Yet, the application would already have been verified by a human resources department. This suspicion of Black people's qualifications is rooted in a history that renders any non-white person a suspect of illegitimacy.

Reading that email I was reminded of how, in 2011, President Barack Obama—a biracial Black man who had succeeded by all the standards of whiteness in the most prestigious white institutions—had to produce his birth certificate to prove his legitimate citizenship. To make matters worse, this proof was demanded by a known failed businessperson without half the academic and professional achievements of the first biracial Black president of the United States. My mind went to the countless unnamed free Black people who, during the antebellum period, had to show their freedom papers to avoid being enslaved. As Douglas A. Blackmon wrote in *Slavery by Another Name*, these people's Blackness is what made them criminal.

My Blackness rendered me a potential liar. The whiteness mindset uses an either/or logic to make sense of the world. This puts whiteness and non-whiteness, Blackness, at odds. Either whiteness is legitimate and trustworthy, or Blackness is natural and honest. Both cannot be true. It is one or the other. Within the whiteness mindset, white ways of being hold power. They are considered *better than* any non-white ways of being. Whiteness must be the appropriate and authoritative way of being, while Blackness is a deceitful and spurious position. So while the credentials of the white cisgender heterosexual male professor at MRU were probably not considered suspicious, mine were.

Second, Dr. Chester Arlington's "as you might expect" hinted that he believed he was talking to an insider who shared his perspective. For Dr. Arlington, my professor shared an understanding of the appropriate place of Black people on the psychology faculty. They are the ones used to fulfill "diversity hire mandates" and serve as the maids of academia. Within the whiteness mindset, Black people have no value except as the Black diversity whisperers.

An examination of any psychology faculty roster and each faculty member's primary specialty will reveal the role Black psychologists are expected to fulfill. You will find it difficult to find any Black faculty who are not expected to teach a course related to some diversity-related issue. This is not because there are not Black psychologists who specialize in general psychology areas like cognitive psychology or clinical disorders. It is—at least partly—due to the ways in which whiteness pigeonholes Black people into playing the "Black role" on psychology faculties.

Playing the "Black role"—or advocating for Black justice, equality, inclusion, and empowerment—is a noteworthy position to occupy. I myself have chosen this position and prioritize it over all others. I am Black first and a psychologist second. Therefore, I use my psychological expertise to help actualize the liberation of the Black mind and the illumination of the human spirit. However, there are some Black psychology professors who wish to move outside of this position and are not allowed to do so by the forces on predominately white psychology faculties that choose to protect their power by siloing the Black faculty member as the "diversity hire."

Third, I was uneasy about the department's restrictive thinking about diversity. Why would the department ask their "diversity and social justice person" to get more information about the Black, same-gender-loving man? Anyone could have done that. Also, why did the department only have *one* designated "diversity and social justice person"? A person who, by the way, was a white cisgender man whose research focused on refugees' mental health. Exactly what qualified him as the "diversity and social justice person"?

Though it may seem innocuous, this email reveals the sickness of the whiteness mindset in that psychology department. Whiteness infected their minds and contributed to them believing that there is only one way to be a legitimate worthwhile candidate. And that way is to be white. If you are not white, then you are other. And if you are other—or worse, Black—then you are unqualified. White is the default, elevated position. The closer you are to this position, the better.

If you are not white—or if you are white but you study, practice, or are even interested in the well-being of people who do not conform to the ideals of the whiteness mindset—then you may be considered a "diversity and social justice person." Often all-white psychology faculties designate the one—at most two—white people who have read *How to Be an Antiracist* or who can give a serviceable definition of *intersectionality* as the advocate for all things diversity. In my experience, this person has often been a white woman or white gay man who occupies a space just off-center of the white ideal. These people become the de facto gatekeepers of what appropriate diversity should look like. This diversity is often superficial at best. Decolonial, antiracist, and anti-capitalistic approaches to psychology and mental health remain scarce in the halls of academia.

We have a society of Black people whose mental health is suffering from oppression and too few Black people allowed access to the required training systems and professional positions to help their communities. The fix is easy: Hire Black people when they interview. Plain and simple. Because guess what? Nine times out of ten they *will* be the best candidate because they've had to be to even get a foot in the door. And even if they are not the *best* candidate, hire the Black person anyway. Lord knows psychology departments have hired countless mediocre white people. Maybe true diversity, equity, and inclusion—or better yet, justice—looks like mediocre Black people getting prestigious jobs in psychology, too.

There will be some people who center the whiteness mindset, those from the global majority and otherwise, who will object to my prescription to hire the Black person, period. They will use the "quality" excuse. They will say that's tokenism and preferential treatment. They will say that is unfair and not based on meritocracy.

To those people, I ask: Do you know American history? The real one? Not the sanitized mythic one they teach in K–12, but the one they are trying to ban in schools across the country and labeling as critical race theory. If you know that history, then you know that white people have been getting things just because they are white since the beginning of Western society.

A reading of Dr. Ronald Takaki's *A Different Mirror*, Dr. Ibram Kendi's *Stamped from the Beginning*, Daniel Golden's *The Price of Admission*, Robert Zieger's *For Jobs and Freedom*, and the anti-literacy laws written into Virginia colonial law will paint a clear picture. This body of literature highlights how, through the centering of the whiteness mindset, white people have shaped the world in their image. They have not had to acknowledge the consequences of that action for themselves or others. They have protected themselves from competition for jobs and access to resources by making it extremely difficult and in some cases illegal for Black and other people from the global majority to even enter their educational and occupational arenas. This is still happening today. The number-one way psychology faculties keep their departments white is by keeping out Black people in the first place. The stress from believing their lies about their value of diversity almost permanently barred me from psychology and everything else. Trusting people who perpetuate the whiteness mindset is killing Black people mentally and physically.

## CHAPTER 12

# Black Boy and the City

The once-little Black boy scared of his shadow took center stage. Five large black leather chairs loomed like monuments. To me, they looked like the marble chair Lincoln sits in at the DC memorial. The stage illuminated from above. The house lights were low in the Langston Hughes Auditorium. About one hundred people peppered the 321-seat space at the historic Schomburg Center for Research in Black Culture.

Ten years prior, I was a twenty-three-year-old entering the Schomburg Center library for the first time. It was a sanctuary of rest after roaming the city, trying to find my way. For the first month I lived in New York, during my time as an AmeriCorps member, I returned to the books, to the computers, to the culture inside those walls every two to three days. I was a scared Southern boy in the big city looking to start my career and find love. A decade later, I had done both. That night, I was about to be interviewed about a major milestone in my profession.

The manager of public programs had agreed to host a panel discussion about my first book, *Black LGBT Health in the United States: The Intersection of Race, Gender, and Sexual Orientation.*

On October 24, 2017, a Tuesday night, my dreams were coming true. My friend, de facto big sister, and co-editor, Dr. Lourdes Follins, also shared the moment with me. The event was moderated by Edward Watkins, a Black, same-gender-loving pioneer, who was the former editor in chief at three major African American magazines. The Black Gay Men Now founder was an inspiration. The panel was rounded out by an award-winning journalist and a Black trans male community activist. I could not believe my sheer good fortune.

Lupe Fiasco's "The Show Goes On" rolled and rollicked in my head. The trumpets made me feel triumphant as I stood backstage waiting to be introduced to the audience. All the whiteness that had tried to hold me back, chain my soul, and whip me into submission had failed. I had achieved all my first-grade goals: become a doctor, write a book, and be considered a renowned expert to help my people. A wide smile lit up my face as Edward read my biography; the crowd clapped as I walked to my chair. I waved, peering out at people in the stadium-style seating. I felt proud that my book and I were now officially in the pantheon of great Black authors whose work had been discussed in that hallowed Harlem space. After an hour and a half, we wrapped the panel and dispersed into the lobby for a reception.

I stood on holy ground, filled with gratitude that so many people came out to see me—a nerd passionate about Black, same-gender-loving people's health—on a Tuesday night. The terrazzo floor beneath my feet was marked by a brass cosmogram with

Langston Hughes's "The Negro Speaks of Rivers" embossed on it. Langston's ashes rested below. I felt lifted up by his spirit.

"Congratulations." A tall, casually dressed, carob-colored man came up and shook my hand.

"Thank you for coming. I hope you got something useful."

"Oh, I sure did. I'm glad you and your friends are doing this work. We need more people talking about our health. Like you said up there, we're not just HIV. You take care now." He smiled and turned to walk away.

"You too," I responded.

Nia, the public programs manager, approached me. "So, how do you think it went?" She smiled and her gingerbread-complected cheeks shined under the lights.

"I think it went well. Thank you so much for doing all of this. For seeing the vision."

"Thank you for reaching out. These are the kinds of events we need in our community. We don't talk about Black gay folks and transgender issues in our communities enough. Thanks for writing the book."

"It was a joint effort," I said, deflecting the compliment.

"Have a good night and feel free to reach out in the future."

"You too and I will." We hugged for a moment and Nia walked away. A few more people congratulated and thanked me before I saw Edward. I went over to him.

"Mr. Watkins. Edward, thank you so much for doing this. You don't know how much this means to have someone of your caliber and commitment to our community moderate this for us. I know I speak on behalf of my co-editor, too, when I say that we are so grateful."

"It truly is my pleasure." He tilted his round, bespeckled face toward me and smiled warmly."

"It means the world."

"You know we really should talk more. It would be good to do a feature on Black Gay Men Now with you."

"I would love that." I stood with awe in my eyes when I felt a hand on my shoulder.

"Mat," Benjamin's lulling voice called. I turned to face him.

"Hi, Benjamin. I'm talking to Edward right now. I'll be ready in just a moment." I turned back around to face Edward, putting Benjamin behind me.

"So, I can just email you and we can set something up?"

"Yes, let's do that," Edward confirmed and looked behind me. "I'm Edward." He reached his hand out to Benjamin. Benjamin extended his pale palm.

"Edward, this is my partner, Benjamin. Benjamin, this is Edward."

"Nice to meet you," Edward said.

"You too," Benjamin said. "The conversation up there was so heartfelt and informative. That's hard to do."

"Thank you," Edward responded. "I know you must be proud of Jonathan."

"He's something special."

"The work is so important. It was nice meeting you. I hate to rush off, but I've got to get home. You two have a good night," he said and excused himself.

"That was Edward Watkins," I said as I turned toward Benjamin, my face beaming. His face matched his red hair. My chest throbbed. My face fell. I knew I was in trouble.

That night, I was living my very best James Baldwin life. I was giving the people all the Black-power excellence they could stand. On the panel, we discussed white supremacy, capitalism, and all the forms of intersectional oppression that negatively impacted the mental and physical health of Black, same-gender-loving and trans people. I raved about the strengths of these communities and railed against the hand of whiteness that tried to control our health care, research, and social spaces. I was a certified Black, same-gender-loving militant nerd. Then Benjamin came and put his hand on my shoulder. I was exposed for loving a skinny, pale, white guy.

Benjamin was the love of my life and had been for nine years at that point. He met and nurtured me when I was new to Manhattan. Unlike other potential suitors who had dismissed me for being too young, too skinny, too nerdy, and too short, Benjamin saw my heart. He cherished my artistic soul, spiritual nature, and intellectual curiosity. With emotional maturity, he encouraged me to be more self-compassionate and embrace my vulnerabilities. He was a sensitive artist. He loved that I had studied ballet, knew who Alvin Ailey was, and could talk about the forefathers of Judaism as much as the writers of the Harlem Renaissance. He did not reject me for being poor. He dated me when I fed myself using food stamps. He loved me when I got medical care through Medicaid. He romanced me when I lived in a building where people addicted to crack smoked in the lobby. Benjamin invited me into his home to cool off when I could not afford an air-conditioning unit and was being steamed by the New York summer. He admired that, when we met, I was in the process of applying to graduate school with the hopes of being a psychologist. Once I was offered admission into graduate school that would take me away to San Francisco, he did not discourage me. Benjamin persuaded me to press on. He whispered words of wisdom when I despaired while on internship in Indianapolis. He was by my side when I defended my dissertation and was called "Doctor" for the first time.

I had never been embarrassed about the love of my life. But on October 24, 2017, for a split second, I wanted Benjamin to disappear. I thought maybe Edward might think less of me for "talking Black and sleeping white." That was the insult hurled at many Black leaders with white romantic partners. I did not want my work delegitimized by my own people because of their belief that I secretly loved the whiteness I protested. True, I loved Benjamin, and he was white. But I did not love whiteness. That was something that I had worked through years prior. But Edward didn't know that. And I was afraid other Black people would not care about that either.

Any Black person serious about resisting the whiteness mindset must reckon with themselves when they find themselves romantically involved with a white person. The whiteness mindset seeps in without much effort and can affect us—often with very little awareness on our behalf—which means dating a white person is not necessarily benign. My reckoning with the interplay of the whiteness mindset and romantic love rolled out through the first two years of dating Benjamin after meeting him in 2008.

✦✦

"He white, ain't he?" Marsae teased me. Marsae was one of my best friends. We had met freshman year of college in 2002. I was enamored by her intelligence, powerful insight, strong spiritual connection, and beauty. I tried to date her. She firmly rejected me.

"You gay," she said matter-of-factly and that was that. Six years later, she was living in Atlanta and I was forging my path in New York City.

"Girl, you won't." I reclined on my wooden IKEA bed in the sixth-floor apartment I shared with three roommates on 125th and St. Nick.

"Am I wrong?"

"I, mean, you not wrong. He's white. Jewish to be exact."

"Mm-hmm, I knew it. You stay dating them white men."

"One, that's not true. I date *all* men who like me." I laughed. "Second, his profile said 'looking for nerds of color.' That's me. No one is looking for that. I've never seen that on the websites. All these profiles be like 'discreet,' or 'no femmes,' or 'looking for big black cock.' And we all know I'm not none of them. But I am a nerd. And he's cute and older, just like I like 'em." Janet Jackson's "Luv" lilted around my room, coming from my CD player. I had been hit by Benjamin's charm big-time. Fully infatuated, I was a wreck, a mess of giddy emotions as I shared details about my new romance.

"If you say so. I just find it interesting that you stay with a white man."

"But it's not me," I protested. "I tried."

"Uh-huh."

"Remember Chauncey? I liked him a lot. But he was DL. And I was willing to stick it out even then. But he dumped me because he said he wanted to be a father and couldn't do that with another man. Donald was Puerto Rican. He kicked me to the curb because I wouldn't have sex with him after one date. And he didn't want to wrap it up. I just went out about a month ago with a cute older Black guy. He was a lawyer and everything. He told me that he didn't see us together because I had dated white guys in the past. I mean, what am I supposed to do? You know me. I will take the next man who meets my requirements and likes me. I'm not trying to be single."

"But even those requirements mean that you're going to end up with a white one."

"What are you talking about, 'Sae?"

"You only want to date a man with a college degree."

"What's wrong with that?"

"You know there are disparities in education, especially for Black men. So you ex-ing out a whole bunch of Black men right there."

"That's not my fault. I have a college degree and am going to get a doctorate. I want someone with a similar education. If I exist, other Black men with degrees exist."

"Then you say you want him to make more money than you and be older."

"I got daddy issues." I laughed.

"You a mess."

"What? I like older guys. That's not exclusive to white men. And I'm going to be a doctor one day, so I need a guy with money, too."

"You don't have money now."

"Even more of a reason to date someone with more money than me. We don't both need to be broke. I'm trying to get upgraded."

"All right, Beyoncé. Ol' gold-digging ass." Marsae laughed.

"Is financial security gold-digging? I don't think so. I don't think there is anything wrong with wanting a man who can do things for you."

"Well, you know Black men are again less likely to be living like that."

"Listen, I can't help that. I need what I need. And I ain't trying to wait forever."

"Anyway, Snow White, I'm just messing with you. Tell me more about this Benjamin." Marsae laughed again.

The conversation with Marsae made me think about my values. Did they make me more likely to be romantically involved with white men than Black ones? Were my values consistent with the whiteness mindset?

Financial security had always been important to me. Growing up in a working-class household, we often experienced financial strain. Whenever I wanted something, my mother would advise me to make sure I asked my father at least two weeks in advance so that he could plan to put the money aside from his upcoming paycheck. Food pantries were the source of our groceries just as often as the local Food Lion. Our clothes frequently came from discount and thrift stores. In the eleventh grade, I wanted to go on a trip with my modern dance class to New Orleans. Despite telling my parents three months in advance, they were still not able to spare the money needed to participate.

When I first moved to New York City in 2007, I was an AmeriCorps Volunteers in Service to America member. I made $900 a month, and was only able to afford living in a building predominately occupied by people suffering with drug addictions. In their inebriated states, they sometimes pissed in the elevator and put trash in the stairwells. So, yeah, I was looking for a way out. To me, that meant making money and marrying money.

*Sex and the City* provided a picture of a pristine privileged life. Carrie, Charlotte, Samantha, and Miranda were women in search of career, coitus, and courtship. Charlotte's ideal partner appealed to me the most. I wanted someone handsome, well-heeled, who could provide a princess life. In my twenty-three-year-old mind, that meant he would need to be highly educated, a white-collar professional, older, and fit.

Statistics supported Marsae's assertion. According to UCLA's Williams Institute, Black, same-gender-loving men are less likely than white gay men to be college educated.[1] They are also more likely to qualify as low-income and be unemployed. Racism and heterosexism ensured a hostile environment that hindered the educational and economic progress of far too many Black, same-gender-loving men. So, looking back, she was right. My wish list was statistically less likely to be fulfilled by a Black man.

One way the whiteness mindset infected me was by making me believe that to have a good life, I needed money and material possessions. A fancy career would give me power and authority. I could be one of Dr. W. E. B. Du Bois's Talented Tenth.[2] Once a member of that elite group, not only would I be able to provide for myself, but I would also then be able to give back. Becoming one of the Talented Tenth was the way to ensure impact and accomplish purpose.

But what was the line between financial security and materialism? Was there a difference? In a world shaped by the whiteness mindset, which insists that you are only as good as the material objects you possess—degrees, money, spouse—how do you avoid confusing the meaning of living and the object of life? In *The Souls of Black Folk*, even Du Bois himself seemed to equate proper education with the learning of Latin and Greek while negating the African traditions, established customs, and strong family ties of Black people. Does desiring these material objects and Western academic achievements equate to a desire of white norms, values, and people, given that these things are only valuable in a system structured by the whiteness mindset? Maybe in other systems being able to live a life of material security would not be tied to money? Perhaps a Eurocentric education would not be required to achieve employment? Maybe even the idea of employment would be nonexistent? Instead of employment, we might think of contributions to and sharing with society. Yet, in the whiteness-based world I was reared in, I believed that to escape poverty I had to embrace the values of whiteness, at least to some extent.

The whiteness mindset showed in many of my actions. Leaving my family of origin to pursue independent advancement demonstrated individualism. My striving to be the top performer in my classes and work environments reflected competitiveness. In seeking to accumulate income to achieve comfort and indulgence, materialism entered my life. In pursuing these values, I sacrificed my connection to my relatives, my health, and my culture. I pursued whiteness-based values in the hope of capturing the benefits of whiteness: power to have autonomy over my life, purpose in knowing I was one of the Talented Tenth, and protection from poverty.

These benefits should not be the sole purview of those who embody the whiteness mindset. They should be human rights that all enjoy. Yet, the whiteness mindset has structured the world in a way that these benefits are most frequently guaranteed through successfully embodying and living it. Again, the Catch-22 of the whiteness mindset is that it has set up a world that simultaneously rewards and penalizes those who perpetuate it.

So Marsae was probably right that my preferences in men—and their achievements—made it more likely that I would be romantically involved with white men rather than Black ones. I was not a snow queen in the sense that I thought white men were more physically attractive than other men. I did not think that somehow white men's customs and interests were better than those of men from other races and ethnicities.

In fact, when I was in high school, I fantasized a lot about my future boyfriend. He was always[3] a Black man like Basil Henderson, one of the main characters from E. Lynn Harris's best-selling books. But after a lot of loneliness and rejection in college by men of all backgrounds, I was eager to have a boyfriend. Even as a child, I wanted to be rescued and shown masculine affection and security. Ever since I saw *The Little Mermaid*, with Ariel singing her heart out on that rock with waves crashing around her, I wanted my own Prince Eric to come and take me away, to make me a part of his world. By the time I was dating in New York, I didn't care if my prince looked like Basil or Eric. What mattered most to me was that he was a prince and provided the life I dreamed of.

I was not interested in waiting around to find the right *Black* man. I just wanted to find the right man, with all the markers of success that I valued. At twenty-three, my dick got hard for a man who would order from a Michelin-starred restaurant menu without looking at prices. I was thrilled by a man who had achieved a white-collar job and six-figure-plus salary. Was I a gold digger? I don't think I was. I do think that the scars of the whiteness mindset made me receptive to any man who could rescue me from the cruelty of harassment, poverty, and unrequited desire. I wanted to be accepted, protected, and cared for. I was not a snow queen; I was desperate. If the man of my dreams happened to be white, his skin color was not important enough for me to give up the promise he offered.

Benjamin was that man who rescued twenty-three-year-old me. Although I identified closely with Charlotte in *Sex and the City*, Benjamin was more like Mr. Big. He was a creative professional who worked at a Wall Street firm, dressed in luxury labels I had never heard of, and was wiser and older. He pampered me and made me feel special with his preparation of Sunday brunch; deep, passionate kisses; candlelight dinners beginning with sparkling water and ending with crème brûlée; and escapes to Cape Cod. He was educated at an expensive college, worked in an office overlooking Lexington Avenue, and was a lover of music, dance, and art. His expertise included everything from Joni Mitchell's catalog and Malcolm X's writings, to the history of the New York City skyline and how to make the savoriest scrambled eggs I had ever tasted. He was also moody and prone to depression. Sometime his emotional storms compelled him to be emotionally distant. As an aspiring clinical psychologist, even that fascinated me. Early on, I knew that he wasn't perfect, but he was perfect for me. I was *the one* for him. He was *my person*. And that was all I needed to sustain my allegiance.

✦✦

"I'll have a ginger ale, please." I smiled at the waiter. Benjamin and I had walked about two blocks to one of the new restaurants that came with the rapid gentrification of Harlem. The menu outside of the Mexican restaurant was enticing enough to encourage us to enter. The place was packed. We sat at a skinny table in between two other couples.

"What?" I asked, knowing I could no longer avoid the topic. Benjamin peered over the small candle melting in between us and met my eyes. Nina Simone's voice rose in the air, coming in and out of perception over the patrons' mumbles. Her lamentation "Black Is the Color of My True Love's Hair" took me out of the moment for a split second. My true love's hair was red, and he was smirking at me across the table.

"So," he spoke slowly. It was torture that brought me back to face my punishment. "What was that about?"

"I mean..." I stammered. "So what had happened was..." I took a deep breath. "I didn't want him to think I was a snow queen," I blurted out.

"I know that's what was going through your head. You're so predictable. Cute. And dumb. Did you think you could hide me by yanking me behind you? I'm almost a foot taller than you, Mat." He smiled.

"I didn't yank you behind me."

"Yes, you did. It was like you were Diana Ross on the *Diana!* special from 1971. And I was Michael Jackson. You yanked me behind you." He laughed. I was embarrassed.

"I didn't mean to yank you. I just... there is no excuse. I'm a horrible person." I looked at him with my best puppy-dog eyes.

"Listen, if people are going to reject you and the things you say because you have a white boyfriend, they're not that intelligent. That's on them."

"I know, but people dismiss Black people with white partners all the time. I just..." The waiter came and put our drinks on the table. I took a sip and continued. "I just don't want to be disqualified before I even make it out the gate."

"You can't control that..."

"I know."

"Let me finish."

"Sorry."

"You can't control that, Mat. It's not like you're advocating white supremacy or that all people should assimilate, or that everyone should have a white partner. You're not with me because I'm white. You're with me because we love each other. The things you and the other panelists were saying tonight are real and need to be highlighted. And you are uniquely qualified as one of the few Black, same-gender-loving psychologists *in the world* to bring attention to Black LGBT mental, medical, and spiritual health. If they reject you, they reject that."

"I hope you're right," I said as the waiter came over with our appetizers.

"I am. Now shut up and try the guacamole, snow queen." We both laughed.

✦✦

I've heard some Black, same-gender-loving people bemoan that it seems that many of our notable figures always have white partners. There is a lot of evidence that this may be true, likely because of the economic and educational systems structured by the whiteness mindset. Many of my favorite Black, same-gender-loving pioneers had white romantic partners. James Baldwin loved Lucien Happersberger. Audre Lorde courted Frances Clayton. Barbara Jordan joined with Nancy Earl. Bayard Rustin bonded with Walter Naegle. Nikki Giovanni gushed over Virginia Fowler. These are just a few of the luminaries who inspired my work. They were wholly committed to Black lives. They also found love in the arms of people who significantly benefited from the whiteness mindset that made their work necessary.

As a young graduate student, I grappled with my proximity to whiteness. Particularly, I wrestled with the rewards I started to reap from whiteness. So much of my early life was about surviving the barbarous effects of the whiteness mindset on my father and our family. After meeting Benjamin, I also started to gain access to the benefits of whiteness. These benefits increased as I advanced in my studies and career as a clinical psychologist. Although the whiteness mindset, and the world it set up, continued to ravage me in big and small ways, I was also able to sample its spoils.

This presented a conundrum for me. Am I a part of the problem? Does the whiteness that contaminates my brain make me more of a hindrance or an asset to Black people? As I rail against the whiteness mindset, am I also assisting its ascension? Joseph Beam, a writer and luminary among culturally conscious Black, same-gender-loving men, wrote in his book, *In the Life*, that "Black men loving Black men is the revolutionary act of the eighties."[4] I agree that Black men, Black people, loving other Black people is the cure to everything that ails us. However, what must that love look like?

Many of the people whom I have heard recite Mr. Beam's quote are often referring to romantic or sexual love only, or primarily. That is too narrow for me. In my personal and professional experience, too much focus has been given to Black men's bodies and not enough to their hearts and minds. I believe that we all should be loving Black people regardless of whether the love is romantic, sexual, familial, platonic, or something else. It seems that's what Joseph Beam had in mind, too, as he described a range of *loving* relationships between Black men. The romantic love that I currently share may not be with another Black man. Yet, my love for Black men, and Black people overall, is unshakable and guides everything I do. My love for Black men is tied to my work for our liberation, mental and physical. Black men sharing romantic and sexual love with other Black men is beautiful. Period. It is not enough. We must consistently work to connect and heal with each other outside of the individualistic, materialistic, and competitive frameworks of the whiteness mindset.

Today, I rely on the work of pioneering Black psychologists to help me judge my own mental health and community impact from African and Black perspectives. I aim to move toward something more liberatory and harmonious—not just *away* from the whiteness mindset. Dr. Linda James Myers's work encourages me to think about how I engage with myself and my community. Am I striving to prioritize communal self-knowledge, increasing my understanding of myself as connected to the divine, my ancestors, future generations, and my communities of origin? In *Skh: From Black*

*Psychology to the Science of Being*, Dr. Wade Nobles informs Black people that we must always be engaged in both affirming our African being and decolonizing our mind. We affirm us when we understand ourselves as spirit and provide opportunities for interpersonal effectiveness, spiritual and cultural consciousness, and collective confidence building. Black people loving Black people looks like minimizing personal trauma by not condemning ourselves and our loved ones based on the narrow definitions of others. Decolonizing our minds requires committing ourselves to specific tasks such as dismantling white Western hegemony, no longer privileging white ideals, and fighting against dehumanizing systems such as racism, sexism, heterosexism, cisgenderism, and classism. Decolonizing our minds includes a commitment to helping Black people love themselves and their heritages first and foremost. My love of Black men looks like my work with my former student Tai, it looks like the psychotherapy I do with my Black male clients, it looks like the research articles I publish about Black, same-gender-loving men's spirituality and health. Regardless of the skin color of the people we date, we must align ourselves with the African-centered standards of mental health and love. That is a revolutionary act. I like to believe that in the grand scheme, I am helping the arc of the universe bend more decidedly away from the whiteness mindset and toward justice.

# Epilogue

## The Work of Healing from the Whiteness Mindset

The whiteness mindset has been and remains a problem, a pathological mindset that leads to harm for everyone regardless of their race and ethnicity, gender, sexual orientation, nationality, ability status, income, or wealth. The whiteness mindset has harmed generations of people, including my family. The whiteness mindset renders my profession of psychology a fraud, given the ways in which whiteness has narrowed its focus to the *white* human mind.

As a person who has achieved many of the life goals that I've set thus far, it is important that I acknowledge that I have been harmed. My achievements do not erase that harm. My accomplishments do not absolve the society responsible for the mechanisms that exact that harm. To some, evidence of "succeeding" means that one has nothing to "complain about." However, systems structured by the whiteness mindset have required me to give up so much to achieve my basic needs. Asking one to divorce themselves from their pain is consistent with a core assumption of the whiteness mindset: fragmentation.

Acknowledging the harm is not weak. It takes insight and fortitude to name the ways one has been harmed and perpetuated that harm. It takes strength to sit with the whiteness mindset and own one's relationship with it. It is likely that people who hear others speak about the whiteness mindset will interpret their testimonies as whining. Their interpretations reveal more about them than they reveal about their target. When we dismiss the exploration and explication of the whiteness mindset as whining, it shows the difficulty and discomfort we have sitting with the internalized whiteness mindset inside of us and the ways we have colluded in the harm of others. Naming the whiteness mindset is the first step toward healing.

I refuse to be silent. I own all parts of myself: the ways in which I have embodied the whiteness mindset to achieve success and the ways in which I have been harmed despite those achievements. I have committed and recommit daily to living my life outside of the whiteness mindset as much as possible.

The whiteness mindset is crazy and crazy making. Of that, we can be sure.

Knowing that the whiteness mindset is crazy is not a cause for despair but relief. Now we understand what the issue is. We have a diagnosis. We can now do the work to get better. This work needs to happen on multiple levels: within ourselves, with our loved ones, and with our communities, businesses, and governments.

Now that we know the whiteness mindset harms those who benefit materially from it and those who don't, we can work to give up seeking whiteness as a means of healing. In the whiteness mindset we are healed when we're once again productive—working and consuming with our emotions tucked away. Healing not guided by the whiteness mindset is found in our relationships and community. This type of healing involves allowing ourselves to feel our emotions—joyful and painful—in the company of our community and is not time limited. We will be healing until the day we die. We must work to give up the hope that whiteness's superficial benefits will ever help us feel whole. These benefits may give us temporary pleasures, but they ultimately disconnect us from ourselves, others, and all the abundance that our connecting life-force energy has to offer. We will never live our best lives embodying and perpetuating the whiteness mindset.

The people with the most power to stamp out the whiteness mindset are the most invested in it, and terrified of relinquishing it. They will never give up the power, purpose, and protection whiteness bestows upon them to heal themselves and the world.

So I want to talk to you, the person who is suffering from the whiteness mindset and subconsciously perpetuating it in your own life and receiving very little of its benefits—that is, people from the global majority.

First, your maladjustment to whiteness is not the problem. The whiteness mindset and its effects are the problem. If you refuse to play by the rules of the whiteness mindset and are then harmed by whiteness-informed systems and people, that is an injustice. That is not your fault. You should not have to adopt a destructive mindset to be respected and rewarded. The people and the systems who require whiteness from you are sick and dangerous.

Second, doing the work of cleansing our minds from the whiteness mindset is a lifelong project. The good news is that there are levels to whiteness and we don't need to be at zero to function in healthier, more connected ways. We just need to consistently work to decrease our reliance on the whiteness mindset. We do this by constantly interrogating the motivation of our actions and refocusing them as needed so that we move away from the assumptions and values of the whiteness mindset and toward liberation for all. Instead of making decisions about who to date, where to go to school, or what law to pass based on what will be the most lucrative or how to one-up the competition, let the principles of Ma'at guide you. The seven principles of Ma'at include: truth, justice, harmony, balance, order, reciprocity, and propriety. Living these principles will look different for each person. Living the principle of truth may look like speaking up honestly in the face of transphobia in the workplace regardless of the individual consequences one might face. Harmony may look like working in collaboration, instead of competition, with your community members—even if it comes at a cost to you individually. You might cultivate order by limiting psychological clutter, tuning out social media use that promotes "happiness through consumption," and distancing yourself from people who predominately perpetuate the whiteness mindset. Living the principles of Ma'at can help people structure their lives in a way that is conducive to peace and deeper connections with others, not centered around whiteness.

Living outside of the whiteness mindset is a process, not a discrete task we can perfect. We will fall into whiteness-influenced patterns of behaving from time to time. That is to be expected as the mindset is so ingrained in all of us and reinforced by our society. Giving up the hope of a full recovery from the whiteness mindset can free us up to do what we can to save ourselves, each other, and the world around us one consistent step at a time.

Third, save your energy. Stop trying to convince people who are invested in, benefiting from, and perpetuating the whiteness mindset to change. Release the expectation that they will ever do anything that is inconsistent with the whiteness mindset. To paraphrase Toni Morrison, stop talking to them. It's a distraction.

Fourth, educate yourself about alternative ways of being not based in the whiteness mindset. These alternative ways of being will give you possibility models of how you might shape your life and reorient yourself to the world. Alternative ways of being will be useful to help you figure out what *to do* and not just what *not to do*. I recommend starting with the work of psychologists like Drs. Linda James Myers, Cheryl Grills, and Wade Nobles to introduce yourself to new paradigms of healing, thinking, behaving, and being.

Finally, educate others about the alternative ways of being you have started to embody in your own life. Show them with your actions how minimizing the influence of the whiteness mindset in yourself can lead to a healthier, more connected life. Share the knowledge, love, and stories of your own healing journey with others to inspire and encourage their growth away from perpetuating the whiteness mindset.

It feels impossible to try to talk to the people who benefit the most from the whiteness mindset about why or how to minimize it. As Cord Jefferson eloquently suggested in his essay "The Racism Beat," the harms of whiteness should be self-evident. Yet, part of the sickness of the whiteness mindset is that it keeps people from seeing its harms. The whiteness mindset encourages avoidance of consequences—for others and for the self. There is an abundance of evidence from history as well as socioeconomic and political policy that white people are willing to suffer for the benefits of whiteness.

Truthfully, I don't have hope for the vast majority of white people. I have decided to primarily invest my energy in helping to agitate and liberate the minds of Black and other people of the global majority from the whiteness mindset. For the fraction of white people at least interested in developing and living outside of the whiteness mindset, the only way to heal from whiteness is to first give up its benefits: power, purpose, and protection. Then learn and live alternative ways of being.

First, you must give up power. This will literally require giving up jobs, housing, and resources. I do not mean that people should relinquish *all* their material gains. It does mean reparations for the years of exploitation of the labor from Black and other people from the global majority. I know that this is appalling to most white people and others who benefit from whiteness, because the whiteness mindset has convinced you that you have legitimately earned these things and have a right to them. News flash: You don't. You have not earned them from your own work alone. You have benefited from a world shaped by the whiteness mindset that structured the world for your success. Step out of the way and do not use your whiteness to limit the work of those seeking to live beyond whiteness. Don't bomb our communities and towns. Don't murder our leaders. Do not infiltrate our social movements and spaces with drugs or force the whiteness mindset on us to destabilize our progress.

Second, you must find a purpose for your life not based on the whiteness mindset. Again, to paraphrase Toni Morrison: Who are you if we take away the myths about yourselves as white people? Would you still have self-esteem if we began history in Ethiopia instead of Greece? What type of person might you be if we moved beyond individualism, competition, and materialism? Would you love yourself without your job title, your hoarded resources, your false claim to intellectual and cultural superiority? Instead of rooting your purpose in materialism and individualism, how can you root your identity in community? In service? In equity?

Third, you must bring down the walls of protection that have, for generations, protected you from having to engage with others outside of the confines set up by whiteness. The whiteness mindset has contributed to the creation of a world where people can buy or demand a world that is fully separate from the things that might distress them. For example, the whiteness mindset allows parents to persuade themselves that they are okay sending their children to schools where anti–critical race theory, "don't say gay," and nullified race-based affirmative action policies actively harm their children's (would-be) classmates. These parents are resistant to how these laws harm their own children, and they don't see themselves as connected to other people who are harmed by such policies. You must leave the tower of unearned material and psychological resources and engage honestly with the reality of the world—both its joy and its profound injustice.

The whiteness mindset also protects people from being judged based on how they treat others. The whiteness-aligned values of individualism and competition hinder people from understanding themselves as part of a global community. Instead of seeking balance and harmony, the assumptions of the whiteness mindset convince them that anyone who presents an obstacle to their individual goals is an enemy. The whiteness mindset protects people from acknowledging others' suffering and taking responsibility for mitigating it.

In the psychology and mental health professions, we must all work to name and root out the whiteness mindset in its various forms in the various settings that it is perpetuated: the classroom, research lab, and therapy office. One essential change is for white-sanctioned professional psychology organizations to relinquish their unearned authority to define mental health for people of the global majority. Black psychologists and other mental health providers of the global majority have the right and should be legally sanctioned to set the standards for rigorous and healthy psychological practices and research for their communities. In addition to the resource list at the end of this book, there are two scholars in particular whose work I highlight for deeper engagement about doing the work of healing from the whiteness mindset. Resmaa Menakem's *My Grandmother's Hands: Racialized Trauma and the Pathway to Mending Our Hearts and Bodies* and Dr. Jennifer Mullan's *Decolonizing Therapy: Oppression, Historical Trauma, and Politicizing Your Practice* are rich resources. These texts provide step-by-step guides for developing one's awareness of one's own internalized oppression, cultivating knowledge about oppression, and increasing one's skills to eradicate the whiteness mindset in the psychology and mental health fields.

Whiteness is a pathological mindset that harms everyone. We must first acknowledge that fact. Second, we have to start diagnosing the whiteness mindset in people, policies, institutions, and governments. Finally, we must place the responsibility for lifelong healing from the craziness of the whiteness mindset on all of us, especially those who benefit from it the most.

# Postscript

## A Letter to a New Psychologist

*Dear Jonathan,*

*They gotta call you Dr. now. You did it. You survived internship. You took their shit, but they didn't break you. They tried and didn't succeed. But guess what, they ain't through tryin it. They gon stay tryin it. But they are the sickos. You will have to continue to endure and triumph. Use your lessons so that you don't make the same mistake twice. Don't ingest the whiteness. Train yourself outside of their value system, their destructive mindset. I know you are wondering what that looks like. How can you train yourself to move against the whiteness mindset given that it is so ingrained in you and the society around you? First, I definitely don't have all the answers. Even ten years in the future, I am still learning how to divest from the whiteness mindset. I am not perfect. I guess in some ways I will always have some part of the whiteness mindset operating within me. But I don't accept it with joy and docility. I fight. You must fight, too. Here are four ways I've learned to fight the whiteness mindset in me and my community.*

*First, you must allow yourself to feel the pain and take responsibility for healing from the whiteness mindset. You have felt a lot of fear, anxiety, and shame due to the ways in which the whiteness mindset through its isms (racism, heterosexism, capitalism, and ableism) have made you feel inadequate. You've done a lot of work to acknowledge your suffering. Don't give in to the temptation to suppress your emotions. Malcolm X is right. The examined life is painful. Yet, self-examination is essential. If you do not consistently check in with the pain of the world structured by the whiteness mindset, you are distancing yourself from it. We are doomed to perpetuate what we do not acknowledge. We repeat what we don't repair. So continue to ask yourself why you work so hard to have a six-figure income. Is it because you are running away from the sting of childhood poverty and the feelings of unworthiness? Are you trying to prove to the people who rejected you because of your race and sexual orientation that you are good enough? Are you trying to prove that you are better than the boys who picked on you in middle school? Are you seeking comfort, validation, self-worth, all of the above? Or something else totally different? Are you wearing your crown that is your birthright or are you coveting someone else's crown because you believe it will make you better? What pain are you still trying to soothe? Are your methods of healing predicated on another person's injury or tied to the well-being of all spirit-filled beings? You must always be checking in with your emotions and motivations. However, that does not mean that you should spend your life worrying about the whiteness mindset, white people, and how the systems created by them might judge or harm you. Your liberation lies in owning your emotions and centering communal ways of being regardless of what the world around you may say and do.*

*Second, ancient indigenous culture is the cure. So much of what the whiteness mindset has done is disconnect you from your birthright of joy and illumination. It has hidden the truth of your origin story. You are spirit at your core. All-encompassing, all-powerful energy courses through you. Your African ancestors and the people who migrated to other parts of the globe and became known as Dravidian, Chinese, and Olmec all knew this. Your roots are in the vastness of the cosmos and the richness of the soil. Your story does not start at your pain. American chattel slavery is only one note in your narrative. Continue to fortify yourself by reading books about pre-colonial African cultures. See if you can find commonalities among world cultures in how they think about what it means to be human. What lessons can you learn from these commonalities? Read books about metaphysics and its connection to spirituality. Read fiction that shows the beauty of Black, same-gender-loving people. Watch films and listen to music that lifts you up and challenges the lies that the whiteness mindset attempts to reinforce. Learn about your ancestors. Who were they? What was important to them? What sacrifices did they make so that you could survive? Maybe you don't know their names. So create their stories for yourself so that you can draw pride from them.*

*Take time in silence to listen to anxiety when it unsettles your mind. What is it trying to tell you? Is fear driving the bus? Too many people driven by their fears of scarcity, fragmentation, and annihilation have worked for centuries to cut off the divinity of the masses so that they could control resources. They have disseminated their rigid and disempowering definitions into the world to protect their ignorance. Don't build your identity on a lie. Reclaim the sacredness of yourself, everything, everyone, and every experience in your world. Use that sacredness as a starting point for all your actions. Begin and end each day asking if you are treating yourself as divine. Question if you use natural resources in a way that honors the sacrifices of those people and things that produced them. Are you seeing beyond the scars of the whiteness mindset in yourself and others to see their potential for god-ness? When you see the god-ness of yourself, everyone, and everything, you will realize that you are all part of the same whole. This requires that you live in the world in a way that accepts your connection to everyone and everything as a reality.*

*Third, heal in community. When thinking about healing, do not think about parts. Focus on the whole. The whole of you: mind, body, and spirit. The whole of your network: you, family, friends, relatives, community members, citizens of your country and the globe. Put your energy and work into your community. This is hard work. But it is not impossible. People will try you. But know that those people are the ones who need healing the most. We help people heal when we diligently cultivate our own healing.*

*Sometimes healing in community will look like volunteering for organizations providing food for hungry people. Sometimes healing in community will look like challenging your best friend to interrogate his self-sabotaging behaviors. At other times, healing in community will look like teaching a class about African-centered psychology. It may also look like saying no when a colleague asks you to join the poorly attended diversity committee meetings. Healing in community will sometimes look like giving your clients what you need. You may be feeling frazzled when you enter a therapy session. Instead of powering through, invite your client to slow down and breathe with you. Even as a therapist, never forget that healing is bidirectional.*

*Understand that you will let people down. You will not always meet their expectations. You will let yourself down. Sometimes you will perpetuate the whiteness mindset in big and small ways. When you share your vulnerabilities, confess your mistakes, and try to correct your errors, you model how others might do so as well. The key is not to disconnect from yourself and your sacredness in an attempt to avoid the pain of these missteps. The whiteness mindset tries to make the world of objects, people, names, and forms appear disconnected from each other. You will find your strength, your bliss, and your healing in the oneness of existence. Always derive your value from inside yourself. Prioritize making people feel loved and cared for in your presence. Don't focus on what you can get from a person, but what you can give. Work on trying to understand others as divine and connected to you.*

*Finally, let the energy of the sun, your breath, movement, and others guide you. All these things have spirit. You are a spirit being. You are not just a collection of cells and electrical pulses. It is important that you unify all the parts of yourself as consistently and often as possible. So get outside and seek divinity in nature. Let the sun nourish your skin. Take deep breaths. You know that people embodying whiteness have literally stopped the breath of too many of us. Take your dance classes. Sing and rap your emotions with a rhythmic flow. Have fun! And let those who love you do so. Don't reject the kindness of strangers. Don't talk yourself out of the warmth of your friends, family, romantic partner, clients, students, and peers.*

*Jonathan, some of these things may sound like no-brainers, too simple, or not consequential enough. You may be asking yourself, how is this connected to the whiteness mindset? The whiteness mindset is all about the belief that resources are scarce, which leads to valuing material possessions. Whiteness convinces too many people that difference is inherently threatening. This leaves us believing we need to compete with each other. The whiteness mindset may try to make you believe that there is no such thing as god or a connecting all-encompassing animating energy in the universe. People who embody whiteness have tried to create a god in their own image. One that is vengeful and concerned about how much money you give in religious houses. Such a god disempowers people. Through these processes the whiteness mindset contributes to oppression that harms everyone's mental health.*

*If you can allow yourself to feel the pain from the whiteness mindset and take responsibility for healing from it, harness ancient indigenous culture as sources for healing, heal in community, and let the energy of the sun, breath, movement, and others guide you, you will be setting up yourself to interpret, feel, and act in a way that connects you with the divine and prioritizes healthy relationships. This way of being is the exact opposite of what existence looks like as defined by the whiteness mindset. Healing from the whiteness mindset requires an intense, consistent intentionality. You can do this. You've got this!*

*Very sincerely yours,*

*Dr. Jonathan Mathias Lassiter*
*from ten years in the future*

# Acknowledgments

Creating a book requires the hard work, expertise, patience, and resources of so many people. I have done my best here to express my gratitude for everyone involved in this project. If I miss you, as they say in the church I was raised in: "Charge it to my head, and not my heart."

First, I've got to thank Cecilia "CeCe" Lyra. I mean... she is the absolute, absolute best literary agent I could have ever prayed for. From beginning to end, 365 days of the year she has been a champion of me and my work. She has been a guardian and hand-holder throughout this process. I will never be able to properly thank her enough. Gratitude to Carly Watters, who did not think my book was right for her but had the vision and generosity to connect me with CeCe. And shout out to everyone at P.S. Literary Agency who has supported this project.

I have had the pleasure of working with several editors on this project. Thanks to Allison Dalafave and Gwen Hawkes who were with me during the first and second versions of this book. The woman responsible for the final version of the book is Krishan Trotman, the Beyoncé of books! It is her vision, investment, patience, and kindness that has helped polish this project. I'm grateful to Leah Lakins for serving as the surgeon of my book: editing it to perfection and believing in its potential. Additional gratitude goes to Mahito Indi Henderson, Carolyn Levin, Sean Moreau, Maya Lewis, Tara Kennedy, Yasmin Mathew, the art department, and all the other fine folks at Legacy Lit Books who have supported this project.

A shout-out to the Hampton Institute, which published the original essay, "Whiteness in the Psychological Imagination," that became this book. Thank you to all the folks who read early drafts of the book: Dani Arigo, Lourdes D. Follins, Johnathan Lay, Sharrell D. Luckett, Marquita Moten, and Michelle Wiltshire.

Immense appreciation goes to my branding, publicity, and film/TV representation teams.

I appreciate all the people who have shown so much support already and are inspirations for this work: Dr. John-Martin Green and others at the Gatekeepers Collective, Dr. Linda James Myers and the Association of Black Psychologists, and all the Black outlets that have been showing so much enthusiasm for this project. Thanks to all my early readers, bookstagrammers, and blurbers. Gratitude goes to all my students and classmates over the years, who have looked to me for inspiration and inspired me to stay and fight in academia.

Finally, my inner circle: mom, dad (R.I.P.), sister, brother, nephews, nieces, and ancestors. And my utmost and unending gratitude goes to my rock, the love of my life: Brian Alex Mindlin.

# Resource List

Below is a list of resources for people interested in learning more about the topics discussed in this book, such as whiteness, mental health, and African-centered psychology.

*Understanding an Afrocentric World View: Introduction to an Optimal Psychology* by Dr. Linda James Myers

*Playing in the Dark: Whiteness and the Literary Imagination* by Toni Morrison

*Black AF History: The Un-Whitewashed Story of America* by Michael Harriot

*Sister Outsider: Essays and Speeches* by Audre Lorde

*Sedated: How Modern Capitalism Created Our Mental Health Crisis* by James Davies

*Post Traumatic Slave Syndrome: America's Legacy of Enduring Injury and Healing* by Dr. Joy DeGruy

*Men, Homosexuality, and the Gods: An Exploration into the Religious Significance of Male Homosexuality in World Perspective* by Dr. Ronald Long

*Boy-Wives and Female Husbands: Studies in African Homosexualities* by Dr. Stephen O. Murray and Dr. Will Roscoe

*The Spirit of Intimacy: Ancient African Teachings in the Ways of Relationships* by Sobonfu Somé

*Egyptian Yoga: The Philosophy of Enlightenment* by Muata Ashby

"Towards an African-Centered Sociological Approach to Africana Lesbian, Gay, Bisexual, Transgender, Queer, and Intersexed Identities and Performances: The Kemetic Model of the Cosmological Interactive Self" by Sekhmet Ra Em Kht Maat (Cher Love McAllister)

*The Egyptian Book of the Dead: The Book of Going Forth by Day* by Dr. Raymond Faulkner, Dr. Ogden Goelet Jr., Carol Andrews, J. Daniel Gunther, and James Wasserman

*Cultural Misorientation: The Greatest Threat to the Survival of the Black Race in the 21st Century* by Dr. Kobi K. K. Kambon

*Seeking the Sakhu: Foundational Writings for an African Psychology* by Dr. Wade W. Nobles

*Skh: From Black Psychology to the Science of Being* by Dr. Wade W. Nobles

*We Real Cool: Black Men and Masculinity* by bell hooks

*The Will to Change: Men, Masculinity, and Love* by bell hooks

*The Falsification of Afrikan Consciousness: Eurocentric History, Psychiatry and the Politics of White Supremacy* by Dr. Amos N. Wilson

*A Race Is a Nice Thing to Have: A Guide to Being a White Person or Understanding the White Persons in Your Life* by Dr. Janet E. Helms

*Akbar Papers in African Psychology* by Dr. Na'im Akbar

*The Developmental Psychology of the Black Child* by Dr. Amos N. Wilson

*Even the Rat Was White: A Historical View of Psychology* by Dr. Robert V. Guthrie

*The Protest Psychosis: How Schizophrenia Became a Black Disease* by Jonathan Metzl

*Madness: Race and Insanity in a Jim Crow Asylum* by Antonia Hylton

*Mental Health, Human Rights, and Legislation: Guidance and Practice* by the World Health Organization and the United Nations

*The Souls of Black Folk: Essays and Sketches* by Dr. W. E. B. Du Bois

*Drug Use for Grown-Ups: Chasing Liberty in the Land of Fear* by Dr. Carl L. Hart

*A Different Mirror: A History of Multicultural America* by Dr. Ronald Takaki

*Stamped from the Beginning: The Definitive History of Racist Ideas in America* by Dr. Ibram X. Kendi

*The Price of Admission: How America's Ruling Class Buys Its Way into Elite Colleges—and Who Gets Left Outside the Gates* by Daniel Golden

*For Jobs and Freedom: Race and Labor in America Since 1865* by Robert H. Zieger

*My Grandmother's Hands: Racialized Trauma and the Pathway to Mending Our Hearts and Bodies* by Resmaa Menakem

*Decolonizing Therapy: Oppression, Historical Trauma, and Politicizing Your Practice* by Jennifer Mullan, PsyD

# Playlist Inspired by the Book

"*Reading Rainbow* Theme Song" by Tina Fabrique
"Order My Steps" by GMWA Women of Worship
"He's Working It Out for You" by Shirley Caesar
"Legend in My Living Room" by Annie Lennox
*Hold On, Help Is on the Way* by Georgia Mass Choir
"Come On in the Room" by Georgia Mass Choir
"Someone to Call My Lover" by Janet Jackson
"I Think I'm in Love with You" by Jessica Simpson
"Love Song for No One" by John Mayer
"When I Grow Up" by Pussycat Dolls
"Damaged" by Danity Kane
"Swagga Like Us" by Jay-Z, T.I., Kanye West, and Lil Wayne
"So What" by Pink
"Womanizer" by Britney Spears
"Over My Dead Body" by Drake
"More Than I Can Bear" by Kirk Franklin
"better in tune with the infinite" by Jay Electronica
*Graduation* by Kanye West

"Barry Bonds" by Kanye West and Lil Wayne
"I Wonder" by Kanye West
"I'm Dat Chick" by Kelly Rowland
"Lost Ones" by Lauryn Hill
"Labels or Love" by Fergie
"Bodak Yellow" by Cardi B
"In the Middle, Somewhat Elevated" by Thom Willems
"99 Problems" by Jay-Z
"Be Good (Lion's Song)" by Gregory Porter
"Doo Wop (That Thing)" by Lauryn Hill
"The Show Goes On" by Lupe Fiasco
"Luv" by Janet Jackson
"Black Is the Color of My True Love's Hair" by Nina Simone

# Notes

**Prologue: Whiteness Makes Us All Crazy**

1. *Global majority* is a collective term that first and foremost speaks to and encourages those so called to think of themselves as belonging to the global majority. It refers to people who are Black, Asian, Brown, dual heritage, indigenous to the Global South, and/or have been racialized as "ethnic minorities." Globally, these groups currently represent approximately 80 percent of the world's population, making them the global majority now, and with current growth rates, notwithstanding COVID-19 and its emerging variants, the global majority is set to remain so for the foreseeable future. It should be noted that I use this term knowing that people of the global majority are not a monolith. My aim is not to flatten the experiences of these groups but to highlight the similarities in our indigenous values (all deriving from East and Nile Valley African pre-colonial groups) and the ways in which whiteness has harmed us and we then collude in that harm. Rosemary Campbell-Stephens, "Global Majority; Decolonizing the Language and Reframing the Conversation About Race," 2020, https://www.leedsbeckett.ac.uk/-/media/files/schools/school-of-education/final-leeds-beckett-1102-global-majority.pdf.

2. I have intentionally used *same-gender-loving* to describe my sexual orientation since I was introduced to the term at a Black Men's Xchange meeting in Harlem, New York, composed of all Black men who were same-sex or bisexually attracted. This term was coined by Dr. Cleo Manago in the 1990s to highlight the unique lived experience of being both same-sex or bisexually attracted *and* prioritizing Black cultural values in a world that is simultaneously anti-Black and anti-gay/bisexual.

3. Donald Moss, "On Having Whiteness," *Journal of the American Psychoanalytic Association* 69, no. 2 (2021): 355–371, https://doi:10.1177/00030651211008507.

4. Jonathan M. Metzl, *Dying of Whiteness: How the Politics of Racial Resentment Is Killing America's Heartland* (Basic Books, 2019).

5. Katie Pavid, "Rethinking Our Human Origins in Africa," Natural History Museum (UK), July 11, 2018, https://www.nhm.ac.uk/discover/news/2018/july/the-way-we-think-about-the-first-modern-humans-in-africa.html.

6. Ana Mari Cauce and Melanie M. Domenech-Rodriguez, "Latino Families: Myths and Realities," in *Latino Children and Families in the United States: Current Research and*

*Future Directions*, ed. J. M. Contreras, K. A. Kerns, and A. M. Neal-Barnett (Praeger/Greenwood, 2002), 3–25.

7. Thomas A. Parham, Adisa Ajamu, and Joseph L. White, *Psychology of Blacks: Centering Our Perspectives in the African Consciousness* (Psychology Press, 2015).

8. Renaud Camus, *You Will Not Replace Us!* (Chez l'auteur, 2018).

9. Kenneth M. Tyler et al., "Black Psychology and Whiteness: Toward a Conceptual Model of Black Trauma Through the Prism of Whiteness," *Journal of Black Psychology* 48, no. 1 (2022): 5–42, https://doi.org/10.1177/00957984211034948.

10. bell hooks, *We Real Cool: Black Men and Masculinity* (Routledge, 2004).

11. Jonathan M. Lassiter, "Extracting Dirt from Water: A Strengths-Based Approach to Religion for African American Same-Gender-Loving Men," *Journal of Religion and Health* 53, no. 1 (2012): 178–189, https://doi:10.1007/s10943-012-9668-8.

12. The definition and diagnosis of whiteness do not represent new revelations or discovery of a new phenomenon. Instead, they are a succinct packaging and explication of ideas that have their roots in the work of several brilliant scholars before me. I ground my definition and diagnosis in the work of African-centered psychologists and whiteness studies intellectuals. Their work is paired with my lived experience to illustrate how whiteness may look in real life. I recommend the following sources for further details: Bobby E. Wright, *Psychopathic Racial Personality and Other Essays* (Third World Press, 1985); Erylene Piper-Mandy and Taasogle Daryl Rowe, "Educating African-Centered Psychologists: Towards a Comprehensive Paradigm," *Journal of Pan African Studies* 3, no. 8 (2010); Frances Cress Welsing, *The Isis Papers: The Keys to the Colors* (CW Publishing, 2004); Judith H. Katz, *White Awareness: Handbook for Anti-Racism Training*, 2nd ed. (University of Oklahoma Press, 2003); Lisa B. Spanierman and Mary J. Heppner, "Psychosocial Costs of Racism to Whites Scale (PCRW): Construction and Initial Validation," *Journal of Counseling Psychology* 51, no. 2 (2004): 249; Mab Segrest, "The Souls of White Folks," in *The Making and Unmaking of Whiteness*, ed. Birgit Brander Rasmussen et al. (Duke University Press, 2001), 43–71.

**Part 1: My Life "Ain't Been No Crystal Stair"**

1. This line references Langston Hughes's poem "Mother to Son," https://www.poetryfoundation.org/poems/47559/mother-to-son.

**Chapter 1: The Impact of Whiteness**

1. Joy DeGruy, *Post Traumatic Slave Syndrome: America's Legacy of Enduring Injury and Healing*, rev. ed. (Joy DeGruy Publications, 2017).

2. Daudi Ajani ya Azibo and Patricia Dixon, "The Theoretical Relationship Between Materialistic Depression and Depression: Preliminary Data and Implications for the Azibo Nosology," *Journal of Black Psychology* 24, no. 2 (1998): 211–225, https://doi:10.1177/00957984980242010.

3. Kobi Kambon, *Cultural Misorientation: The Greatest Threat to the Survival of the Black Race in the 21st Century* (Nubian Nation Publications, 2003).

4. Geraldine Pinch, *Egyptian Mythology: A Guide to the Gods, Goddesses, and Traditions of Ancient Egypt* (Oxford University Press, 2004).

5. Sobonfu Somé, *The Spirit of Intimacy: Ancient African Teachings in the Ways of Relationships* (Berkeley Hills Books, 1997; repr. Quill, 2002).

6. "How Being Trauma-Informed Improves Criminal Justice System Responses—Fact Sheet: Historical Trauma," SAMHSA's GAINS Center for Behavioral Health and Justice Transformation, https://healthandlearning.org/wp-content/uploads/2017/11/Historical-Trauma-SAMHSAs-Gains-Center.pdf.

**Chapter 2: Who God Wants Me to Be**

1. "Black Religion Statistics," Black Demographics, https://blackdemographics.com/culture/religion/.

2. Albert J. Raboteau, *Slave Religion: The "Invisible Institution" in the Antebellum South*, 2nd ed. (Oxford University Press, 2004).

3. Philip Neri, "Baptism and Manumission of Negro Slaves in the Early Colonial Period," *Records of the American Catholic Historical Society of Philadelphia* 51, no. 3 (1940): 220–232.

4. Kelly Brown Douglas, *Sexuality and the Black Church: A Womanist Perspective* (Orbis Books, 1999).

5. Milton C. Sernett, *Harriet Tubman: Myth, Memory, and History* (Duke University Press, 2007).

6. C. Eric Lincoln and Lawrence H. Mamiya, *The Black Church in the African American Experience* (Duke University Press, 1990).

7. Keith Boykin, *One More River to Cross: Black & Gay in America* (Anchor Books, 1997).

8. Elias Frajajé-Jones, "Breaking Silence: Toward an In-the-Life Theology," in *Black Theology: A Documentary History, Volume Two: 1980–1992*, ed. James H. Cone and Gayraud S. Wilmore (Orbis Books, 2003), 139–159.

9. "Religious Affiliation & Behaviors—Religious Preference," GSS Data Explorer, NORC, University of Chicago, https://gssdataexplorer.norc.org/trends?category=Religion%20%26%20Spirituality&measure=relig_rec.

10. "Sex & Sexual Orientation—Is It Wrong for Same-Sex Adults to Have Sexual Relations," GSS Data Explorer, NORC, University of Chicago, https://gssdataexplorer.norc.org/trends?category=Gender%20%26%20Marriage&measure=homosex.

11. Stephen O. Murray and Will Roscoe, eds., *Boy-Wives and Female Husbands: Studies in African Homosexualities* (Palgrave Macmillan, 2001), 6.

12. Marc Epprecht, *Heterosexual Africa? The History of an Idea from the Age of Exploration to the Age of AIDS* (Ohio University Press, 2008); Murray and Roscoe, *Boy-Wives and Female Husbands.*

13. Murray and Roscoe, *Boy-Wives and Female Husbands.*

14. Lynne Ellsworth Larsen, "Wives and Warriors: The Royal Women of Dahomey as Representatives of the Kingdom," in *The Routledge Companion to Black Women's Cultural Histories*, ed. Janell Hobson (Routledge, 2021).

15. Boykin, *One More River to Cross.*

16. Audre Lorde, *Sister Outsider: Essays and Speeches* (Crossing Press, 1984; Penguin Books, 2020).

17. Other works that have informed my thinking about the topics in this chapter are: M. T. Fullilove and R. E. Fullilove III, "Stigma as an Obstacle to AIDS Action: The Case of the African American Community," *American Behavioral Scientist* 42, no. 7 (1999): 1117–1129, https://doi.org/10.1177/00027649921954796; Dwight McBride, *Why I Hate Abercrombie & Fitch: Essays on Race and Sexuality* (New York University Press, 2005); Cornel West, *Race Matters* (Vintage, 1994); Calvin C. Hernton, *Sex and Racism in America* (Anchor, 1992); Eddie Donoghue, *Black Breeding Machines: The Breeding of Negro Slaves in the Diaspora* (AuthorHouse, 2008); Marc Ferro, *Colonization: A Global History* (Routledge, 1997); Bonnie G. Smith, *Imperialism: A History in Documents* (Oxford University Press, 2000); Afaf Lutfi Al-Sayyid Marsot, *A History of Egypt: From the Arab Conquest to the Present*, 2nd ed. (Cambridge University Press, 2012).

**Chapter 3: You Can't Buy Whiteness**

1. People with sickle cell anemia often experience delayed puberty. My small body was a source of insecurity for a very long time. Melissa Rhodes et al., "Growth Patterns in Children with Sickle Cell Anemia During Puberty," *Pediatric Blood & Cancer* 53, no. 4 (2009): 635–641, https://doi.org/10.1002/pbc.22137.

2. McBride, Dwight A. 2005. *Why I Hate Abercrombie & Fitch: Essays on Race and Sexuality.* New York: NYU Press.

3. Cedric X. Clark et al., "Voodoo or IQ: An Introduction to African Psychology," *Journal of Black Psychology* 1, no. 2 (1975): 9–29, https://doi.org/10.1177/009579847500100202.

4. "Race, Materialism, and the False God of Western Civilization," Chalmers (blog), July 29, 2020, https://chalmers.org/blog/race-materialism-and-the-false-god-of-western-civilization/.

5. Aye Ochai and José Soto, "The Effect of Adultification on Empathy for Black Individuals," *McNair Scholars Journal* 25 (Summer 2020–2022): 225–235, https://gradschool.psu.edu/assets/uploads/mcnairJournals/Ochai.pdf; Rebecca Epstein et al., *Girlhood Interrupted: The Erasure of Black Girls' Childhood* (Georgetown Law Center on Poverty and Inequality, 2017), https://genderjusticeandopportunity.georgetown.edu/wp-content/uploads/2020/06/girlhood-interrupted.pdf; Erik M. Hines et al., "Preserving Innocence: Ending Perceived Adultification and Toxic Masculinity Toward Black Boys," *Journal of Family Strengths* 21, no. 1 (2021), https://doi.org/10.58464/2168-670X.1444; Amir A. Gilmore and Pamela J. Bettis, "Antiblackness and the Adultification of Black Children in a U.S. Prison Nation," *Oxford Research Encyclopedia of Education* (2021): 1–32, https://doi.org/10.1093/acrefore/9780190264093.013.1293.

6. Christian Grov et al., "Challenging Race-Based Stereotypes About Gay and Bisexual Men's Sexual Behavior and Perceived Penis Size and Size Satisfaction," *Sexuality Research and Social Policy* 12 (2015): 224–235, https://doi.org/10.1007/s13178

-015-0190-0; Alvin Tran et al., "'It's All Outward Appearance-Based Attractions': A Qualitative Study of Body Image Among a Sample of Young Gay and Bisexual Men," *Journal of Gay and Lesbian Mental Health* 24, no. 3 (2020): 281–307, https://doi.org/10.1080/19359705.2019.1706683; Jared Hudson, "Why All the Limp Wrists? Black Gay Male Representation and Masculinity in Film," *Ursidae: The Undergraduate Research Journal at the University of Northern Colorado* 5, no. 2 (2019): 1–13, https://digscholarship.unco.edu/urj/vol5/iss2/2; Naveen Kumar, "For Queer Men of Color, Pressure to Have a Perfect Body Is About Race Too," Them, August 19, 2019, https://www.them.us/story/queer-poc-body-image.

7. Amos N. Wilson, *The Falsification of Afrikan Consciousness: Eurocentric History, Psychiatry and the Politics of White Supremacy* (Afrikan World InfoSystems, 1993).

**Chapter 4: "Cause We Niggas and That's All We Ever Gonna Be"**

1. "Black," Dictionary.com, https://www.dictionary.com/browse/black; Malcolm X and Alex Haley, *The Autobiography of Malcolm X* (Grove Press, 1965; repr., Ballantine Books, 1992).

2. Leon Lam et al., "Research: The Unintended Consequences of Pay Transparency," *Harvard Business Review*, August 12, 2022, https://hbr.org/2022/08/research-the-unintended-consequences-of-pay-transparency.

3. Rachel Ferguson, "The Union Movement Was Anti-Black from the Beginning," Acton Institute, August 9, 2022, https://rlo.acton.org/archives/123721-the-union-movement-was-anti-black-from-the-beginning.html; Paul D. Moreno, *Black Americans and Organized Labor: A New History* (Louisiana State University Press, 2008); Herbert Hill, "Labor Unions and the Negro: The Record of Discrimination," *Commentary*, December 1959.

4. Vinay Baskhara, "Americans Don't Like Affirmative Action—Higher Ed Has to Deal with It," *Forbes*, July 10, 2023, https://www.forbes.com/sites/vinaybhaskara/2023/07/10/americans-dont-like-affirmative actionhigher-ed-has-to-deal-with-it; Students for Fair Admissions, Inc. v. President and Fellows of Harvard College, 600 U.S. ___ (2023), Justia, accessed May 18, 2024, https://supreme.justia.com/cases/federal/us/600/20-1199.

5. Deirdre Cooper Owens, *Medical Bondage: Race, Gender, and the Origins of American Gynecology* (University of Georgia Press, 2017).

6. "Intersections of Black and Japanese American History: From Bronzeville to Black Lives Matter," Densho, Feburary 17, 2016, https://densho.org/catalyst/japaneseamericanandblackhistory.

7. Dion Lim, "Coming Together: Understanding the History of Tension Between the Black and Asian Communities," July 10, 2020, ABC7 News, KGO-TV (San Francisco), https://abc7news.com african-american-asian-history-black-lives-matter/6309505.

8. Harvey Dong, "Third World Liberation Comes to San Francisco State and UC Berkeley," *Chinese America: History and Perspectives* (2009): 95–106, 157, https://www.proquest.com/openview/0bbb678ea8601ce1493169485b8c9798/1?pq-origsite=gscholar&cbl=32930.

9. Kimmy Yam, "Officer Who Stood By as George Floyd Died Highlights Complex Asian American, Black Relations," June 1, 2020, NBC News, https://www.nbcnews.com/news/asian-america/officer-who-stood-george-floyd-died-asian-american-we-need-n1221311; Hansi Lo Wang, "N.Y. Police Shooting Case Divides City's Asian-Americans," NPR, May 14, 2015, https://www.npr.org/sections/codeswitch/2015/05/14/406444625/n-y-police-shooting-case-divides-citys-asian-americans; Michael Corkery, "A Korean Store Owner. A Black Employee. A Tense Neighborhood," *New York Times*, October 17, 2020, https://www.nytimes.com/2020/10/15/business/beauty-store-race-protests.html; Felix B. Chang, "Ethnically Segmented Markets: Korean-Owned Black Hair Stores," *Indiana Law Journal* 97, no. 2 (2022), https://www.repository.law.indiana.edu/cgi/viewcontent.cgi?article=11443&context=ilj; Jay Caspian Kang, Where Does Affirmative Action Leave Asian-Americans?," *New York Times Magazine*, July 29, 2021, https://www.nytimes.com/2019/08/28/magazine/where-does-affirmative-action-leave-asian-americans.html; Neil G. Ruiz et al., "Asian Americans Hold Mixed Views Around Affirmative Action," Pew Research Center, June 2023, https://www.pewresearch.org/wp-content/uploads/sites/20/2023/06/RE_2023.06.08_Asian-Americans-Affirmative-Action_Report.pdf; Students for Fair Admissions, Inc. v. President and Fellows of Harvard College, 600 U.S. ___ (2023).

10. Chong-suk Han, "They Don't Want to Cruise Your Type: Gay Men of Color and the Racial Politics of Exclusion," *Journal for the Study of Race, Nation and Culture* 13, no. 1 (2007): 51–67, https://doi.org/10.1080/13504630601163379; C. Shawn McGuffey, "Intersectionality, Cognition, Disclosure and Black LGBT Views on Civil Rights and Marriage Equality: Is Gay the New Black?," *Du Bois Review* 15, no. 2 (2018): 441–465, https://doi.org/10.1017/S1742058X18000218.

11. Ta-Nehisi Coates, "Prop 8 and Blaming the Blacks," *The Atlantic*, January 7, 2009, https://www.theatlantic.com/entertainment/archive/2009/01/prop-8-and-blaming-the-blacks/6548/; Marisa Abrajano, "Are Blacks and Latinos Responsible for the Passage of Proposition 8? Analyzing Voter Attitudes on California's Proposal to Ban Same-Sex Marriage in 2008," *Political Research Quarterly* 63, no. 4 (2010): 922–932, https://www.jstor.org/stable/25749260; Pam Spaulding, "The N-Bomb Is Dropped on Black Passersby at Prop 8 Protests," *HuffPost*, December 11, 2008, https://www.huffpost.com/entry/the-n-bomb-is-dropped-on_b_142363.

12. Elizabeth Fernandez, "Thousands in S.F. March to Protest Prop. 8," *SFGate*, November 8, 2008, https://www.sfgate.com/bayarea/article/Thousands-in-S-F-march-to-protest-Prop-8-3262717.php.

13. Outtraveller Staff, "San Francisco Finds Gay Bar Owner Discriminated Against Blacks," *Advocate*, April 28, 2005, https://www.advocate.com/news/2005/04/28/san-francisco-finds-gay-bar-owner-discriminated-against-blacks-15860/.

14. John M. Glionna, "Assault Heightens Tensions in S.F.," *Los Angeles Times*, July 23, 2007, https://www.latimes.com/archives/la-xpm-2007-jul-23-me-castro23-story.html.

15. Bobby E. Wright, *The Psychopathic Racial Personality and Other Essays* (Third World Press, 1984).

16. Patrick A. Wilson et al., "Race-Based Sexual Stereotyping and Sexual Partnering Among Men Who Use the Internet to Identify Other Men for Bareback Sex," *Journal of Sex Research* 46, no. 5 (2009): 399–413, https://doi.org/10.1080/00224490902846479.

17. Sam Worley, "The Battle in Boys Town," *Chicago Reader*, July 14, 2011, https://chicagoreader.com/news-politics/the-battle-in-boys-town.

18. Juan Battle et al., *Social Justice Sexuality Survey: The Executive Summary for the Black Population* (New York, 2012), https://socialjusticesexuality.com/files/2014/09/SJS BLACK_ExSum_2012.pdf.

19. Janet E. Helms, *A Race Is a Nice Thing to Have*, 2nd ed. (Microtraining Associates, 2007).

20. Osagyefo Uhuru Sekou, "Gays Are the New Niggers," *Killing the Buddha*, June 26, 2009, https://killingthebuddha.com/mag/damnation/gays-are-the-new-niggers.

**Chapter 5: A Good Match Is Hard to Find**

1. "Directory Statistics & Trainee Stipends," Association of Psychology Postdoctoral and Internship Centers, September 16, 2024, https://www.appic.org/Directory/Directory-Statistics-Trainee-Stipends.

2. James M. Stedman, "What We Know About Predoctoral Internship Training: A Review," *Training and Education in Professional Psychology* no. S2 (2006): 80–95, https://doi.org/10.1037/1931-3918.S.2.80.

3. "2012 APPIC Match: Survey of Internship Applicants Part 2: Summary of Applicant Placement by Applicant and Program Characteristics," Association of Psychology Postdoctoral and Internship Centers, https://www.appic.org/Internships/Match/Match-Statistics/Applicant-Survey-2012-Part-2.

4. "The Black Alone Population in the United States: 2012," United States Census Bureau, https://www.census.gov/data/tables/2012/demo/race/ppl-ba12.html.

5. June Liang et al., "Mental Health Diagnostic Considerations in Racial/Ethnic Minority Youth," *Journal of Child and Family Studies* 25, no. 6 (2016): 1926–1940, https://doi.org/10.1007/s10826-015-0351-z.

6. Megan-Brette Hamilton and Laura DeThorne, "Volume and Verve: Understanding Correction/Behavioral Warnings in Teacher–Child Classroom Interactions Involving an African American Kindergarten Student," *Language, Speech, and Hearing Services in Schools* 52, no. 1 (2021): 64–83, https://doi.org/10.1044/2020_LSHSS-19-00105.

7. James M. Jones, "TRIOS: A Model for Coping with the Universal Context of Racism," in *Racial Identity in Context: The Legacy of Kenneth B. Clark*, ed. G. Philogène (American Psychological Association, 2004), 161–190.

8. Danielle Wexler et al., "What's Race Got to Do with It? Informant Rating Discrepancies in Neuropsychological Evaluations for Children with ADHD," *Clinical Neuropsychologist* 36, no. 2 (2022): 264–286, https://doi.org/10.1080/13854046.2021.1944671.

9. Robert C. Schwartz and David M. Blankenship, "Racial Disparities in Psychotic Disorder Diagnosis: A Review of Empirical Literature," *World Journal of Psychiatry* 4, no. 4 (2014): 133, https://doi.org/10.5498/wjp.v4.i4.133; Linda A. Teplin et al., "Racial and

Ethnic Biases and Psychiatric Misdiagnoses: Toward More Equitable Diagnosis and Treatment," *American Journal of Psychiatry* 180, no. 6 (2023): 402–403, https://doi.org/10.1176/appi.ajp.20230294; Liang et al., "Mental Health Diagnostic Considerations in Racial/Ethnic Minority Youth"; Supriya Misra et al., "Structural Racism and Inequities in Incidence, Course of Illness, and Treatment of Psychotic Disorders Among Black Americans," *American Journal of Public Health* 112, no. 4 (2022): 624–632, https://doi.org/10.2105/AJPH.2021.306631.

10. Alfiee Breland-Noble and the AAKOMA Project, *State of Mental Health for Youth of Color 2022* (AAKOMA Project, 2023).

11. Sam Levin, "'A Talented, Goofy Kid': Family of Ryan Gainer, Autistic Teen Killed by Police, Speak Out," *Guardian*, March 21, 2024, https://www.heguardian.com/us-news/2024/mar/21/ryan-gainer-autistic-teen-police-killing-california; Jessica Gertler, "'She Didn't Deserve to Die the Way She Did.' Questions Surround Woman's Death After Police Interaction During Mental Health Crisis," WREG (Memphis), March 14, 2024, https://wreg.com/news/investigations/she-didnt-deserve-to-die-the-way-she-did-questions-surround-womans-death-after-police-interaction; "Walter Wallace Jr. Struggled with Mental Health Issues, Family Says," NBC10 Philadelphia, WCAU, October 27, 2020, https://www.nbcphiladelphia.com/news/localwalter-wallace-jr-struggled-with-mental-health-issues-family-says/2575493.

12. John Paul Wilson et al., "Racial Bias in Judgments of Physical Size and Formidability: From Size to Threat," *Journal of Personality and Social Psychology* 113, no. 1 (2017): 59–80, https://doi.org /10.1037/pspi0000092.

13. Jennifer L. Eberhardt et al., "Seeing Black: Race, Crime, and Visual Processing," *Journal of Personality and Social Psychology* 87, no. 6 (2004): 876–893, https://doi.org/10.1037/0022-3514.87.6.876.

14. "2012 APPIC Match: Survey of Internship Applicants Part 1: Summary of Survey Results," Association of Psychology Postdoctoral and Internship Centers, https://www.appic.org/Internships/Match/Match-Statistics/Applicant-Survey-2012-Part-1.

**Chapter 6: How I Know White People Are Crazy**

1. "Apology to People of Color for APA's Role in Promoting, Perpetuating, and Failing to Challenge Racism, Racial Discrimination, and Human Hierarchy in U.S.," American Psychological Association, October 29, 2021, https://www.apa.org/about/policy/racism-apology.

2. David K. Mosher et al., "Cultural Humility: A Therapeutic Framework for Engaging Diverse Clients," *Practice Innovations* 2, no. 4 (2017): 221–233, https://doi.org/10.1037/pri0000055.

**Chapter 7: Shiny Object Syndrome**

1. ABFE and Candid, *Philanthropy and HBCUs: Foundation Funding to Historically Black Colleges and Universities* (ABFE and Candid, 2023), https://www.issuelab.org/resources/41808/41808.pdf.

2. Glenn Gamboa, "Ivy League Schools Received Billions from Top Foundations. HBCUs Got Less than $50M," Associated Press, May 2, 2023, https://apnews.com/article/hbcus-underfunded-ivy-league-college-3b2a1f3cb6ddf93baf66cea47b902657.

3. Jennifer M. Johnson et al., "Ivy Issues: An Exploration of Black Students' Racialized Interactions on Ivy League Campuses," *Journal of Diversity in Higher Education* 17, no. 2 (2024): 165–175, https://doi.org/10.1037/dhe0000406.

4. Transcript of Toni Morrison speech at Portland State University, May 30, 1975, https://www.mackenzian.com/wp-content/uploads/2014/07/Transcript_PortlandState_TMorrison.pdf.

5. Chandler Brossard et al., "HBCU vs. Ivy League Schools," Prezi, July 30, 2018, https://prezi.com/srxut8t5wida/hbcu-vs-ivy-league-schools/.

6. Sharron Scott et al., "Investigating Ivy: Black Undergraduate Students at Selective Universities," *Journal of Postsecondary Student Success* 1, no. 2 (2021): 72–90, https://doi.org/10.33009/fsop_jpss128468.

7. Johnson et al., "Ivy Issues."

8. Felix Boateng, "Combating Deculturalization of the African-American Child in the Public School System: A Multicultural Approach," in *Going to School: The African-American Experience*, ed. Kofi Lomotey (State University of New York Press, 1990), 73–84.

9. Ebony O. McGee and David Stovall, "Reimagining Critical Race Theory in Education: Mental Health, Healing, and the Pathway to Liberatory Praxis," *Educational Theory* 65, no. 5 (2015): 491–511, https://doi.org/10.1111/edth.12129.

10. "Black Student at Lehigh University Harassed and Assaulted on His Way to His Dormitory," *Journal of Blacks in Higher Education*, May 5, 2023, https://jbhe.com/2023/05/black-student-at-lehigh-university-harassed-and-assaulted-on-his-way-to-his-dormitory/.

**Chapter 8: "I Feel Like They Don't Want Me Here"**

1. "Full-Time Faculty in Degree-Granting Postsecondary Institutions, by Race/Ethnicity, Sex, and Academic Rank: Fall 2020, Fall 2021, and Fall 2022," US Department of Education, National Center for Education Statistics, November 2023, https://nces.ed.gov/programs/digest/d23/tables/dt23_315.20.asp.

2. Jinann Bitar et al., *Faculty Diversity and Student Success Go Hand in Hand, So Why Are University Faculties So White?* (The Education Trust, 2022).

3. Linda James Myers, *Understanding an Afrocentric World View: Introduction to an Optimal Psychology* (Kendall/Hunt Publishing, 1993).

4. Kenneth I. Maton et al., "Experiences and Perspectives of African American, Latina/o, Asian American, and European American Psychology Graduate Students: A National Study," *Cultural Diversity & Ethnic Minority Psychology* 17, no. 1 (2011): 68–78, https://doi.org/10.1037/a0021668.

5. Stanley Milgram, "Behavioral Study of Obedience," *Journal of Abnormal and Social Psychology* 67, no. 4 (1963): 371–378, https://doi.org/10.1037/h0040525.

6. Jerry M. Burger, "Replicating Milgram: Would People Still Obey Today?" *American Psychologist* 64, no. 1 (2009), 1–11, https://doi.org/10.1037/a0010932.

7. "The 50 Most Influential Psychologists in the World," TheBestSchools, https://www.taosinstitute.net/images/WhatsNewImages/Ken%20Gergen%20-%20Top%2050%20psychologists%20today%201-2018.pdf.

8. Shawn M. Bergman et al., "Millennials, Narcissism, and Social Networking: What Narcissists Do on Social Networking Sites and Why," *Personality and Individual Differences* 50, no. 5 (2011): 706–711, https://doi.org/10.1016/j.paid.2010.12.022; Christine E. Rittenour and Colleen Warner Colaner, "Finding Female Fulfillment: Intersecting Role-Based and Morality-Based Identities of Motherhood, Feminism, and Generativity as Predictors of Women's Self Satisfaction and Life Satisfaction," *Sex Roles: A Journal of Research* 67, no. 5–6 (2012): 351–362, https://doi.org/10.1007/s11199-012-0186-7; Timothy Barrett, "Friendships Between Men Across Sexual Orientation: The Importance of (Others) Being Intolerant," *Journal of Men's Studies* 21, no. 1 (2013): 62–77, https://doi.org/10.3149/jms.2101.62.

**Chapter 9: "Dr. Lassiter Is Intimidating"**

1. Dana A. Williams, "Examining the Relation Between Race and Student Evaluations of Faculty Members: A Literature Review," *Profession*, 2007, 168–173, https://www.jstor.org/stable/25595863; Bettye P. Smith and Billy Hawkins, "Examining Student Evaluations of Black College Faculty: Does Race Matter?," *Journal of Negro Education* 80, no. 2 (2011): 149–162, https://www.jstor.org/stable/41341117; Armon R. Perry et al., "Understanding Student Evaluations: A Black Faculty Perspective," *Reflections: Narratives of Professional Helping* 20, no. 1 (2015): 29–35, https://ir.library.louisville.edu/faculty/15.

2. Anish Bavishi et al., "The Effect of Professor Ethnicity and Gender on Student Evaluations: Judged Before Met," *Journal of Diversity in Higher Education* 3, no. 4 (2010): 245–256, https://doi.org/10.1037/a0020763.

3. Bavishi et al., "The Effect of Professor Ethnicity and Gender on Student Evaluations."

4. Heidi J. Nast, "'Sex', 'Race' and Multiculturalism: Critical Consumption and the Politics of Course Evaluations," *Journal of Geography in Higher Education* 23, no. 1 (1999): 102–115, https://doi.org/10.1080/03098269985650; Williams, "Examining the Relation Between Race and Student Evaluations of Faculty Members."

5. TaLisa J. Carter and Miltonette O. Craig, "It Could Be Us: Black Faculty as 'Threats' on the Path to Tenure," *Race and Justice* 12, no. 3 (2022): 569–587, https://doi.org/10.1177/21533687221087366.

6. John Paul Wilson et al., "Interactive Effects of Obvious and Ambiguous Social Categories on Perceptions of Leadership: When Double-Minority Status May Be Beneficial," *Personality and Social Psychology Bulletin* 43, no. 6 (2017): 888–900, https://doi.org/10.1177/0146167217702373.

7. Jessica D. Remedios et al., "Impressions at the Intersection of Ambiguous and Obvious Social Categories: Does Gay + Black = Likable?," *Journal of Experimental Social Psychology* 47, no. 6 (2011): 1312–1315, https://doi.org/10.1016/j.jesp.2011.05.015.

8. Justin P. Preddie and Monica Biernat, "More Than the Sum of Its Parts: Intersections of Sexual Orientation and Race as They Influence Perceptions of Group Simi-

larity and Stereotype Content," *Sex Roles* 84, no. 9–10 (2021): 554–573, https://doi.org/10.1007/s11199-020-01185-3.

9. Remedios, "Impressions at the Intersection of Ambiguous and Obvious Social Categories."

10. Steve O. Michael, "American Higher Education System: Consumerism Versus Professorialism," *International Journal of Educational Management* 11, no. 3 (1997): 117–130, https://doi.org/10.1108/09513549710164014; Rajani Naidoo and Ian Jamieson, "Empowering Participants or Corroding Learning? Towards a Research Agenda on the Impact of Student Consumerism in Higher Education," *Journal of Education Policy* 20, no. 3 (2005): 267–281, https://doi.org/10.1080/02680930500108585; Louise Bunce et al., "The Student-as-Consumer Approach in Higher Education and Its Effects on Academic Performance," *Studies in Higher Education* 42, no. 11 (2016): 1958–1978, https://doi.org/10.1080/03075079.2015.1127908.

11. Michael Tomlinson, "Student Perceptions of Themselves as 'Consumers' of Higher Education," *British Journal of Sociology of Education* 38, no. 4 (2017): 450–467, https://doi.org/10.1080/01425692.2015.1113856.

12. Rebecca Gross, "Toni Morrison: Write, Erase, Do It Over," *NEA Arts* 4 (2014): 1–3, https://www.arts.gov/stories/magazine/2014/4/art-failure-importance-risk-and-experimentation/toni-morrison.

13. Pinch, *Egyptian Mythology*; Tonia Renee Durden, "African Centered Schooling: Facilitating Holistic Excellence for Black Children," *Negro Educational Review* 58, no. 1–2 (2007): 23–34, https://digitalcommons.unl.edu/cyfsfacpub/16.

14. Michael S. Merry and William New, "Constructing an Authentic Self: The Challenges and Promise of African-Centered Pedagogy," *American Journal of Education* 115, no. 1 (2008): 35–64, https://doi.org/10.1086/590675.

15. "Kanye West Stirs Up TMZ Newsroom over Trump, Slavery, Free Thought," TMZ, May 1, 2018, https://www.tmz.com/2018/05/01/kanye-west-tmz-live-slavery-trump/.

**Chapter 10: Nice White Women**

1. Gwendolyn Puryear Keita et al., *Women in the American Psychological Association: 2006* (American Psychological Association, 2006); "Data Tool: Demographics of the U.S. Psychology Workforce," American Psychological Association, 2022, https://www.apa.org/workforce/data-tools/demographics.

2. Fred Bemak and Rita Chi-Ying Chung, "New Professional Roles and Advocacy Strategies for School Counselors: A Multicultural/Social Justice Perspective to Move Beyond the Nice Counselor Syndrome," *Journal of Counseling & Development* 86, no. 3 (2008): 372–381, https://doi.org/10.1002/j.1556-6678.2008.tb00522.x.

3. Colleen Flaherty, "The Souls of Black Professors," *Inside Higher Ed*, October 20, 2020, https://www.insidehighered.com/news/2020/10/21/scholars-talk-about-being-black-campus-2020.

4. Stanley J. Huey Jr. et al., "The Contribution of Cultural Competence to Evidence-Based Care for Ethnically Diverse Populations," *Annual Review of Clinical Psychology* 10 (2014): 305–338, https://doi.org/10.1146/annurev-clinpsy-032813-153729.

5. Renée A. Middleton et al., "Racial Identity Profile Patterns of White Mental Health Practitioners: Implications for Multicultural Counseling Competency in Research and Practice," *International Journal of Psychology and Psychological Therapy* 11, no. 2 (2011): 201–218, https://www.researchgate.net/publication/328968872_Racial_identity_profile_patterns_of_white_mental_health_practitioners_Implications_for_multicultural_counseling_competency_in_research_and_practice.

6. Cirleen DeBlaere et al., "Multiple Microaggressions and Therapy Outcomes: The Indirect Effects of Cultural Humility and Working Alliance with Black, Indigenous, Women of Color Clients," *Professional Psychology: Research and Practice* 54, no. 2 (2023): 115–124, https://doi.org/10.1037/pro0000497; Chavella T. Pittman, "Racial Microaggressions: The Narratives of African American Faculty at a Predominantly White University," *Journal of Negro Education* 81, no. 1 (2012): 82–92, https://doi.org/10.7709/jnegroeducation.81.1.0082.

7. "Does DEI Training Work?," Clearinghouse on DEI Research, Stanford Law School, https://law.stanford.edu/clearinghouse-on-diversity-equity-inclusion-research/does-dei-training-work/#slsnav-overview.

8. Lorraine T. Benuto et al., "Training Culturally Competent Psychologists: A Systematic Review of the Training Outcome Literature," *Training and Education in Professional Psychology* 12, no. 3 (2018): 125–134, https://doi.org/10.1037/tep0000190.

9. Lisa B. Spanierman et al., "Psychosocial Costs of Racism to Whites: Understanding Patterns Among University Students," *Journal of Counseling Psychology* 56, no. 2 (2009): 239–252, https://doi.org/10.1037/a0015432.

10. Janet K. Swim and Deborah L. Miller, "White Guilt: Its Antecedents and Consequences for Attitudes Toward Affirmative Action," *Personality and Social Psychology Bulletin* 25, no. 4 (1999): 500–514, https://doi.org/10.1177/0146167299025004008.

11. Lisa B. Spanierman et al., "Psychosocial Costs of Racism to White Counselors: Predicting Various Dimensions of Multicultural Counseling Competence," *Journal of Counseling Psychology* 55, no. 1 (2008): 75–88, https://doi.org/10.1037/0022-0167.55.1.75.

12. Irene H. Yoon, "The Paradoxical Nature of Whiteness-at-Work in the Daily Life of Schools and Teacher Communities," *Race Ethnicity and Education* 15, no. 5 (2012): 587–613, https://doi.org/10.1080/13613324.2011.624506.

13. David R. Williams, "Stress and the Mental Health of Populations of Color: Advancing Our Understanding of Race-Related Stressors," *Journal of Health and Social Behavior* 59, no. 4 (2018): 466–485, https://doi.org/10.1177/0022146518814251.

**Chapter 11: Killing Me Softly with Diversity**

1. Roy L. Brooks, "Life After Tenure: Can Minority Law Professors Avoid the Clyde Ferguson Syndrome?," *University of San Francisco Law Review* 20 (1986): 419–427, https://hls.harvard.edu/wp-content/uploads/2022/10/life-after-tenure.pdf; Lauren Turman, "Emails Surface from LU's VP of Student Affairs Sent the Day She Died by Sui-

cide," January 12, 2024, KRCG TV, https://krcgtv.com/news/local/emails-surface-from-lus-vp-of-student-affairs-sent-the-day-she-died-by-suicide.

2. Kiara Alfonseca and Jade Lawson, "HBCU President Reinstated After Investigation Following Administrator's Suicide," ABC News, March 21, 2024, https://abcnews.go.com/US/hbcu-president-reinstated-after-investigation-administrators-suicide/story?id=108356070; Andrew Lawrence, "'She Endured Cruelty': What Led to a Leader's Death at a Historically Black University?," *The Guardian*, February 28, 2024, https://www.theguardian.com/us-news/2024/feb/28/antoinette-candia-bailey-lincoln-university-death.

3. Joanna N. Lahey and Douglas R. Oxley, "Discrimination at the Intersection of Age, Race, and Gender: Evidence from an Eye-Tracking Experiment," *Journal of Policy Analysis and Management* 40, no. 4 (2021): 1083–1119, https://doi.org/10.1002/pam.22281; Costas Cavounidis and Kevin Lang, "Discrimination and Worker Evaluation," NBER Working Paper No. 21612 (National Bureau of Economic Research, October 2015).

4. Samuel L. Gaertner and John F. Dovidio, "The Aversive Form of Racism," in *Prejudice, Discrimination, and Racism*, ed. John F. Dovidio and Samuel L. Gaertner (Academic Press, 1986), 61–89.

5. Marybeth Gasman, "The Five Things No One Will Tell You About Why Colleges Don't Hire More Faculty of Color," *The Hechinger Report*, September 20, 2016, https://hechingerreport.org/five-things-no-one-will-tell-colleges-dont-hire-faculty-color.

6. Carl L. Hart, *Drug Use for Grown-Ups: Chasing Liberty in the Land of Fear* (Penguin Books, 2022).

**Chapter 12: Black Boy and the City**

1. "Race and Well-Being Among LGBT Adults," Williams Institute, UCLA School of Law, accessed May 18, 2024, https://williamsinstitute.law.ucla.edu/visualization/lgbt-races/#Social.

2. W. E. Burghardt Du Bois, "The Talented Tenth," in *The Negro Problem: A Series of Articles by Representative American Negroes of Today*, ed. Booker T. Washington (James Pott, 1903), 33–75.

3. E. Lynn Harris, *Just As I Am* (Anchor Books, 1995).

4. Joseph Beam, ed., *In the Life: A Black Gay Anthology* (Alyson Books, 1986; 2nd ed., RedBone Press, 2008).